POINT ME TO JESUS

365

Devotions for Parents and Children

TARA McCLARY REEVES

BroadStreet
PUBLISHING

For the three reasons I've written this book:

Caroline Fraley Reeves,
Daniel Cleburne Reeves, and
Harrison McClary Reeves.

This is my prayer: that your love may abound more and more in knowledge and depth of insight, so that you may be able to discern what is best and may be pure and blameless for the day of Christ, filled with the fruit of righteousness that comes through Jesus Christ—to the glory and praise of God.

—Philippians 1:9–11

JANUARY

Go Ahead, Make My Day

In the beginning God created the heavens and the earth.
GENESIS 1:1 NASB

Every creation has a creator. Our twins love to craft. Sometimes they design homemade cards. At other times they sculpt. Whatever it is they use their imaginations to construct, Caroline and Daniel know their ideas won't just appear and tape themselves to our refrigerator door. They first require work.

But amazingly, just by His word, our awesome Creator brought into existence all the planets, the sky, the stars, the oceans, the galaxies, the seahorse, the platypus, grapes, puppies, kittens, watermelons, the moon, the sun, rainbows, coconuts, hummingbirds, the firefly, moose, hamsters, mountains, roses, starfish, Adam and Eve, and night and day. God made everything in six days, and He did it without a supply box.

In the New Testament, we are reminded that Jesus, who is God, was right there calling time and matter into being in creation week. John 1:1 tells us, "In the beginning was the Word [Jesus], and the Word was with God, and the Word was God." Without Jesus, the Bible says, nothing was made that has been made (v. 3). That includes you, who He fashioned in His own image.

Jesus literally made your day when He first selected your birth date and then laid out the days of the week. By putting your trust in Him, you will, in a sense, make His day too.

Why do you think Jesus made you and wants to be your Savior?

A Godly Growth Chart

*Jesus kept increasing in wisdom and stature,
and in favor with God and men.*

LUKE 2:52 NASB

We have a giraffe in our house. No, not a real giraffe, but a painting of the tallest animal in the jungle hanging upstairs. What makes this mammal so special to me are the little marks and dates I've made up his long neck. It's a growth chart, tracking my children's height over the years.

At one time, Jesus was a child like you. His growth chart of sorts is found in Luke 2:52, which tells us He grew taller and wiser, loving both God and other people well. He grew mentally by studying and memorizing Bible verses and praying. Physically, He became tall and strong. Perhaps He did that by eating the healthy foods prepared, instead of chips and cookies. Spiritually, He made wise choices in what He watched, listened to, in what He did, and where He walked. Socially, He was friendly with everyone, but was careful about who He called His friend.

God's Word says, "Jesus kept increasing" in all these things. That means He never got tired of listening and learning. He had a teachable spirit. When He was twelve, we're told that one day, Mary and Joseph found Jesus "sitting among the teachers, listening to them and asking them questions" (Luke 2:46). That's where He chose to be. Make a commitment to monitor your "growth" by seeking to follow the example of Jesus.

What is something you can do to grow more like Jesus?

Love Does

"To obey is better than sacrifice."
1 Samuel 15:22

I asked my children, Caroline and Daniel, to clean the playroom. It was a big job. LEGO® sets, dollies, and trains were scattered everywhere. But they said, "Yes, ma'am." Upon my return, I got quite a surprise. Sitting in their little chairs around the wooden craft table, still surrounded by all the toys I'd requested they tidy up, my twins were beaming, each holding up beautiful artwork. "Look what we made for you, Mommy!" Not wanting to break their spirits, I sat next to them and let them explain each detail of their master-piece. However, I knew I had to address their disobedience. "Mommy loves your drawings," I replied, "but my heart is sad." I explained that their pictures would have meant so much more to me had they first obeyed what I had asked them to do and cleaned the room.

Many times, we justify our decisions based on the same reasoning my children used to postpone their obedience. We know what the Lord has instructed us to do. But we translate His instructions into: *This feels more comfortable. Maybe He will like this better.* Jesus honored His Father through His obedience (John 6:38). Our goal should be the same. Anything else is just a disobedient heart drawn on pretty paper.

Discuss a time in your life when God clearly instructed you to do one thing, but you chose another. What happened as a result of your choice?

Beware of I

"If you love me, obey my commandments."
JOHN 14:15 NLT

In *Willy Wonka and the Chocolate Factory*, Veruca Salt is a spoiled brat who thinks of no one but herself. She is disrespectful to her parents, even shoving and hitting her father. Veruca's final scene in the movie takes place in the Golden Egg Room, where she wants her father to buy her a goose that lays golden eggs. "I want it now, Daddy!" she demands. With his checkbook in hand, Veruca's father ignores Willy Wonka's claim that none of the geese are for sale. When Veruca doesn't get what she wants, she goes wild, tearing up the room and ruining the Oompa-Loompas' work. Her tantrum ends with her disappearance down a chute into the furnace holding room.

Veruca's actions show us what sin can look like. Sin is a little word with a big *I* in the middle, and its side effects are serious. When we are unkind and disrespectful to our parents and others, God is never pleased. When we sin, we are being disrespectful to God as well.

Obedience is one of the surest ways to show God that we love Him. When He says, "Be kind to one another" (Ephesians 4:32 ESV), He means that we should love those around us and not demand our own way. Doing what God says reveals how much we love Him.

Recall a time you made a choice to show God how much you loved Him by doing what He said.

The War Room

"But you, when you pray, go into your room."

MATTHEW 6:6 NKJV

Upon his election as prime minister of Great Britain, Winston Churchill entered the Cabinet Room and declared, "This is the room from which I will direct the war." The Cabinet Room eventually expanded into other rooms in the basement of Whitehall and became the brain center of operations during World War II. These rooms were in use twenty-four hours a day. Leading government officials, top military experts, and Prime Minister Churchill met here in what became known as Churchill's "war rooms." For six years a light shone in the room, which housed the maps. Because of the highly sensitive nature of the business addressed in these rooms, they were off limits to the public.

In Matthew 6:6, Jesus teaches us the importance of establishing our own "war room." Though He was not talking about a room from which we direct a war, He encouraged us to find a special, quiet place where we can talk to God so He can direct us. When we come humbly before Him, wanting to follow God's plan, instead of our own, victory is certain.

Where is your war room, and what concerns do you want to bring to God right now?

Sniff Test

We are the aroma of Christ.
2 CORINTHIANS 2:15 ESV

Just south of the Balkan Mountains is a valley famous for growing roses. During May and June, the scent is incredibly sweet and strong. Even if you're only in the garden for a brief period of time, for the rest of the day everyone will know where you've been. You carry the fragrance of the garden along with you.

In the fourth chapter of Acts, Peter and John stand before an extremely powerful, educated group of men called the Sanhedrin. (They were kind of like our modern-day Supreme Court.) Peter and John had spent three years in Jesus' presence and those observing them that day noticed hints of Jesus' teachings and ways evident in the two men who stood trial. Peter and John had experienced the forgiveness of their sins through Jesus' death on the cross. They'd witnessed His empty tomb and been challenged by Jesus in person after He'd risen from the dead. This made Peter and John unstoppable in their desire to make the living Christ known. Though Peter had denied knowing Jesus three times the night before Jesus died on the cross, there was no denying Him now.

God's Holy Spirit, who lived inside these friends of Jesus, helped them boldly witness in front of this very intimidating audience. And "when [the Sanhedrin] saw the courage of Peter and John and realized they were unschooled, ordinary men, they were astonished and they took note that these men had been with Jesus" (Acts 4:13).

What is the fragrance others encounter after you are with them?

The Great Pretender

"Not everyone who says to Me, 'Lord, Lord,'
will enter the kingdom of heaven."

MATTHEW 7:21

Tony Evans shares a story about a bodybuilder visiting a tribe in Africa.[1] Blown away by his guest's muscular body, the tribe's chief asked, "What do you do with all those muscles?" The man replied, "Well, it's probably easier to show you than explain." Immediately, the bodybuilder went into different poses, showcasing his triceps, biceps, obliques, quadriceps, and back. Afterwards, the tribal chief exclaimed, "Wow! Impressive. But what else do you do with all those muscles?" The bodybuilder admitted, "Well, that's pretty much it. I work out to pose." Shaking his head in dismay, the chieftain said, "What a waste."

How many of us are like this bodybuilder? We attend church, try to keep the Ten Commandments, go to Sunday school or Bible study, pray, and may even have been baptized. We work out spiritually to look good in the eyes of others. Yet, we're just posers. Life isn't about who's looking at us, but *who* we're looking to for strength and guidance. When we have a real relationship with Jesus, it creates a longing to stay close to Him, to believe what He says in the Bible, and to trust in His power to change us. We won't be content to just look good on the outside. We will want to be the real deal inside and out, not posers.

Share a time when you chose to please others instead of choosing to please God.

---

1 Tony Evans. *Tony Evans' Book of Illustrations* (Chicago: Moody Publishers, 2009).

The Sign of the Cross

*Beginning with Moses and all the Prophets,
he interpreted to them in all the Scriptures
the things concerning himself.*

LUKE 24:27 ESV

My parents wisely taught me the dangers of reading horoscopes, playing with Ouija boards, and visiting fortune tellers. I'll never forget being asked in middle school, "What's your sign?" Because my parents had been so careful to guard my sister and me against negative spiritual influences, I had no idea what my friends at the lunch table were talking about. On the way home, I asked my mom. She told me about the zodiac symbols and how the only focus of our faith should be the Lord Jesus Christ. She replied, "You tell them tomorrow that your sign is the cross!"

Jesus never used any teaching other than the Word of God, the Bible, when He talked about faith. We shouldn't either. The Bible is our source of truth for all situations.

I've always been amazed how close the horoscopes are placed near the comics in a newspaper. My parents taught me to fold the paper so I couldn't see them, so I wouldn't even be tempted to read anything that didn't line up with God's truth. The enemy is persistent and we are powerless to fight him in our own strength. First Corinthians 15:57 reminds us we don't have to: "But thanks be to God! He gives us the victory through our Lord Jesus Christ."

Name a specific way you can be more careful today to avoid doing something that goes against God's truth.

Semper Fidelis

"I glorified You on the earth, having accomplished the work which You have given Me to do."

JOHN 17:4 NASB

As you grow up, at times you may feel stressed out because it seems you don't have enough time to do what you feel you were put on this earth to do. It helps to remember just how much we can accomplish when we make the most of the hours God gives us. Jesus was thirty when He began His ministry on earth and thirty-three when He went to the cross. For three years He was completely faithful to the mission His Father gave Him. He accomplished everything His Father asked.

My father is a marine. "Semper Fidelis" is the Marine Corps' motto. It's Latin for "always faithful." The wedding ring I placed on my husband's finger is engraved with those same words. "Semper Fidelis" reminds me that no matter what gets in my way, tempts me, distracts me, or threatens disaster, nothing should take my eyes off the mission God's given me—to live for Jesus. Time is short. I need to live with focus.

If you get married when you grow up, being faithful means not flirting with anyone other than your spouse. At home, it means honoring your parents' authority and responding to them with respect. At school, it means obeying the rules and completing your assignments. With your friends, it means making good and loving choices in your relationships. A life "always faithful" to the Lord has enough time to accomplish His purposes.

What does it mean for you to be Semper Fidelis, always faithful, to God?

Unstoppable Love

*Only goodness and faithful love will pursue me
all the days of my life.*

PSALM 23:6 HCSB

Jennifer Wilbanks went missing four days before her wedding, leaving her engagement ring behind. Three days later, Jennifer called her fiancé, John Mason, and said she'd been kidnapped, but was safe. Police soon learned Jennifer's story was a lie to avoid her wedding. After Jennifer's return, John knelt down and slipped the same ring onto her finger for the second time. The depth of this guy's love for his fiancée may seem crazy considering what she did, but it reminds me of Jesus' radical love for us.

Though John was willing to forgive his runaway fiancée, Jennifer rejected his love. "I don't want to give myself to John until I feel like I'm the right person for him," Jennifer said in an interview, "and right now, I don't." She felt she didn't deserve his love.

Many people hear about Jesus' wide-open arms of acceptance and sincere invitation to accept His love, but they think they've done too many bad things. So they reject His proposal. They've missed the point. Jesus chases after us in spite of ourselves. He knows the only way we can be forgiven and enjoy the loving-kindness of God is through Him. Salvation's not about what we've done for Jesus. It's about accepting what He's done for us: "But God demonstrates his own love for us in this: While we were still sinners, Christ died for us" (Romans 5:8).

What is one way God shows his love for you?

A Modern Day Parable

*While a large crowd was gathering and people
were coming to Jesus from town after town,
he told this parable.*

LUKE 8:4

The Good Samaritan. The Prodigal Son. The Good Shepherd. Jesus often taught in parables, which are earthly stories with a heavenly lesson. Many times my mom would encourage us with her own parables of truth. One was about our dog, Fancy.

My mother and father love animals—especially dogs. For seventeen years, they had a little mutt named Fancy who knew to sit on command. One day, after my father spoke at a church, my dad walked across the road with the pastor. Fancy followed behind. Once across, Fancy looked back and saw my mom on the other side of the road, talking to some ladies. Mom could tell Fancy was thinking about dashing toward her and she feared she'd get hit by a passing car. "Sit, Fancy!" she yelled across the street. Fancy sat. Fancy's disciplined response saved that adorable dog's life.

Each of us is a little like Fancy, running through life, unaware of the dangers around us. Often it takes an automatic, disciplined response to God's Word to avoid trouble. Just as Fancy knew to sit because she was familiar with the command, we can know what is right, and obey it faithfully, the more familiar we are with God's Word. Whatever God asks of us in Scripture, we can be sure it is for our good.

What Bible truths have you learned that can help keep you out of trouble?

Regifting

He said to them, "Go into all the world
and preach the gospel to all creation."
MARK 16:15

Regifting is passing a gift we've been given on to someone else. Seldom do people regift a treasured item of great value. Yet, our Lord commands us to be "regifters" by telling others that forgiveness cannot be earned. It's free, thanks to Jesus. What's more, no matter how many times we give this gift away, we never have any less to keep for ourselves.

The Bible tells us that Saul (whose Greek name was Paul) became a chronic regifter after his encounter with Jesus on the road to Damascus. He stopped killing those associated with Christ and began preaching to the public that life is only found in a relationship with Him. Paul's desire for others to know Jesus was unstoppable, because he'd experienced firsthand God's radical love for him. He knew he'd been spared a life of eternal separation from a living and loving God. Paul was willing to walk, run, and sail thousands of miles because of his conviction about the life-changing message of the good news of Jesus Christ. He confidently proclaimed, "The gospel … is the power of God for salvation to everyone who believes" (Romans 1:16 ESV).

Jesus paid the ultimate price for us to have the greatest gift of all. Salvation's too big for any box, but telling others how the power of Christ's love can change their life, and eternity, is the only present truly worthy of regifting.

Who are you willing to share the greatest gift with today?

WWJD?

*"When you pray, do not be like the hypocrites,
for they love to pray standing in the synagogues and
on the street corners to be seen by others."*

MATTHEW 6:5

As the vain queen in *Snow White and the Seven Dwarfs* calls out to the mirror to see who is the fairest of them all, she expects to see her own image, because she thinks of herself as the most important, beautiful person in the kingdom. Sadly, our culture often encourages us to view the face we see in the mirror as the center of everything too. But it's the Lord who should be the center of our attention—even when it comes to prayer.

Prayer isn't about placing attention on ourselves, listing our wants, and talking about our desires. It's about focusing on the character of God. The disciples themselves witnessed the difference between the showy prayer lives of the religious leaders of their day (who loved nothing more than keeping attention focused on themselves) and how Jesus prayed. So the disciples asked Jesus to teach them how to pray as He did. Jesus responded by shining the spotlight on the holiness of God: "When you pray, say this: Father, let your name be kept holy" (Luke 11:2 GW).

God is holy and hates sin, including our selfishness. So let's challenge ourselves to see if we can stamp "Holy be Your name" on everything we do, from choosing TV shows and music to being careful about the way we treat His name.

Without praying to get it over with, to impress Mom, or to submit your list of wants, pick out something you love about God, and then thank Him for who He is.

Bubble Wrap

"On that day you will realize that I am in my Father,
and you are in me, and I am in you."

JOHN 14:20

When my son decided to play football, I purchased every imaginable piece of safety equipment. I bought so much that when the cashier at Dick's Sporting Goods looked at my overflowing buggy, she stated matter-of-factly, "Honey, you're in the wrong store. I think you meant to visit Lowe's. We don't sell Bubble Wrap® here!"

She called me out. I just wanted to make sure my son was safe from all possible injury.

Safety and security seem incredibly important as we seek to live the best lives possible, but ultimately, our well-being rests in the hands of the Lord. To help us remember that truth, Bible teacher Denise Glenn suggests illustrating John 14:20 by drawing four circles, one inside the other.[2] Label the largest circle God, the second circle Jesus, the third circle me, and the fourth circle Jesus. As you look at your drawing, you can rest assured knowing that when you become God's child by inviting Jesus into your heart, you are protected on all sides. He's on the inside of us and on the outside of us. No matter what life throws at us, we are safe within the "Bubble Wrap" of His love.

How do you feel, knowing that God is protecting you inside and out?

---

2   Denise Glenn, *Wisdom for Mothers* (Houston, TX: Kardo International Ministries, 2004), 60.

Respect Authority

"Honor your father and mother…
that it may go well with you."

EPHESIANS 6:2–3 ESV

With long hair, big muscles, and a name meaning "sun child,"[3] Samson was a star from the moment of his miraculous birth announcement. For years, though, Samson got so caught up in his looks and abilities that he failed to make wise choices. The brightness of the future God planned for Samson was dimmed by selfishness and foolishness. His sad downfall began with his decision to dishonor his parents.

Samson hid things from his mom and dad (Judges 14:6). When he did speak to them, his tone was rude, demanding, manipulative, and disrespectful (Judges 14:2). The way Samson responded to their authority reflected what he thought about God's authority. Both Samson's ministry and life were cut short, because he didn't want to answer to anyone.

God placed people in authority over you to help you learn how to make wise decisions and avoid bad ones. Since Jesus instructs you to honor your parents, you must choose not to pout when disciplined or resist directions from them. Never plug your ears with your fingers and stomp off when they give you an answer you don't like. Instead, remember God gave you parents to help guide and protect you. By honoring them, you honor Jesus.

What specific things can you do to honor your parents and please Jesus?

---

3 SHEKNOWS BabyHold, http://babynames.allparenting.com/list/Hebrew_Baby_Names/Samson/details/.

Go Fish

He said to them, "Follow me,
and I will make you fishers of men."
MATTHEW 4:19 ESV

The twins and I went fishing the other day. With every fish we reeled in, Daniel kept asking me to remove it from the hook for him. "Daniel," I stated, "one day you may be somebody's daddy. You'll be responsible for showing him how to do this. What are you going to do?"

"We just won't go fishing," Daniel replied.

Unlike my son, the first four men Jesus called into ministry with Him were career fishermen. Matthew 4:20 reports their response to His call: "At once they left their nets and followed Him." I think it's interesting that the Bible points out how quickly they were ready to obey. It also mentions what they left behind—their nets.

"Nets" like worry, fear of failure, or fear of what others will think are all examples of obstacles to following Christ. But Jesus desires our willingness to leave our "nets," trusting that our futures and the catch are up to the Holy Spirit. He wants us to step away from our concerns in order to become fishers of men. That means we're ready to share with anyone we meet that God loves them so much that He sent Jesus to take their place on the cross. The punishment our sins deserve was placed on Him. Once we have accepted Jesus as our Lord and Savior, refusing to fish is not an option.

Talk about any "nets" that keep you from sharing about Jesus with others.

Remember
It's Not about You

We don't tell people about ourselves.
But we tell people that Jesus Christ is Lord.

2 Corinthians 4:5 ERV

While Paul was teaching daily about the cross of Christ, false teachers were spreading their own theories about how to get to know God. They enjoyed having the attention of the crowd—whether there was any truth to what they said about spiritual matters or not.

Their tendency to favor being the center of attention, over knowing and proclaiming truth, was not a problem confined to their time. In the 1800s, a gentleman visiting London heard some great teaching from the most gifted preachers of the day. When he got home, he told his wife about the two services he attended. On Sunday morning, he'd heard Dr. Lewis. That evening he'd listened to Charles Spurgeon. "Darling," he recounted, "I was impressed with them both. Dr. Lewis is a great preacher, but Mr. Spurgeon has a great Savior."[4] The man recognized that only one preacher had focused his message on Jesus. The other had done little more than draw attention to his own public speaking abilities.

Our culture encourages us to spend lots of time discussing empty topics that don't lead anyone closer to Christ. But one purpose God has for you is to share with others how great God is, to tell people the gospel truth about Jesus. Life really isn't all about you.

What have you taught others about Jesus?

---

4 Ron Hutchcraft, "The Only Impression that Matters," Ron Hutchcraft Ministries, https://hutchcraft.com/a-word-with-you/your-hindrances/the-only-impression-that-matters-5982.

Hear Ye, Hear Ye

*"My sheep hear My voice, and I know them,
and they follow Me."*

JOHN 10:27 NASB

The story is told of a Native American man who walked alongside a stock broker in New York City. He stopped abruptly and said to the broker, "Listen, I hear a cricket." The city dweller laughed and said, "In the middle of this busy city and afternoon traffic? You have got to be kidding." The Native American man bent down and turned over a clump of debris next to a building. Sure enough, there was a cricket. Then he stood up, took a handful of coins from his pocket, and dropped them on the ground. People in both directions stopped and started looking for the money. The wise man said, "See, it all depends on what you are trained to hear."

We too are faced with the daily question: To what will we tune our ears? Will we listen for tips on how to be popular? Follow advice on getting wealthy? Or will we zero in on the beautiful sound of God's voice as He calls us to live for Him? Jesus tells us we can know His voice through His written love letter to us, the Bible. If you read God's Word and obey what He says, you pass the hearing test. You are tuned into the right thing.

Pay attention to what you listen to today. Then, before bedtime, share what voices you heard most clearly.

Picked for a Purpose

Christian brothers,
we know God loves you and
that He has chosen you.

1 Thessalonians 1:4 NLV

Caroline ran toward me after tennis camp, beaming ear to ear. I hugged her and asked, "What was the kindest thing anybody said to you today?" "Mommy, one of the other players pointed to me and said, 'I want her on my side.'" As we drove the short distance between the tennis club and home, I thought about the joy we give the Lord when we delight in "being on His side."

Colossians 3:12 declares, "Therefore, as God's chosen people, holy and dearly loved, clothe yourselves with compassion, kindness, humility, gentleness and patience." Like this verse says, Jesus has chosen us to be on His squad and He's given us a uniform!

We show others we are on God's team by the kind words we say to them, the thoughtful things we do for them, the caring hug we provide at just the right time, and the forgiveness we offer, even when it's not deserved. Remember, no matter how difficult the challenges are in life or how lonely we may feel, Jesus is with us and has placed us on His winning team.

What does it mean to you to know the Lord has chosen you to be on His side?

Empathy vs. Sympathy

Since He Himself was tempted in that which He has suffered,
He is able to come to the aid of those who are tempted.

HEBREWS 2:18 NASB

As I waited for the nurse to call my son Daniel's name, the exit door was held open for a mom pushing her son in his wheelchair. His skin was extremely pale. It seemed like it took all the energy he had just to draw his breath. His mother looked as if she needed the wheelchair as much as her son did. I felt an emotional bond with her that came as a result of sharing familiar, sad experiences. I smiled at another momma with a child battling cancer. I didn't have sympathy, a feeling of sorrow for her; I had empathy. I truly shared her grief, because I walked a similar path.

A vast difference stretches between sympathy and empathy. Both are based on compassion and imply genuine concern for another. But with empathy, you feel the weight of what the other person is enduring, because you've been through it, or something like it, yourself.

Daily, we face pressures in life. Many are in the form of desires that go against God's will. Giving into those urges is sin. Jesus was tempted, yet He never sinned. On the other hand, because the Lord knows firsthand what it's like to be tempted to lie, to cheat, and to disobey, He can empathize with us in our struggles. And since He resisted temptation and chose to do the right thing, we can too.

How can you empathize with someone who doesn't know Jesus?

Lean on Thee

"The eternal God is your refuge,
and his everlasting arms are under you."
DEUTERONOMY 33:27 NLT

When my children were close to walking on their own, they leaned heavily on me for balance. They'd hold onto my arm for stability, and I would lead them. Eventually, Caroline, Daniel, and Harrison each built up confidence enough to balance themselves and walk confidently across the room. But when it comes to their spiritual lives, I pray they'll never stop leaning on the Lord and the biblical truths their dad and I have taught.

In his book on the life of King David, Chuck Swindoll explains that every person is "built to be a leaner."[5] But he warns about the danger of leaning on other people, other things, or even ourselves, rather than the Lord. In Proverbs 3:5–6, God's Word reminds us, "Trust in the Lord with all your heart, and lean not on your own understanding; in all your ways acknowledge Him, and He shall direct your paths" (NKJV). When we are small, we naturally and rightly lean on our parents. As we grow, however, we must learn to lean on the Lord Jesus Christ. He's the only Friend who will never fail us or let us fall.

What is one way you can "lean" on the Lord?

---

5 Charles R. Swindoll, *A Man of Passion & Destiny: David* (Nashville, TN: W Publishing Group, 1997), 70.

Fruit Filled

The fruit of the Spirit is love, joy, peace, patience, kindness,
goodness, faithfulness, gentleness, self-control.
GALATIANS 5:22–23 ESV

Have you ever noticed how several days of bad weather or hearing negative stories on the news can make people cranky? Have you watched a friend's attitude sour when she feels like she's having a bad hair day? It's easy to let minor things push us toward feeling anxious or blue. That's a big problem, because life is full of opportunities that hold the potential to bring out our worst.

Sometimes, life hurts and everything seems to be falling apart. Psalm 75:3 says, "When the earth quakes and its people live in turmoil, I am the one who keeps its foundations firm" (NLT). God doesn't say *if* the earthquakes come or *if* people will go through days of confusion. He says *when* they do. Why? Because of Adam's sin we live in a broken world. But Jesus is our hope: "In this world you will have trouble. But take heart! I have overcome the world" (John 16:33).

In Ephesians 5:18, Paul reminds Christians to "be filled with the Spirit." That means instead of focusing on the negative, we should ask Jesus to fill us with the good things that come from His Spirit. As Christians, we can pray that the Holy Spirit will flow through us even when we are shaken by the annoyances of this world, allowing His love, joy, peace, patience, kindness, goodness, faithfulness, gentleness, and self-control to characterize us.

Would you rather be surrounded by people living by the Spirit or living in anxiety? Why?

Real "Selfie"

*Then Jesus declared, "I,
the one speaking to you—I am he."*

JOHN 4:26

Recently, Oxford Dictionary's word of the year was *selfie*, defined as "a photograph that one has taken of oneself, typically with a smartphone or webcam and uploaded to a social media website." It's part of God's plan that Jesus walked the earth before cell phones. Can you imagine the chaos of all those people wanting to pose for a "selfie" with Jesus?

I've been to events where celebrities were present. Often, few people really want to talk to them; they'd rather have a picture taken with them so they can publicize their encounter. What would have happened if the woman at the well had a camera? She might have missed Jesus' message—God in the flesh—as He looked into her soul. Thankfully, because she focused on Him, she left that face-to-face encounter a transformed woman, a child of God.

When I choose to let my self-centeredness, self-pity, self-promotion, or self-reliance distract me from focusing on the One who loves me most and has the best in store for my life, I am being selfish. That "selfie" attitude inevitably leads to restlessness, frustration, fear, insecurity, and discouragement—giving ugly snapshots of what's going on in my heart. However, when I make time to really talk to Jesus and to read His Word, my focus changes. I stop caring so much about me, and I start honoring Him for who He is. Now, that's a picture worth posting.

What is one thing you can do to help you focus on Jesus this week?

Mission Possible

"All things are possible with God."

MARK 10:27

When Nehemiah received word that the walls surrounding his homeland were in ruins and that his people were in trouble, he was surely tempted to think that trying to do anything about it would prove an impossible mission. But Nehemiah fasted and prayed. He knew Israel's only hope was in the Lord's help, and in his own willingness to follow God's orders as His faithful servant.

A few days later, Nehemiah was in the presence of the Persian king. Nehemiah served as his cupbearer, someone who tasted the king's food and drink before he ate to make certain one of his enemies hadn't tried to poison him. When the king noticed Nehemiah's sadness, he wanted to know what was wrong. So Nehemiah explained his concerns and said he wanted to help. "Then, go," the king commanded, sending Nehemiah to Judea with royal requests for protection and building supplies.

Nehemiah journeyed to Jerusalem and—incredibly—he led the inhabitants there to rebuild the wall in only fifty-two days! The mission was accomplished so well, in fact, that Nehemiah's enemies, who'd bullied workers during their rebuilding project, were "frightened and humiliated" when they saw what the Lord had done through His people (Nehemiah 6:16 NLT).

Perhaps God is stirring your heart to take on what may seem like an impossible mission. Like Nehemiah, pray before you plan, and remember: "With God, all things [really] are possible."

Talk about a time when you have faced a big problem and chosen to focus on our big God.

Guess Who's Coming to Dinner

[Jesus] looked up at Zacchaeus and called him by name!
"Zacchaeus!" he said. "Quick! Come down!
For I am going to be a guest in your home today!"
LUKE 19:5 TLB

At 5'6", basketball player Spud Webb prayed nightly that God would make him tall. Each morning he found his size hadn't changed. Finally, Webb asked, "Lord, if you're not going to make me bigger on the outside, please make me bigger on the inside." In time, Webb, described by one sports writer as "a sapling in a forest of sequoias," went on to win a college scholarship and eventually became a powerhouse in the NBA. He's most famous for winning a slam dunk contest against six-foot-eight Dominique Wilkins.

Like Webb, Luke 19 suggests the tax collector Zacchaeus was "small in stature." But Zacchaeus didn't seem upset that God made him small. Instead, he used his size to his advantage. He wanted to see Jesus so much that he climbed a tree so he could see over the pressing crowds welcoming Christ into Jerusalem. When the Creator saw His child Zacchaeus, He called him by name.

You may feel small and unnoticed, but Jesus sees you and knows your name too. When Jesus called out to Zacchaeus, the Bible says, "He hurried and came down and received Him joyfully" (Luke 19:6 ESV). Jesus desires to make a difference in your day today too—no matter your size. Don't miss out on His invitation to do something big in your life.

What would you like to see Jesus do through you?

Face the Book

Draw near to God and He will draw near to you.
JAMES 4:8 NASB

Every day, Americans spend 4.4 hours on screen time, entertaining themselves with TV, computers, tablets, or smartphones.[6] For many people, this time is like a drug used to cover up their sense of isolation and lack of purpose. This habit may make us feel good for a while, but it doesn't provide any lasting value. In truth, it isolates us from those we love and keeps us from using that time to mature and grow in God's ways.

Psalm 1:1–2 says, "Blessed is the one … whose delight is in the law of the Lord, and who meditates on His law day and night." When we use our free time to grow, by delighting in the Word of God and obeying what He says, there is victory over loneliness and bad habits. Psalm 1:3 describes the person who reads, and thinks about, God's Word as "a tree planted by streams of water, which yields its fruit in season and whose leaf does not wither—whatever they do prospers."

Is it time you cut back on your screen time? Instead, you could use that time to focus on God's Word—maybe even memorize a new verse. Perhaps you'd like to set the amount of time spent in front of all screens, whether a computer monitor, handheld device, or television, to one hour a day. If you need help sticking to a time limit, ask a parent to hold you accountable.

Discuss how you think Jesus might feel when you choose entertainment over spending time with Him.

---

6 Cara Pring, "216 Social Media and Internet Statistics (September 2012)," http://thesocialskinny.com/216-social-media-and-internet-statistics-september-2012/.

Free Build

*This Jesus is the stone that was rejected by you, the builders,
which has become the cornerstone.*

ACTS 4:11 ESV

Back in the days when the Bible was written, stones served as the chief construction material for a wall or a building. The cornerstone was the most important of these, because it was the largest and strongest. It held all of the other stones up. Without that foundation piece, the other stones lacked the stability to stand together as a sound structure.

The Bible talks a lot about building and about stones. In fact, the book of Acts explains the relationship between Christ, called the "Cornerstone," and the church, made up of individuals who believe in Him and are described as "living stones." My toddler and I built a tower of blocks one day. We observed that when I carefully removed blocks from the top of the tower, it remained standing. But when I took away blocks at the base of our structure, the entire tower crashed to the ground. When this happened, my daughter Harrison frowned and said, "Uh-oh, Mommy!"

Uh-oh is right. The world will lie to you and try to get you to think you can build your life on being liked by others, excelling at sports, or making good grades in school. But if we try to build our lives without Jesus as the cornerstone of our foundation, we'll be a toppled-over tower, unable to stand.

Can you think of anything else you're building your life on other than Jesus?

The Simple Life

"Unless you turn to God from your sins and become as little children, you will never get into the Kingdom of Heaven."
MATTHEW 18:3 TLB

Many people think following God is about earning points by doing good things or gaining a great reputation. But Jesus taught that no one can get into heaven through their own effort or because of the applause of others. Instead, we come to God by turning away from our sin and turning to Christ in faith. How do we become great? Jesus said that being as honest and humble as a little child and trusting what God says, are what really count.

In Hans Christian Anderson's "The Emperor's New Clothes," an emperor is approached by two thieves claiming to be tailors. "Our cloth is so wonderful," the con men claim, "that it will be invisible to anyone who's dumb or unfit for his position in the kingdom. Every ruler needs one of our suits."

The emperor hires the tricksters immediately, and when he sees nothing on the tailor's looms, he remains silent—not wanting to appear unworthy. When the suit is finished, every adult in the kingdom applauds the king's invisible clothes as he parades down Main Street. After all, who wants to appear dumb? But then a little child blurts out the truth: "He hasn't got anything on!"

Children are usually open-minded, honest, and not readily swayed by what others think. They trust in King Jesus, not trying to earn His love but accepting it as the gift it is. This is the childlike faith Jesus wants us to have.

How can you have a childlike point of view on something you are dealing with today?

Dandelion Dilemma

"I tell you, on the day of judgment people will give account for every careless word they speak."

MATTHEW 12:36 ESV

Dandelions are fluff balls of fun in springtime. Blowing on them and watching their little seeds spread across the neighborhood can be a source of entertainment. What I didn't know about the dandelion when I was little is that it's a pesky weed. Millions of dollars are invested annually by homeowners hoping to eliminate dandelions from their lawns. Although the dandelion, when grown, produces a beautiful little yellow flower, looks can be deceiving. The tap root of the dandelion can grow 2–3 feet deep, strangling the growth of healthy grass and trees.

The dandelion reminds me of one of my favorite VeggieTales® videos, *LarryBoy and the Rumor Weed*. Bumblyburg becomes infested by a large group of rumor-spreading weeds. Roads are torn up. Houses are destroyed. The more Bumblyburgers talk badly about each other, the stronger and more powerful the rumor weed's hold on the city.

Our words can be like those weeds. Jesus says we are going to have to stand before Him and admit to each one. We can disguise our gossip. But just like the pretty little yellow flower of the dandelion, we know what it is underneath—a destroyer. The Bible warns against unwise words in Proverbs 16:28: "A troublemaker plants seeds of strife; gossip separates the best of friends" (NLT).

What is a "seed" of gossip you wish you hadn't spread? Is there anything you need to do set things right?

Me, Myself, and You

*"In everything, therefore, treat people
the same way you want them to treat you."*
Matthew 7:12 NASB

If you've seen the movie *Finding Nemo*, you'll recall the chorus the seagulls chant: "Mine! Mine! Mine! Mine!" Despite who or what was before them, these birdbrains thought only of what they wanted, disregarding the feelings of everybody around them.

Jesus teaches us something pretty radical in His "Golden Rule" of Matthew 7:12. "Mine, mine" is not a chant Christ's followers should sing. Instead, we should think of the needs of others.

Let's say your buddy on the football team fumbles the ball, forcing a turnover and, ultimately, your team's loss in the championship game. Put yourself in his cleats and think of how you can encourage him. When you're invited to a birthday party, don't give the gift you'd like to receive. Rather, think of something that person would want and give them that special gift. If your sister's notebook runs out of paper, surprise her by cheerfully sharing some of yours. Plus a few sheets more.

True friendship means knowing what other people need and giving it to them when they need it most.

What "gift" can you give to a friend who is in need?

No Other Option

*"Abba, Father! All things are possible for You.
Take this cup away from Me. Nevertheless,
not what I will, but what You will."*

MARK 14:36 HCSB

One of the most common causes for traffic accidents is the failure to yield the right of way. When a driver doesn't yield, that means he does not slow down, move over, or stop for anyone else. He demands his own way.

Jesus lived for no other reason than to yield to the will of His Father. The "cup" Jesus refers to in Mark 14:36 was His fast-approaching death. Jesus was fully God, but He was also fully human. He did not want to endure the pain of being separated from His heavenly Father because of the sins of the world He would bear on our behalf. Yet, our Savior, because of His great love for us, chose to do His Father's will and not His own. So we could live, Jesus would have to die.

Many times God asks us to do things in life that are not easy. It takes courage to bow to pray before your meal in the cafeteria before eating your lunch. It takes a champion not to buy a ticket to the movie you know would not please the Lord. But every time we choose to yield to God's will in our lives, He rewards our faithfulness by accomplishing something bigger in our lives and in the lives of others than we can see.

Share a recent example of when you yielded to God's will by choosing to do something you knew would please Him when you wanted to do something else.

FEBRUARY

Jesus Loves the Little Children

"Let the children come to me."
MATTHEW 19:14 NLT

Research by Barna Group suggests that by age thirteen most people know what they believe about the Bible and have decided what they believe about Jesus. So how does Jesus feel about His youngest followers?

One of my most vivid childhood memories is of Sunday visits to my grandparents' church. Behind the pulpit where the preacher preached and the loft where the choir sang was a huge stained glass window of a smiling Jesus on a grassy hillside surrounded by children. His hands were placed on their little heads, signaling their special place in God's heart. Since my parents taught me about Jesus and the truth of His Word on a daily basis, I'd often picture myself as one of those children, getting a big grin and hug from Jesus after running down that hill with Him. I'd be the one sitting on His lap, wrapped in His strong arms, eager to hear another story.

Jesus invites even the smallest of us to "come." I don't know about you, but when I get an invitation in the mail for a party, it makes me feel warm inside. That person cares about including me. We don't always get that party invitation we're hoping for. But guess what? The King of the universe, the Creator of the stars and galaxies daily asks you, His special creation, to be His friend and get to know Him a little better today.

Why do you think the opportunity to be God's friend is the best invitation of all?

Know Pain, Know Gain

*Let perseverance finish its work
so that you may be mature and complete.*

JAMES 1:4

A man watched a moth's cocoon. As the creature's process of metamorphosis progressed, the moth inside struggled to push its body through a small hole in the silk. After hours of great effort, the moth stilled.

Using a pair of scissors, the man snipped open the remaining bit of cocoon to reward the creature for his perseverance. He felt sorry for him in his long battle. But the man didn't realize that the struggle out of a cocoon forces fluid from the creature's body and into the wings to make it flight ready. So out fell the moth—body swollen and wings shriveled. Without completing the struggle God designed for its benefit, the moth could never fly. He could never mature as he should.

We too need struggles. They refine our faith and help us grow spiritually. First Peter 5:10 promises that "after you have suffered a little while, [God] will Himself restore you and make you strong, firm and steadfast." So if you find yourself in the midst of struggle, don't look for a shortcut. Allow God to use your difficulties as a tool to refine you. Ask Him to help you persevere, so that one day you might soar.

What struggle has God used in your life to help make you stronger?

No "I" in Team

You are all one in Christ Jesus.
GALATIANS 3:28 NLT

On this date in 2002, the New England Patriots surprised thousands of football fans by beating the favored St. Louis Rams by a field goal in Super Bowl XXXVI. It was the first Super Bowl victory for New England, but it made the history books for another reason too.

Prior to this, the Super Bowl was the only game of the year when each team's individual starters, for both the offense and defense, were introduced. This gave each player a moment in the spotlight at one of the world's most watched events. However, Coach Bill Belichick thought the New England Patriots would play better without this individual emphasis.

Before the game, he asked NFL officials if his players could be announced all together, as a team. His idea and their decision helped the teammates play with unity. Instead of thinking about how each individual could build up his own name, they concentrated on how they could defeat the opposition—together.

All who confess their sins before God and believe Jesus took their punishment when He died on the cross have a shared bond. We're a team whose goal is to bring honor to the name of Jesus. Each day we should trade our individual hope to be the center of attention for an attitude that puts Christ in the spotlight and chooses to respect our fellow Christians as teammates.

Share a positive experience you've had working as a team with others who follow Jesus.

Follow the Yellow Brick Road

"Enter through the narrow gate;
for the gate is wide and the way is broad
that leads to destruction. …
The gate is small and the way is narrow
that leads to life, and there are few who find it."

MATTHEW 7:13–14 NASB

Dorothy Gale, her little dog Toto, and their newfound friends follow the yellow brick road to get to the Wizard of Oz, who may be able to get Dorothy back home to Kansas. In the original story, the group gets off the path and ends up lost, surrounded by deadly poppies. They finally reach Oz, but the detour proves costly.

Staying on the right road in life is important. Throughout the Bible, many people messed up by heading down a path other than the one God had directed them to follow. In Jonah 1:3, we're told, "Jonah ran away from the Lord and headed for Tarshish. He went down to Joppa." Samson, a man with tremendous physical strength, went "down to Timnah" (Judges 14:1), away from where the Lord wanted him to go. Anytime we walk in disobedience to God, we can anticipate trouble ahead.

In contrast, after Jesus transformed Paul from a murderer, he was instructed to get up and go to Straight Street. There he became a missionary. Paul did exactly what Jesus told him to do. When we make a choice to live for Jesus, we're on the straight street, too. Our path may not be a road of yellow bricks, but one day we will walk on streets of gold!

Share how the Bible can be a road map to help you stay on the road God's chosen for your life.

Light for a Dark World

"I have come as a light into the world, that whoever believes in Me should not abide in darkness."

JOHN 12:46 NKJV

Just as the sun brings light to our days, Jesus, God's Son, brings light to our hearts. And just as certainly as the moon reflects the sun's radiance, you and I are meant to reflect His. Christ's love at work within us should shine like a moon in our sin-darkened world, ever pointing people to the greater light of Jesus.

Importantly, the moon does not generate any light of its own. Its glow is actually the result of the sun reflecting off the moon's surface. But if you pay attention to the night sky, you'll notice that some days we can see a full moon and other times it practically disappears as the earth moves between the sun and moon—leaving the world in shadows.

You and I should constantly reflect the Savior's love. But sometimes, we can be just as unhelpful as that darkened moon. We let other things get between us and God. When we get impatient, moody, lazy, worried, or jealous, we flat out fail to shine. Jesus wants us to confess our sin daily to Him so there is nothing blocking His brilliance in us: "For God who said, 'Let light shine out of darkness,' has shone in our hearts to give the light of the knowledge of God's glory in the face of Jesus Christ" (2 Corinthians 4:6 HCSB).

What can you do to reflect the light of God's love today?

Cheater in Church?

*"You are the ones who justify yourselves
in the eyes of others, but God knows your hearts."*
LUKE 16:15

Jesus tells a story about two men from very different walks of life. One was a religious man. The other was not. They both went to the temple to pray. The nonreligious man—likely a fellow who spent little time at the temple—fell to his knees in a quiet corner, crying and humbly confessing his sins: "God, have mercy on me, a sinner" (Luke 18:13). In contrast, the religious man—who probably never missed services—stood up, bowed his head proudly, and loudly listed all of the good things he'd done for God that week, so everyone nearby could hear. He even pointed out the nonreligious man in the corner and said, "Lord, I'm better than *that* guy!"

The religious man proves that just going to church doesn't make you a Christian and reminds us that Satan is behind every cheat. He wants us to think that if we pray louder and longer than anyone else, become a leader in youth group, go to church more often, or serve hot meals to the homeless, we can earn more gold stars with God. "You're okay," Satan tells us. "You aren't that bad. God's lucky to have you!" Then, he encourages us to compare ourselves favorably to everyone else. Listening to all of these lies leads us to take our eyes off Jesus and focus on what others think. In the end, it's what God thinks about us that matters.

Why is it important to keep God's gifts of grace and forgiveness in mind when we attend church?

Rebirth Certificate

"I tell you, no one can see the kingdom of God unless they are born again."

JOHN 3:3

Your arrival was so important that the government documented the exact day, hour, minute, and place that you left the comfort of your mother's womb to make your entrance into the world. Births are noteworthy occasions. Even more so are spiritual rebirths.

Nicodemus got a lesson about being born again when he approached Jesus at night to learn more about His teaching. Nick was a Pharisee, a member of a group of religious leaders that wanted Jesus dead, but something in his heart was drawn to Jesus. He paid attention when Jesus said, "You must be born again to be a part of God's kingdom." That's the only way, Nick learned, that people can receive spiritual rebirth certificates, so they can enjoy God's forgiveness and favor, and one day live with Him in heaven.

But at first Nick was confused. He'd long thought the good works he was doing made him a member of God's kingdom, a person who had God's approval. But Jesus explained that no one enters heaven based on being good. Instead, people receive eternal life—spiritual rebirth— only by believing in Him, the One God sent (John 3:16).

Just like Nick, you can receive rebirth by accepting God's free gift of forgiveness from your sins through the blood of Jesus. As soon as you do, your spiritual rebirth is recorded forever in the Lamb's Book of Life (Revelation 3:5).

What's the difference between physical birth and spiritual rebirth?

The Box

"On the outside you seem righteous to people,
but inside you are full of hypocrisy and lawlessness."
MATTHEW 23:28 HCSB

Our family hosts Backyard Bible Club at our home. One day, I surprised the neighborhood children in attendance with a huge box, beautifully wrapped with the finest wrapping paper and ribbon. I asked for a volunteer to open the box and many hands went up. The children could hardly wait for the mystery to be revealed.

Imagine their disappointment when inside the beautiful package they found four-day-old garbage: rotten bananas, tomatoes, dried orange peels, coffee grinds, mushy apples, moldy cheese, and sour milk. It smelled as bad as it looked. A wave of disappointment crashed over the crowd.

Until we know Jesus, we're like that pretty package filled with trash. Our hearts are sinful and rebellious toward God. He wants us to admit the bad things we've done and come to Him to be made clean and fresh. We may be able to fool some people for a little while, but we cannot hide anything from His eyes. He even says that if we think we've never done anything to break His rules, "we deceive ourselves and the truth is not in us" (1 John 1:8).

Thankfully, when we're honest about who we are and what we've done, "[Jesus] is faithful and just and will forgive us our sins and purify us from all unrighteousness" (1 John 1:9). He removes the trash and fills us with His unspoiled fruit.

Next time you take out the trash, think about how you're going to remain pure in Christ.

The Lamb's Book of Life

*Nothing evil will be permitted in [heaven]—
no one immoral or dishonest—but only those whose
names are written in the Lamb's Book of Life.*

REVELATION 21:27 TLB

When I worked as personal assistant to the First Lady of South Carolina, my office was in the Governor's Mansion. I had to drive through a large security gate with guards who'd check to make certain my name was approved and the first family knew I was coming. I was a friend of the governor, so my name was on the list.

The moment we agree with God that we've broken His rules and invite Him into our hearts as our Savior and Lord, we're approved too. Our names are then written on the most important list of all: the Lamb's Book of Life.

Throughout Scripture, Jesus is referred to as the Lamb, an animal that was often used as a sacrifice to cover the sins of God's people. John the Baptist said of Jesus, "Behold, the Lamb of God, who takes away the sin of the world!" (John 1:29 ESV). That's because God made Jesus to be the perfect sacrifice for the world's sins. When God looks at us and sees we've accepted the truth about why Jesus' blood was shed, we're safe. We're assured a spot in heaven—the beautiful home He's created for all who trust Him. In John 17:24 Jesus says, "Father, I want those you have given me to be with me where I am." Once we receive God's free gift of salvation, our names are never removed from His book.

Discuss how easy it is to reserve your place in heaven and get your name in the Lamb's Book of Life.

Blue Light Special

Nothing in all creation is hidden from God's sight.
Everything is uncovered and laid bare before the eyes
of him to whom we must give account.

HEBREWS 4:13

Police officers have a clever way of enforcing the speed limits in our city. Occasionally, they'll position police cars in neighborhoods. Drivers hit their brakes when they come around a corner and see the patrol car. But what a nice surprise it is to discover there's no one in the car: it's empty. The joy this practice gives speeders is a false sense of security, because they're not getting "caught."

What's interesting in this new strategy of our local law enforcement officials is that it provides a visual reminder of the existing law. How differently we behave when we think the police are watching. Jesus is always watching. He warns us in Proverbs 16:18 "Pride leads to destruction. A proud attitude brings ruin" (ICB). Often we think, *Oh, I can get away with this little sin. Nothing bad will ever happen to me*. That may work if we only consider the world's opinion. But it never truly "works."

Our heavenly Father sees and will hold us accountable. Not only that, but the first compromise only paves the way for bigger mistakes. Consider your life as front-page news and seek to have a headline you would be proud to have Jesus read.

Share a recent news story that you think might have ended differently if the people involved knew Jesus was watching.

To Tell the Truth

Pilate said to him, "What is truth?"
JOHN 18:38 ESV

The television game show *To Tell the Truth* featured celebrity judges trying to correctly identify the contestant who had an unusual job or life experience. The twist was that while one of the contestants was sworn to tell the truth, two impostors tried to fool the panelists with lies. In the end, each member of the panel voted on who they thought was the truth-teller. Then, the host would say to the three contestants, for instance, "Will the real circus performer please stand up?"

The Roman governor, Pilate, wanted to know the truth about Jesus. He interviewed Jesus shortly before His death and tried to determine whether he believed Christ's claims about being God's Son. In the end, Pilate said, "I find no basis for a charge against him" (John 18:38). In other words, he was at least open to the possibility that Jesus' words were true. But instead of inviting "the way and the truth and the life" (John 14:6) into his heart, and working to set an innocent man free, Pilate put more value on his own approval rating. In doing so, he ensured Jesus' death.

We must be careful to recognize and honor the truth of Christ's claims. Jesus is God and God can never lie. He can only say what is true because He is absolutely holy and perfect. When God says it, that settles it.

What do you think Jesus meant by, "I am the truth"?

Beware of Self-Importance

*If anyone thinks that he is important when he
is really not important, he is only fooling himself.*

GALATIANS 6:3 ICB

Self-importance, thinking everything will fall apart without your oversight, robs you of peace and stands in the way of what God wants to accomplish. I experienced this firsthand, shortly after Daniel's cancer diagnosis. The phone was ringing off the hook with offers of help. But my Mom overheard me decline assistance from all callers. Finally, she scolded, "Tara, you want to look like you have it all together and you don't. You are letting pride rob people of their ability to share their gifts of service." I soon discovered how right she was. As I allowed people to bring meals and help bear our family's load, our week got a lot more restful. It also reminded me that the Lord was still in charge.

Moses too wore himself out thinking he could be everything to everybody, when his father-in-law, Jethro, finally asked why. Moses insisted everyone needed him, but Jethro lovingly taught Moses the importance of letting others help (Exodus 18:13–24).

Pretending we have it all together when, in fact, we feel like we're drowning in stress is a sign that self-importance has crept into our lives. So we need to be willing to ask for and accept help. By letting others partner with us, we'll be more likely to remember who is really in charge.

How can you avoid letting self-importance take control in your life?

Extreme Makeover

If anyone is in Christ, he is a new creation.
The old has passed away; behold, the new has come.
2 CORINTHIANS 5:17 ESV

After buying their lake house, Tom and Cindy took us on a tour to show us the property. The view was spectacular, but the house was old and falling apart. It had been empty for years—maybe even decades—and the needed repairs were obvious. There were broken windows, uneven floors, a caved-in ceiling, and doors hanging off their hinges. Lee and I looked at each other with concern. Both of us felt tired just thinking about the amount of work there was to be done. Then, our friends explained they weren't planning to repair the house. They were going to tear it down and construct a whole new home.

Similarly, when you give your heart to Jesus, He removes the old and builds something new. Psalm 103:12 tells us that God "has removed our sins as far away from us as the east is from the west" (TLB). How far is the east from the west? So far that they can never touch each other. Thanks to Jesus, all of your bad choices, mistakes, and regrets can no longer touch you. This means you are not just repaired, renovated, and redecorated. You are recreated into a brand-new you! Your sins are forgiven and you have a bright future with Jesus.

Why is it better to be a new creation than an old one that's been fixed up to look like new?

God's Valentine

This is love: not that we loved God,
but that he loved us and sent his Son
as an atoning sacrifice for our sins.

1 JOHN 4:10

For many, today is not a day of candy hearts and glossy Valentines. Some have been hurt by the death of a family member, by disease, or by the fallout that comes when loved ones turn their back on God. But when we trust Jesus as our Savior and obey what He says in His Word, we have His assurance that He's working everything out for something better than we can see at the moment—even when things are sad. May our hearts be so filled by God's love that when things do not work out the way we desire or plan, our trust will be in the One whose plan is perfect.

While the love notes written by human hands this Valentine's Day will eventually fall apart or fade away, the love letter of God's Word never will. In Isaiah 49:16 God says, "See, I have engraved you on the palms of My hands." His love for us never fades or fails. Victor Hugo wrote, "The greatest happiness in life is the conviction that we are loved—loved for ourselves, or rather, loved in spite of ourselves." Valentine's Day is among my favorite holidays because it's a time to reflect on the Lover of my soul. I am God's Valentine! And so are you!

If you were to send God a Valentine's Day card, what would it say?

The Sun's Bully

What then shall we say to these things?
If God is for us, who can be against us?
ROMANS 8:31 ESV

The morning was overcast and dreary. In my rearview mirror, I noticed Daniel's head tilting up toward the sky. "Mommy," he asked, "have you ever thought how the clouds are the sun's bullies?"

"No, sweetheart, I haven't," I replied. "But isn't it comforting to know even when we cannot see the sun, it still shines? The sun *always* wins."

In life, storm clouds are always on the horizon. We get a bad grade on a test we thought we did well on. Dad gets fired. We catch the flu and miss an important game. Our best friend moves away.

But we need these cloudy days to keep our faith fit. If everything goes our way all the time, we'd most likely be centered on ourselves and not on our Savior. Psalm 121:2 is a good reminder: "My help comes from the Lord, who made heaven and earth" (ESV). Even though we may not see the Lord during those gray days, the fact is He is there and He sees us. We delight Him most when we choose to march by faith in the rain—beneath the rainbow—knowing He loves us and has His best in store for us. Remember, the Son always wins.

Talk about a time when life felt like a dark, stormy day, but knowing God made it brighter.

Word Power

When the Lord saw her,
his heart went out to her and he said, "Don't cry."
LUKE 7:13

A man sat on a busy street corner holding a sign that read, *I'm blind. Please help.* The tin cup in his hands held only a few pennies and dimes from the busy passersby. About midmorning, he heard the *click-click* of high heels stop next to him. He caught a whiff of sweet perfume as a woman gently pulled the cardboard from his hands, explaining that she had no cash to give, but wanted to use her skills in marketing to help him. He heard rapid scribbling, and then the sign was placed back into his grip. She left as quickly as she came.

In no time at all, the man's tin grew heavy with donations. Dollar bills were being stuffed into his pockets. Three businessmen offered to buy him lunch, and a little girl and her mother brought him a milkshake.

A little while later, the beggar noticed a familiar scent as the woman returned and knelt at his side. "What did you write on my sign?" he asked. "It's a beautiful day," she whispered. "Wish I could see it."

We please Jesus when, like this thoughtful woman, we take time to notice the needs around us, to imagine ourselves in the place of a person in need, and then use the unique gifts Jesus has given us to do something to help.

Think of a specific person in your neighborhood who could use a hand. What special way has God equipped you to help?

The Real Superhero

The Lord is my strength and shield. I trust him will all my heart.
He helps me, and my heart is filled with joy.

PSALM 28:7 NLT

I ron Man, Hulk, Thor, and my favorite, Captain America, are all agents of S.H.I.E.L.D., a band of superheroes protecting earth and its inhabitants against evil villains. Though these characters are make-believe, there's one true Superhero and His name is Jesus. He's our Savior and shield of protection.

David was just a young shepherd boy when he volunteered to take on Goliath, a nine-foot giant of a man who mocked God and all who worshiped Him. Rather than run away from Goliath's taunts and threats, David stood upon the promises of what God was going to do through him: "All those gathered here will know that it is not by sword or spear that the Lord saves; for the battle is the Lord's, and He will give all of you into our hands" (1 Samuel 17:47).

Every day we're in a battle. Our sinful nature shouts like the giant Goliath to cheat on that test, lie to our parents, compromise in our conviction about doing what is right. However, just like David, we can take up our shield of faith (Ephesians 6:16), which means putting our complete trust in the Lord Jesus' protection. Anytime we choose to put our trust in anyone else, whether it be Captain Cool or Captain America, we're always going to be disappointed. Our true Superhero, Jesus, will never let us down.

What do you need to put down before you can fully pick up the shield of faith?

Speak Life

Do not let any unwholesome talk come out of your mouths,
but only what is helpful for building others up according
to their needs, that it may benefit those who listen.

EPHESIANS 4:29

Skinny!" "Crooked nose!" "Buck teeth!" "Freckle face!"
The children on my school playground could be cruel
in what they said to me. Even though I'd reply, "Sticks and
stones may break my bones, but words can never hurt me!"
I didn't mean it. Their words wounded me.

At home, I'd stand in front of the mirror studying my face,
convincing myself that what I'd heard was true. And I'd cry.
Thankfully, my parents led me to the Bible. There, I learned
to replace lies about myself with God's truth. For instance,
Psalm 139:14 says, "I have been remarkably and wonder-
fully made" (HCSB).

Getting into the bad habit of criticizing, cursing, or
speaking disrespectfully clashes with the way Jesus wants us
to speak. He was known for the pleasant words He shared.
Luke 4:22 reports, "All … spoke well of [Jesus] and were
amazed by the beautiful words that fell from his lips" (TLB).
When we carefully choose the words we use, people are
drawn to us—and they'll be more willing to listen when we
share how they too can belong to our Lord.

Think of someone you may have offended recently with
your words. How can you speak life (say something good
and true) to that person this week?

The Hole in My Bucket

*"Sir," said the woman, "You don't even have a bucket,
and the well is deep. So where do You get
this 'living water'?"*

JOHN 4:11 HCSB

Jesus offered "living water" to the woman at the well. And He promises this same abundant and eternal life ("living water") to all who will place faith in Him. But oftentimes people think real living comes not through faith in Jesus but as a result of what they accomplish. As long as we hold onto that misunderstanding, there will be a hole in our lives that will keep us from experiencing all the Lord offers.

In the song, "There's a Hole in the Bucket," Henry's bucket has a hole and his friend, Liza, tries to tell him how to repair it. But, by the time Liza's finished sharing her idea for fixing the bucket, she acknowledges that Henry will first need to draw water from the well before he can put the repair plan into action. The situation seems hopeless.

Like Henry's leaky bucket, we're born with a hole in our lives. While the world, like Liza, offers suggestions such as becoming more popular, getting money, winning beauty pageants, finding a boyfriend or girlfriend, or making the honor roll as ways to fix it, these methods will leave us empty. It is only when we make Jesus our Savior and Lord that He plugs that hole in our hearts once and for all so He can fill us to overflowing with His living water.

Share one way you've tried to fill that empty place in your heart with something other than Jesus.

One Out of Ten

Then one of them, when he saw that he was healed, turned back, praising God with a loud voice; and he fell on his face at Jesus' feet, giving him thanks.

LUKE 17:15–16 ESV

Ten men were living in isolation, meaning they couldn't live in comfortable houses with their families or friends who loved them. They had a contagious disease called leprosy; it marked their skin with painful spots and sores.

One day these men saw Jesus, the Great Physician, in the distance. They cried out to Him for healing, and He stopped. Jesus told them to go show themselves to the priests, who would see the men weren't sick anymore. Right away, the ten men trusted what Jesus told them to do—even before they saw their spots disappear. By the time they arrived at the temple, their bodies showed no evidence of the disease. Giving each other high fives, they celebrated the miracle of being healed. Then, nine of the ten hurried off to reunite with their families and friends. Only one man sprinted back to Jesus to say thank you!

Not a day goes by that Jesus doesn't do great things for each of us. He provides us with the food we eat, the places we rest our heads, our pets, our toys, the air we breathe, and, greatest of all, healing from the dark spots on our hearts caused by sin. It makes the Lord glad when we give thanks to Him too.

Name three things you can thank Jesus for right now. Then, take time to thank Him.

A Little Boy's Lunch

*"Here is a boy with five small barley loaves
and two small fish, but how far will
they go among so many?"*

JOHN 6:9

Have you ever been so excited you forgot to eat? That's exactly what happened to over five thousand people who followed Jesus up a mountainside to hear Him teach. They were in such awe of Him they didn't even notice their hunger, until the sun started to set. In that day, there were no restaurants along their paths toward home. The disciples worried that the people might faint from hunger on their way down the mountain in the dark. But what could be done?

One little boy, his stomach probably growling, decided to help. He gave Jesus the basket of food he'd brought from home that day. While Jesus could have simply taken the food for Himself or just shared it with the boy, He decided to work a miracle through a child's generosity.[1] He told the disciples to have everyone sit down. Then, after thanking His heavenly Father for making the food they were about to eat—and for the little boy's unselfish heart—Jesus divided up the bread and the fish. Miraculously, that one meal multiplied to feed the masses!

Anytime we choose to put anything into the hands of Jesus, we give it to the Miracle Worker. Our hearts, our hurts. Our time, our talents. When we give Jesus all we've got, He takes even our "little" and makes a lot.

What's something you can trust Jesus with that you've been holding on to? How might He use it to bless others?

---

1 *Favorite Bible Stories 2* (Pensacola, FL: A Beka Book, 2005).

The Leftovers

They all ate and were satisfied,
and the disciples picked up twelve basketfuls
of broken pieces that were left over.

LUKE 9:17

Reheated spaghetti from the weekend. Odds and ends from a meal eaten last night. None of that sounds very appetizing to me, but it's often on the menu. If I'm honest, I'm not much for leftovers—unless they come from the hand of the Master Chef.

In yesterday's reading, we talked about Jesus feeding over five thousand people. This story is recorded in all four gospels. After Jesus hears His disciples' concern over what the huge crowd is going to eat for supper, Jesus tells the Twelve, "You give them something to eat" (Luke 9:13). Puzzled, the doubting dozen holds up what appears to be a skimpy meal for one or two hungry stomachs. Surely, they stood in awe as Jesus used that meager meal to feed thousands!

But what really amazes me about this passage is verse 17. After the miracle meal, the disciples picked up twelve whole baskets of leftovers! I don't believe it was an accident that God left a basket of scraps for each of the Twelve to carry home—visible proof that He's more than enough to meet every need.

Our memories can serve as leftovers of Christ's work in our lives, reminding us of all the good things He did in the past and helping us look forward to what He'll do in the future.

Share a "leftover" about something good God has done in your life.

Life Is Not a Picnic

Those who were in the boat worshiped him,
saying, "Truly you are the Son of God."
MATTHEW 14:33

Jesus instructed His twelve friends to get into a boat and head out across the lake to the other side. Though they'd just picked up baskets full of leftovers at the miraculous picnic, "their hearts were hardened" (Mark 6:52). They'd seen what Jesus could provide and were likely thinking what an excellent king He'd make for their nation. But ahead lay an important lesson about their Leader: Jesus didn't come to set up a kingdom on earth. He came to rule as King over each individual's heart.

During the night, when the disciples were out in the middle of the deep lake, Jesus, who'd stayed behind on the shore, caught up with their boat on foot. When Peter saw Jesus walking on the water, he asked to join Him. But as the disciple made his way out to Jesus, "when he saw the wind, he was afraid," and he started to sink (Matthew 14:30)! In taking his focus off Jesus, he saw only the lake and its stormy depths.

The Bible points out that the disciples' hard hearts were softened in the storm. I think that's a reminder that God will use our difficult times to remind us of our greatest need—not to assure we'll never miss a meal or to have a national leader who will grant our desires. Suffering reminds us we need Jesus to be the Savior of our lives and the King who reigns over our thoughts.

Tell about a time when something difficult drew you closer to Jesus.

Soul Quencher

For You are great, and do wondrous things;
You alone are God.
PSALM 86:10 NKJV

King Ahab's disobedience to God brought a famine. But the problem didn't just affect the soil. It reflected what was happening in people's souls. Israel ignored the Lord's command not to worship false gods, called idols. So in time they forgot that He alone can do miracles, like sending rain.

Elijah met the idolatrous prophets for a contest; it was an opportunity for God to remind the people that He was the only deity who could quench their thirst. Both Elijah and the false prophets were supposed to prepare burnt offerings without lighting fires. Instead, they'd ask God and Baal, an idol, to light them. All day, the idol worshipers pleaded with their false god, but nothing happened. Elijah even teased them, saying, "Maybe he had to go to the bathroom!" (1 Kings 18:27).

By nightfall, Baal's altar still hadn't caught fire. So, in the perfect timing for God to display His splendor, Elijah soaked his sacrifice with water. Immediately, fire fell from heaven, licking up the whole sacrifice and even the last drops of water. Everyone there agreed the Lord is God: He alone could do such great things.

Maybe you've known someone who depends on lucky charms, crossing her fingers, or saying "magic" words to try and influence events. None of these holds any power. Such things are designed to take our hearts off the only one worthy of our faith and prayers. Look to Jesus instead. Only He can prevent drought, literal or spiritual.

How does your courage to trust Jesus influence those around you?

Supernatural Response

I have been crucified with Christ and I no longer live,
but Christ lives in me. The life I now live in the body,
I live by faith in the Son of God, who loved me
and gave himself for me.

GALATIANS 2:20

On a black bracelet my husband wears are four letters: WWJD (What Would Jesus Do?). The acronym reminds him to constantly consider what Jesus would do. The answer is always simple, because Jesus said, "I always do the things that are pleasing to [God]" (John 8:29 ESV).

When someone hurts us, the sinful part of us wants revenge. It pushes us to say mean things or lash out at the person who was unkind. But if we're going to do what Jesus our Savior did, we must love our enemies (Luke 6:35). Daily, we must choose forgiveness over trying to get even.

This may seem impossible, but it's a supernatural way of life that shows the world that we do indeed belong to Jesus. When we realize that our sin hurts God, but that He loved us so much He sent His own Son to take the punishment we deserve for our sins—it grows easier.

Offering grace to others by letting them off the hook can help make them eager to know God. True, showing such love is beyond what comes naturally to us. But doing what Jesus would do shows God's supernatural power at work within us through His Holy Spirit. God will empower us to the right thing. All we need do is ask for His help.

Give an example of how you will love like Jesus this week.

Choose Freedom

We have freedom now because Christ made us free. So stand strong. Do not change and go back into … slavery.

GALATIANS 5:1 ICB

In *Open Season 2*, Mr. Weenie the dachshund flees confinement to discover freedom in the forest. He doesn't want to go back to life as a pet, but his owners pursue him, tempting him with doggie treats. Mr. Weenie sees these snacks as "the food of oppression," knowing he must be strong. As he sniffs the first treat, Mr. Weenie looks away, trying to resist. But finally he weakens. He ends up eating the whole trail of treats, winding up where he didn't desire to go: back to life as a pet![2]

Weenie's war, though fictional, is a great picture of the battle that rages within every believer (Romans 7:15). Daily, you will have struggles between your sin nature (which always wants to lure you right back into living as if you never met Christ) and the spirit of God in you (which wants to keep you free from sin's bondage).

Thankfully, unlike Mr. Weenie who was left to fight his battle with only his willpower, we have the Holy Spirit's help. So ask Him to strengthen your determination, and faithfully run from any temptation disguised as a "treat." Sin makes you a slave; choose freedom.

Talk about a time Jesus gave you the strength to resist sin.

---

2 *Open Season 2*, directed by Matthew O'Callaghan (Culver City, CA: Sony Pictures Animation, 2015), DVD.

A Heart Ablaze

*"Were not our hearts burning within us
while he talked with us on the road
and opened the Scriptures to us?"*

LUKE 24:32

As the disciples walked from Jerusalem to Emmaus, they talked about recent events. Three days earlier, Jesus had been crucified. Now, there was a rumor He'd risen from the dead. Along the road, the disciples were joined by a stranger who contributed some mind-blowing truths from Scripture to their conversation. After He departed, they finally figured out that it was Jesus Himself who they'd been talking to the whole time. The two reflected on their journey. They exclaimed the Lord's teaching had been so powerful that "their hearts felt on fire" as the living Word (John 1:14) walked with them and opened Scripture to them.

These traveling companions were locked in sadness and doubt before their encounter with Jesus and the truth of His Word. But as they spent time with Him and applied themselves to grasping more about Scripture, something amazing happened. Their confusion and unrest melted away, and their hearts were set ablaze with new passion for following Jesus.

In Jeremiah 23:29 the Lord asks, "Is not my word like fire?" If you are feeling doubtful or unsure about what you believe, spend some time with Jesus in His Word. An encounter with Him can set your heart ablaze, giving you the passion and fuel you need to serve Him and share about Him.

Who do you know who is on fire for Jesus? How do they show their commitment to Him?

The Unexamined Life

*"These people come near to me with their mouth
and honor me with their lips, but their hearts
are far from me. Their worship of me is based on
merely human rules they have been taught."*

ISAIAH 29:13

My father says he went to church "nine months before" he was born, because that's what his parents wanted. He had perfect attendance in fact. And every Sunday morning, an elderly woman patted him on his back as she passed by: "Clebe, what a fine Christian boy you are!" Daddy said so many people told him he was a Christian that he assumed he was one. But while he had a lot of Bible stories in his head, he was missing the Savior in his heart.

Some people believe they're Christians because they were born in the United States or because they have Christian parents. Many think attending church makes them a Christian. But all of these beliefs are wrong. Until you trust in Christ for the forgiveness of your sins, you are unsaved. You aren't a Christian.

Jesus quoted Isaiah 29:13 when He met with some big-time church leaders of His day, men who never missed a service and who knew all about Scripture. But they'd never accepted how sinful they were or how much they needed God. Jesus told them they were just going through the motions. His words warn us that rule following can never replace a relationship with our Creator. That connection is only made when we place our faith in Jesus Christ.

Are you a Christian? If so, what makes you one?

The Cure for Stinkin' Thinkin'

Brothers and sisters, whatever is true, whatever is noble,
whatever is right, whatever is pure, whatever is lovely,
whatever is admirable—if anything is excellent
or praiseworthy—think about such things.

PHILIPPIANS 4:8

In the Bible, the Lord uses truth to direct our thoughts, since thoughts often drive the train that takes us to how we feel about life. So just what kinds of things does the Lord suggest we ponder? Those that are true, noble, right, pure, lovely, admirable, and worthy of praise.

Jesus is truth, so we can always think about Him. "Noble" knights protected the weak and defenseless against evil villains. "Right" thinking is based on God's righteousness. He commands us, "Be holy, because I am holy" (1 Peter 1:16), so we need to think about what is good and what pleases God. When things are pure, they don't have any dirt; our thoughts should be pure, free of ugly words, images, and things that scare us.

The word *lovely* made our son, Daniel, think of Daddy kissing Mommy, but the word really reminds us to think of beautiful things. *Admirable* is when "mommies and daddies love each other!" daughter Caroline suggested. She's right. Admirable things are things worth cheering for. Excellence appears in God's creation: sea otters, starfish, sunrises, puppies, and certain unique qualities about ourselves. Excellence is found in everything that reminds us of how worthy of praise our Creator God is.

Suggest one example to help you define each of the eight characteristics of godly thinking.

MARCH

Don't Run and Hide

*They heard the sound of the Lord God walking
in the garden in the cool of the day, and the man
and his wife hid themselves from the presence
of the Lord God among the trees.*

GENESIS 3:8 ESV

When my two-year-old covers her eyes, she thinks she's hidden. We laugh at her confidence in having escaped our sight, but she's serious, convinced she's disappeared. In the same way, Adam and Eve, after they disobeyed God's instruction not to eat of the forbidden tree, thought they could not be seen either. But God sees everything. The Bible says, "Nothing in all creation is hidden from God's sight. Everything is … before the eyes of him to whom we must give account" (Hebrews 4:13). God sees the good we do—and the bad—because He is with us all the time.

Oftentimes, when we break God's rules, we want to cover it up or pretend it didn't happen. But the Bible says, "If we claim to be without sin, we deceive [only] ourselves" (1 John 1:8). It makes God sad when we do things that go against what He says—and there are always consequences for our bad choices. Adam and Eve were no longer allowed to live in the special garden God had created for them. Although their sin messed up their perfect relationship with Him—and ours, as well—He still loves us all. He sent Jesus to show us just how big His love is for Adam, Eve, you, and me.

What have you been trying to hide from God? Why?

As I Am

*True love is God's love for us, not our love for God.
God sent his Son to die in our place to take away our sins.*

1 John 4:10 ICB

Have you ever said, *I'll love you, if …*? Or, how about, *I love you, but …*? God doesn't place any conditions on His love. Instead, He says, *I love you, although …* That's because God knows everything we've done and loves us anyway.

When I was little, I liked to watch the Billy Graham Crusades. These were televised events held in a stadium where thousands of people gathered together to hear the gospel. I loved seeing large crowds of people decide to accept Jesus after Reverend Graham said, "God's not waiting to condemn you or judge you. He's waiting with open arms to receive you and forgive all your sins as you come to Him in repentance and faith." Then, a choir would sing, "Just as I am, without one plea, but that Thy blood was shed for me, and that Thou bidst me come to thee, O Lamb of God, I come."[1]

The Lord loves us as we are. We don't have to wash up or change our habits or look a certain way before saying yes to Jesus. He accepts us in spite of our messes, and then does something amazing in our hearts. He gives us the desire to "go and sin no more" (John 8:11 NKJV). By coming "just as we are," we're never the same.

Why do you think God chooses to love us in spite of our sins?

---

1 "Just As I Am," by Charlotte Elliott and William B. Bradbury, Public Domain, 1849.

Loving "No"

Sin will not be your master,
because you are not under law but under God's grace.

ROMANS 6:14 ICB

When my daughter Caroline was two, she'd run through the house loudly singing, "Jesus loves me. This I know. For the Bible tells me, 'No.'" She'd misheard the words to the song, which is not surprising when I think of how often a toddler must hear the word *no*. The lyrics really say, "For the Bible tells me *so*." But Caroline's mistake is a reminder that many people are so convinced that the Bible is just a book of rules and don'ts, that they completely miss out on the fact that God came to offer us grace and to teach us the best way to live.

No is an expression of love. When Jesus tells us no to disobeying our parents, no to cursing, no to stealing, no to gossiping, it's not because He doesn't love us or doesn't want us to enjoy life. Instead, the Lord, always the best parent, wants to protect us from doing things that would harm us or make us miss out on His plans. How do we know? Because the Bible tells us *so*: "How happy are those whose way is blameless, who live according to the Lord's instruction! Happy are those who keep His decrees and seek Him with all their heart" (Psalm 119:1–2 HCSB).

When you're told no by a parent or teacher, what is your first response? What might need to change?

The Widow's Might

"She, out of her poverty, put in all she owned,
all she had to live on."
MARK 12:44 NASB

In the classic TV cartoon *Mighty Mouse*, the main character always arrives with a song: "Here I come to save the day!" Flying in to defeat the evil cats and critters in his town, the heroic mouse takes on the big guys. Tiny as he is, he gives all he has and finds success.

Jesus was watching people place their offerings in one of the temple's collection chests. The rich dropped in their money, not considering their giving a big deal at all. But a widow (a woman whose husband has died) put in two small coins worth only about two pennies. Because she gave all she had to the Lord, Jesus said her two cents were worth more than the hundreds the others had put in. She may have seemed unimportant to anyone else watching her, but the woman greatly pleased God when she gave her all out of mighty faith.

The widow trusted in the strength and provision of her Lord, confident He would provide her next meal. When we are obedient to God's command to "look to the Lord and his strength; seek his face always" (1 Chronicles 16:11), we demonstrate might too.

What is something big you are trusting Jesus for today?

Poor Little Rich Ruler

The love of money is the root of all kinds of evil.
1 TIMOTHY 6:10 NLT

The Bible does not say money is wicked; it's loving money that can become a problem. Money can be used to accomplish lots of good things. But some people make money an idol, placing it higher than God in importance. That's what happened in the case of a rich young ruler, who chose his wealth over following the Lord.

Jesus knew this man's true love, telling him to sell all that he had and come and follow Him (Luke 18:22). But when he heard this, the Bible says the rich young ruler "became very sad" (v. 23 NASB). He didn't want to give up what had become so comfortable to him. Following Jesus, in his mind, just wasn't worth the sacrifice. But the Bible says of his foolishness, "What do you benefit if you gain the whole world but lose your own soul?" (Matthew 16:26 NLT)

One day the rich man died, and he did not take his wealth with him. If only he had realized how much more is gained when we stop putting our faith in money, popularity, and the things we own, and instead put our all in the trustworthy hands of our Savior who loves us so much He paid for us with His life. That gift is beyond price.

The worst evil of all is anything that draws us away from surrendering our hearts to Jesus.

Why do you think it's so easy to follow things more than Jesus?

Keeping Jesus in First Place

Dear children, keep yourselves from idols.
1 John 5:21

Anything we think about more than Jesus is an idol in our lives. If you're constantly making a list in your mind of video games you want to purchase, then "things" may be an idol in your life. If you're concerned all the time about what your friends may be texting or talking about when you're not around, then your friends' opinion of you may be an idol. If it makes you mad to miss an episode of your favorite TV show, then guess what may be your idol? Idols have to be dealt with radically. If not, they hurt our most important relationship of all. Our love for Jesus.

Daniel was a teenager living in one of the most idol-filled places in the world, Babylon. "But Daniel purposed in his heart" not to bow to any idols or give in to pressure to worship anything other than God (Daniel 1:8 KJV). That means Daniel planned out a strategy to help him say no to anything he might be tempted to treat as an idol. He wasn't going to let anything or anyone come between him and his relationship with the Lord.

Jesus is pleased when we, like Daniel, decide in advance what we're going to do when we're faced with the temptation to put anything in His place.

What do you want to do to make sure Jesus comes first in your life?

The Secret of Life

"There is only one thing worth being concerned about. Mary has discovered it, and it will not be taken away from her."
LUKE 10:42 NLT

*H*oarders is a reality TV show that follows the struggles of people whose homes and lives are a mess, because they hold onto too much stuff.

Scripture doesn't label Martha a "hoarder" in her housekeeping, although it does reveal another messy habit hiding in her heart. In Luke 10:41, Jesus says to her, "Martha, Martha, you are worried and upset about many things" (HCSB). Like Martha, most of us spend a lot of time cluttering our hearts with worries over many things. But Jesus wants to come in and clean house. He challenges us all to act more like Martha's sister, Mary, by concerning ourselves with Him.

Jesus reminds us that we should set apart time each day to talk to Him and to think about His Word, applying what we learn to every task we're asked to do. The last time we meet Martha in Scripture, we see she's applied what Jesus taught her. Once again, she's hosting a dinner for Jesus. While little sister Mary is anointing Jesus' feet with expensive oil, the Bible says, "Martha served" (John 12:2 ESV). This time, her service isn't filled with worried frenzy, but is an act of worship. She's learned the secret of life: keeping Jesus first in her heart. Martha traded in a bad habit for a good one, trusting her Savior.

What is a bad habit you can break that may be taking your focus off Jesus?

The Wilderness Way

*Then Jesus was led up by the Spirit
into the wilderness.*

MATTHEW 4:1 ESV

When new airplanes roll off the assembly line, aeronautical engineers set up "test flights" to observe how the aircraft will perform. The creators of these multimillion dollar planes are quite confident their machines are going to fly, but they still need to be tested. God also tests His creation—us. He even allowed His own Son, Jesus, to be tested by Satan.

Imagine Jesus wandering through the desert—hot, hungry, and horribly thirsty. His own Father led Him there to test Jesus' faithfulness to Him. Jesus went through this experience to show every human on earth how to handle the tricks and lies of Satan, God's enemy and ours.

The wilderness is usually a place outside our comfort zone. Throughout Scripture we see God taking His people into challenging places to show them that their safety and security is in Him. We are never alone in whatever struggle we are facing. The Bible says, "But with us is the Lord our God to help us and to fight our battles" (2 Chronicles 32:8). God may allow us into an uncomfortable spot in life, not to destroy us but to demonstrate His power through us. Like a new airplane, God designed us to soar.

Talk about a time when God's power helped you through a difficult situation.

What's in a Name?

*"Salvation is found in no one else,
for there is no other name under heaven
given to men by which we must be saved."*
ACTS 4:12

Calvin Klein. Jimmy Choo. Kate Spade. Tony Hawk. Chuck Taylor: these are all sought-after names, designer brands people like to wear. Many people think that by wearing clothing with these labels, they will feel happier and be more liked, respected, and powerful. But in reality, choosing to wear names like these only gives the labels power. They don't give us any. We may think we'll be "saved" from social embarrassment or rejection by wearing them. The sad reality is none of these names can give us lasting joy and satisfaction. Certainly, none of them can save us. In fact, buying clothes with these labels may well blow our budget.

There's only one name that truly empowers us—giving us hope for new life and power over the temptation to do wrong. That name may not alter our looks, but it will change the way we look at things. It's the name of Jesus. What you choose to do with His name is the most important decision you can make: "For 'whoever calls on the name of the Lord shall be saved'" (Romans 10:13 NKJV).

What does the name of Jesus mean to you?

Seeing Jesus

Answering him, Jesus said,
"What do you want Me to do for you?"
MARK 10:51 NASB

Bartimaeus. The name's just fun to say. The Bible tells us Bartimaeus had a problem. He was blind; he couldn't see. One day as he was sitting in his usual spot by the road to Jericho where he begged for bread, Jesus, the Bread of Life (John 6:35), passed by. Immediately Bartimaeus grew excited: he'd heard Jesus was a great healer, and he didn't want to miss the chance to meet Him. So he cried out, "Jesus! Son of David! Have mercy on me!" The crowd was heavy and irritated by all of Bart's noise. "Hush!" they demanded. Had Bartimaeus listened, he would've missed out on a miracle.

God is never annoyed by a cry for help; He doesn't dismiss the distress of those who trust in Him. "The helpless call out to him," Scripture says, "and he answers; he saves them from all their troubles" (Psalm 34:6 GNT). Jesus always knows exactly where we are and what we need. Many times, though, He will prompt us to tell Him in our own words. When Jesus asked Bartimaeus what he wanted, the man cried, "I want to see!" (Mark 10:51). And while he wanted to watch the sun cross the sky, see the birds singing in the trees, and look into the eyes of friends, what he wanted most was to see Jesus. Knowing this, and touched by Bart's heartfelt plea, the Lord granted his request.

What might you cry out to Jesus for right now?

Overstuffed

The Lord answered, Behold,
he hath hid himself among the stuff.
1 Samuel 10:22 KJV

A frantic mother looked everywhere for Sally, her two-year-old, who'd made it clear she didn't want to go shopping. Finally, she glanced over at the arcade games. To her horror, she found her daughter was sitting inside a crane game, playing with the stuffed animal prizes. Apparently, the toddler had squeezed through the game's chute where the toys are dropped for winners to receive. Firefighters had to rescue her. But Sally didn't want to leave. "No dresses!" she cried.

Saul was chosen by God as the king over Israel—an honor and gift by anyone's standards. But instead of embracing what God was doing in his life, Saul tried to run away from it—just like Sally. When it was time for him to receive his crown, he hid "among the stuff," doing all he could to escape his destiny.

We can be like Saul and Sally too when we settle for hiding among "stuff" rather than embracing God's plans and promises for us. Jesus died so we might live—not for more toys or so we could carry on with our own selfish plans—but so we could work together with Him and receive "the blessings God has for his children. These blessings are kept for you in heaven. They cannot be destroyed or be spoiled or lose their beauty" (1 Peter 1:4 ICB).

What "stuff" do you tend to hide behind when you don't want to obey or step up to do as you've been told? What does God want you to do instead?

Your Serve

"The greatest among you shall be your servant."
MATTHEW 23:11 ESV

When warts appeared on my little boy's feet and I had to bend over them nightly to treat them, I pictured Jesus washing the feet of his disciples. Though their toes were surely caked with mud, He wasn't disgusted. He loved the men who allowed Him to clean up their lives and who joined Him in telling the world of His love.

When the Lord finished washing His disciples' feet, He said, "Now that I, your Lord and Teacher, have washed your feet, you also should wash one another's feet" (John 13:14). In other words, He wanted His followers to see the beauty of one another as fellow believers. As they worked on a mission to tell others about God, He wanted them to become servants to one another.

Each morning when we wake up, we are in service to someone—either to ourselves or to our Savior and His people. So even before we roll out of bed, we have to "choose this day whom [we] will serve" (Joshua 24:15 ESV). Jesus sacrificed everything for us. We can certainly serve Him by using our hands, feet, and hearts to help others get to know Him better.

No. I haven't warmed up to warts. But in caring for Daniel's feet, I am in the position God wants me to be—on my knees in service and obedience to the Lord.

What's a creative way you can share the love of Jesus by serving someone today?

If the Crown Fits

*"He must become greater and greater,
and I must become less and less."*
JOHN 3:30 NLT

John the Baptist never had to be the center of attention. Instead, even before he was born, John lived to shine the spotlight on Jesus. The Bible tells us he did backflips in his mother's tummy when he heard the voice of Jesus' pregnant mother, Mary. Luke 1:41 says, "At the sound of Mary's greeting, Elizabeth's child leaped within her" (NLT).

Getting over self is key for victorious living. Surrendering our desire to make life all about us is the only option that works in our relationship to Jesus Christ. We can't agree to follow Him without including those times it proves inconvenient. We can't obey God's Word on all matters and then exclude those with which we disagree. In fact, any time we put a "but" after "Yes, Lord," we're still trying to give orders and interfering with God's work within us. We're fighting Him for the spotlight.

Revelation 5:13 says, "Blessing and honor and glory and power belong to the one sitting on the throne and to the Lamb forever and ever" (NLT). God will not share His glory. There is only room on the throne for One. We don't wear the crown. He does. And that is why you and I, like John, will find that less of me plus more of Jesus is the only path to real joy, peace, and fulfillment.

What is something you've done to try to share God's spotlight?

Eenie, Meenie, Miney, Mo

*If you want to know what God wants you to do,
ask him, and he will gladly tell you.*

JAMES 1:5 TLB

Have you ever heard the phrase "Her opinion carries a lot of weight"? That suggests a woman is respected in her field of work, and what she says is important. She carries influence.

No one's words should carry more weight in our lives than the Word of God. What He tells us is the opposite of an opinion. He speaks in fact. An opinion can be formed based on how you feel about something; facts never change.

When our children were small, my friend Jackie and I were laughing about how her seven-year-old daughter, Mason, and five-year-old daughter, Kaitlyn, would one day fight over which sister would marry my son, Daniel. Over-hearing our conversation, seven-year-old Daniel exclaimed, "Oh, that decision is easy. I will just do, 'Eeny, meenie, miney, mo!'"

Sadly, many people make life decisions this way, allow-ing even childish opinions or the results of games to carry much weight. Rather than trusting God's Word, which tells us, "I will instruct you and teach you in the way you should go" (Psalm 32:8), we persist in our own stubborn ways and methods—even when doing so is foolish.

Jesus loves us so much that He gives us the Holy Spirit as our helper, a guide for every decision in life. So remember there's no need for "Eeny, meenie, miney, mo." Ask Jesus to show you the way you should go!

For what decision do you need wisdom this week?

Kai

"Greater love has no one than this,
that one lay down his life for his friends."

JOHN 15:13 NASB

During the Vietnam War, the North Vietnamese soldiers killed many people in an effort to spread Communism across the country. Brave American soldiers set up orphanages for the boys and girls who lost their parents in the struggle. Sadly, enemy soldiers targeted one of the orphanages. An eight-year-old boy was badly wounded in the attack and needed a blood transfusion. It was explained to the other orphans that he would die if no one volunteered to donate blood.

Kai, a six-year-old, raised his hand to give his own blood to help his friend. That afternoon, lying on a stretcher next to the wounded child, Kai began to cry. A kind American soldier, Lieutenant Bruce Bickel, walked over to the boy as he donated his blood. "Kai, why are you so sad?" he asked. Wiping his eyes, Kai looked up at the lieutenant and asked, "Sir, when am *I* going to die?"[2]

Kai didn't understand that when a person donates blood, he gives only a pint. When he volunteered to give his blood to save the life of his friend, Kai expected to give it all. He thought he would die in his friend's place.

Jesus loves you and me so much that He willingly gave all of His blood, and His life, so that we might live.

How did Jesus' sacrifice on the cross show us how much He loves us?

---

2 Clebe McClary, *Living Proof* (Clebe McClary Incorporated, 1979).

FIDO

*One thing I do: forgetting what lies behind
and straining forward to what lies ahead.*

PHILIPPIANS 3:13 ESV

My father developed an acronym based on this verse. It grew so popular that NFL teams had shirts printed with the letters, and certain MLB leagues put the letters on baseball caps. Some politicians have even quoted it. The letters F-I-D-O stand for "Forget It and Drive On."

Christians shouldn't dwell on past troubles or regrets. Rather than beating ourselves up about a situation where we felt embarrassed or getting angry all over again when we remember something someone said or did to us, we need to release it and move on. This allows us to focus on what God wants to do in us and through us today—after all, we are not promised tomorrow.

God never wastes anything we've been through. He can use hurts to shape us and draw us closer to Him. But He also sets a standard we should follow: He continually forgives and forgets. In spite of all the times we as followers of Christ hurt Him and fail, He looks on us and says, "I will remember their sins and their lawless deeds no more" (Hebrews 10:17 ESV).

Had the apostle Paul, a murderer, not chosen to "FIDO" his past, the greatest missionary the world has ever known might have wasted his life by having a pity party instead. When you're tempted to wallow in what happened yesterday, ask yourself: *What might I miss by clinging to what Jesus wants me to forget and leave behind?*

What do you need to "FIDO" today?

My Father's Eyes

He had no beauty or majesty to attract us to him,
nothing in his appearance that we should desire him.

ISAIAH 53:2

Society often equates how a person looks on the outside with what he is like on the inside. Outward beauty, however, isn't a reflection of a heart. A girl with nice clothes and a pretty face can be a mean-spirited terror; a charming, handsome boy might be a bully at heart. And that "plain" individual who's always kind? In truth, she may be the most beautiful person you know.

Jesus didn't have movie-star looks. No one followed Him because they liked His dimples. Jesus lived to serve, always putting the needs of others above His own. He modeled obedience, constantly listening to direction from His heavenly Father. He was kind and compassionate, never looking down on the poor or playing favorites with those the world would call "beautiful." He saw the world through His Father's eyes. As He continually acted in love, He modeled inner beauty.

Highlights in our hair are nothing compared to the light of Jesus shining in our hearts as we seek to help and encourage every person He puts in our path. Look at yourself—and others—as people Jesus loves, unique creations designed for His special purpose.

My grandmother always said, "Pretty is as pretty does." It's far more important to treat others with kindness—a mark of true beauty—than it is to be good looking.

Who in your life models inward beauty? Explain.

His Eye Is on the Sparrow

"Look at the birds of the air; they do not sow or reap or store away in barns, and yet your heavenly Father feeds them. Are you not much more valuable than they?"

MATTHEW 6:26

Have you ever felt unloved? All of us do sometimes. But a woman named Ethel Waters had good reason. Today, she's best remembered for her jazzy rendition of the song "Stormy Weather." She was also the first African American woman to star in her own TV show. The public adored her. But her childhood was incredibly sad. She was never cuddled by a parent or even liked by her own family. Ethel Waters was born to a thirteen-year-old mother who rejected her and a father who had nothing to do with her. Ethel never lived in the same place for more than a year and a half.

Her extremely difficult childhood made her believe she was unloved—until she heard about the love of Jesus. She accepted Him and with His love warming her heart, she said, "I am somebody 'cause God don't make no junk."

Ethel's favorite hymn, and the title of her autobiography, was "His Eye Is on the Sparrow." It was inspired by the words of Jesus: "Are not two sparrows sold for a penny? And not one of them will fall to the ground apart from your Father. But even the hairs of your head are all numbered. Fear not, therefore; you are of more value than many sparrows" (Matthew 10:29–31 ESV).

The Lord's eyes are always on us. We *are* loved because we are His.

What should you do the next time you feel unloved?

The Bible Is Not a Fairy Tale

*These things happened to them as examples for others,
and they were written down as a warning for us. For we
live at a time when the end is about to come.*

1 Corinthians 10:11 GNT

Fairy tales are made-up stories. In contrast, every word in the Bible is true. It was written down by people, but it was inspired by God, whose every word is truth (John 17:17). It's truth meant to teach us.

Many people question the Bible's stories. Was Jonah really swallowed by a whale (Jonah 1:17)? Was Lot's wife really turned into a pillar of salt (Genesis 19:26)? Could Noah have built a boat big enough for all those animals (Genesis 6:14)?

When Jesus spoke to His disciples about His death and the time of His return, He reminded them of the world history they'd been taught since childhood: about Noah, who listened and obeyed God's warning, and about Lot's wife, who did not (Luke 17:26, 32). About Jonah, He said, "As Jonah was a sign to the Ninevites, so also will the Son of Man be to this generation" (11:30). Jesus did that because throughout the historical stories printed in Scripture, God was revealing *His story*. The whole of the Old Testament pointed to Jesus. Those who have faith in Him will be saved, as Noah was when he built an ark in preparation of a flood. Those who refuse to believe will be judged, like Lot's wife. Those who run from the Lord will bring sorrow on themselves, but God's plans will not be stopped.

Why is it important for us to accept what the Bible says is true?

Trashing God's Name

*"You shall not misuse the name of the
Lord your God, for the Lord will not hold anyone
guiltless who misuses his name."*

EXODUS 20:7

Casual Friday is a trend in the American business world. Some businesses that typically require their employees to wear coats, ties, or nice dresses allow more comfortable attire, like jeans and tee shirts, on Fridays. This reflects the increasingly casual preferences of our culture. Though there is nothing wrong with stocking our closets with comfortable clothing, we must take care never to grow casual in our attitude toward Christ's holiness.

Sadly, many people take a very casual attitude toward Jesus, particularly in their speech. To take the Lord's name in vain means to say—or type—His name in a useless or empty way. When you text *Oh-Em-Gee* to a friend, for instance, you are breaking the third commandment, failing to keep God's name holy. When you feel like you want to fit in with the crowd at school and are pressured to say God's name in a casual way, don't. The name of Jesus, too, should always be said with respect, because Jesus is God (John 10:30).

If you've gotten into the habit of this sin, ask God to forgive and help you. He promises He will: "For I am the Lord your God who takes hold of your right hand and says to you, Do not fear; I will help you" (Isaiah 41:13).

How would you feel if your name were used as a swear word?

Making Christ at Home

*I pray that Christ will make his home
in your hearts through faith.*

EPHESIANS 3:17 GNT

In his popular book *My Heart—Christ's Home*, Robert Munger talked about his heart as if it were a house that Jesus moves into at the moment of our salvation. But Munger realized that often we tend to treat Jesus more like a guest in our lives, than as Master. The trouble is that we want to deny Jesus access to the parts of our hearts that embarrass us or feel messy.[3]

In the same way that we wouldn't flinch over showing a guest a display room, like a fancy parlor or library, we welcome Jesus into the living room of warm fellowship. Similarly, we are happy to show off the workroom where we use our talents and abilities for His glory. But as sure as we don't want guests peeking into messy closets, we tend to fight giving Jesus access to the deepest corners of our hearts—those places where we keep unpleasant memories and hurts and a record of all the ways we've failed.

Don't try to confine Jesus to only certain areas of your life. Instead, ask Him to air out and clean up every space in your heart. When you allow Jesus to be in charge of every room, closet, and drawer, you allow Him to make Himself at home.

Since making Jesus Master of the "home" of your heart, what changes have you experienced?

---

3   Robert Boyd Munger, *My Heart—Christ's Home* (Madison, WI: InterVarsity Press, 1954).

Making the Cut

This small and temporary trouble we suffer
will bring us a tremendous and eternal glory,
much greater than the trouble.

2 CORINTHIANS 4:17 GNT

We are Jesus' treasure, His gemstones: "And they shall be mine, saith the Lord of hosts, in that day when I make up my jewels" (Malachi 3:17 KJV).

The process a master gem cutter uses to transform a rough stone into a gem of great worth is called "cutting." Two prepared stones can seem very similar, yet be very different. One may shine brightly and the other look dull. Jewelers will tell you it's because of the all-important "cut" of the stone. The gem cutter may have forced one stone to "suffer" seventy cuts and the other just seven. Seven cuts sound preferable to seventy, but it's the stone that is worked by the gem cutter the longest that shines the brightest.

In a similar way, Jesus uses the hard times that come into our lives to help us focus on our forever future with Him. He shapes us to shine, never wasting the tough things we go through. Waiting, and hanging in there when times are hard, makes us more patient. Hurting makes us more compassionate toward others' pain. Losses make us more grateful. All of these things make us more like Jesus, fitting jewels for our King's crown.

How does knowing there is purpose in painful times make it a bit easier to endure those difficult situations?

911

*I have hidden your word in my heart
that I might not sin against you.*

PSALM 119:11

The Bible provides an important emergency message in Psalm 119:11. It reminds us that memorizing Scripture gives us a weapon we can use to fight against temptation. God's Word is truth and no matter how many years go by, it never changes. God has given us the Bible so we can live for Him—even when it isn't easy. We can always rely on God's Word for help.

Jesus obeyed every one of God's words. He resisted the devil's temptations by quoting Bible verses (Matthew 4:1–11). He could do this because He knew Scripture well, and with it, He was equipped to defeat the devil.

Even though Christians are forgiven, we still struggle with sin. The devil is continually tempting us to do wrong. He may try to convince you that lying is not such a big deal. Or, that it's okay to take that candy bar when no one is looking. But God has promised that when we take His Word to heart and choose to live by what He says, He will show up on the scene as our defender. He'll help us through the power of His Holy Spirit and provide a way to escape whatever is tempting us (1 Corinthians 10:13). The key is to know and trust His Word.

Memorize today's verse, remembering you are less likely to sin when you hide God's Word in your heart.

Take Your Medicine

"These instructions are not empty words—
they are your life!"
DEUTERONOMY 32:47 NLT

Knowing how much time her son would spend outdoors during his camping trip, my friend Melissa carefully packed her boy's allergy pills. Miller would be miserable without his medicine. He needed it to enjoy the trip. Melissa made sure to put the pills in an obvious place where he couldn't miss them—his toothbrush case.

Three days later, Miller returned home complaining of itchy eyes and constant sneezing. It turned out that because Miller was more interested in playing than in personal hygiene, he had neglected to brush his teeth for the whole trip. He suffered with allergies all weekend, because he failed to take care of a basic need. If he had, he would have found the treatment for what was ailing him.

You and I can be a lot like Miller. We suffer needlessly with worry, depression, jealousy, and anger, because we ignore the daily necessity of seeking Jesus in prayer and through His Word. God has carefully packed the spiritual medicine we need in the Bible. Psalm 19:7–8 tells us, "The instructions of the Lord are perfect" (NLT). They refresh our soul, make us wise, fill our hearts with joy, and provide insight for living. So make spending time with Jesus a daily habit. You will find relief in His Word.

Talk about a time you found relief by spending time in Scripture.

Dip Protector

"In me you may have peace. In this world you will have trouble. But take heart! I have overcome the world."

JOHN 16:33

For school, my twins created ideas for new inventions. My daughter suggested "Caroline's Clip-Clop Conditioner," which, she claimed, kept flies off horses, while adding sparkle to their manes. Daniel, who hates roller coasters as much as I do, created "Daniel's Dip Detector." Pitched as a "must-pack" item for traveling to amusement parks, the idea was to hold his telescope-like device up to the eye at each ride. Doing so warned of dips, plunges, drops, or rapid downward movements in advance so a person could avoid unpleasant riding experiences.

Wouldn't it be nice to have a "dip detector" in life, something that could warn you that down times are around the bend? Some of us have been on rides in life that would put any roller coaster to shame. Parents divorce. Cancer comes. Friendships crumble. Even when we belong to Jesus, our lives are often marred by pain, suffering, difficulties, and other "dips" this fallen world brings.

In His Word, our heavenly Father prepares us for the fact that our human experience is as much about the "downs" as it is the "ups." But God promises, "He who watches over you will not slumber" (Psalm 121:3). We can trust the Lord as our constant safety harness for every dip life brings.

Why do you think God promised to be with us through life's dips, rather than protecting us from them altogether?

Look and See

"Behold my hands and my feet."
LUKE 24:39 KJV

Every Easter my parents hide eggs. We all get tickled when the little grandchildren stare into a bush filled with eggs and fail to see what they're searching for. My parents point out the obvious. "Look," they say, "and see." Soon, the children realize that the very thing they want is right in front of them.

After Jesus' crucifixion, He appeared to His disciples on the first Easter week. He found them hiding in fear. And though they were soon staring right at Him, they completely missed the truth they so craved. Their Savior really had returned to life just as promised!

So in much the same way my parents help children appreciate what's right in front of them at Easter time, Jesus said, "Behold My hands and feet." In other words, He told the group who'd lived alongside Him for years to study Him. To recognize that His hands were the same hands that healed the sick. His feet were the sandaled feet they'd seen walk beside them on their shared journey, in perfect obedience to God. As they leaned in closer, perhaps grinning as they made connections like these, they couldn't help but notice Jesus' scars—nail marks bearing evidence of His love.

Picture Jesus' scarred hands and feet. But then, really *see*. Recognize that these marks announce the whole point of Easter: Jesus died for our sins and rose again so we can live with Him forever.

What do you see when you imagine Jesus?

Jesus Never Leaves Me

*"Be sure of this: I am with you always,
even to the end of the age."*

MATTHEW 28:20 NLT

When the lights are off and you can't sleep, counting smelly sheep doesn't do any good, but counting on Jesus, the Shepherd, does.

King David's psalm reminds us that the Lord, our Good Shepherd, is with us at all times. David wrote in Psalm 23:4 (ESV), "Even though I walk through the valley of the shadow of death, I will fear no evil, for [God] is with me." David's words remind us the Lord is always present. He was there at the moment of your birth and He'll be present when you take your last breath. He is with you on the playground and on the playing field. At home and in the hospital. He is with you when you feel safe, and in the times you are afraid. Whether you're in a hurricane or a calm day, in the crowd or in a time out, Jesus never leaves. He'll even be with you if that boy or girl you really like should hurt your heart.

Sometimes, it's easy to spend the nighttime hours staring at the ceiling, feeling lonely and replaying things that hurt. But Jesus doesn't want us to get caught up in feelings. He wants us to talk to Him, to rely on Him, and to remember He promised, "Never will I leave you" (Hebrews 13:5). Jesus is a faithful friend.

Why do you think Jesus sticks by you so closely?

Crossroads

[Jesus] told them what was going to happen to him. …
"The Son of Man will be delivered over. … [They] will mock
him and spit on him, flog him and kill him.
Three days later he will rise."

MARK 10:32–34

Jesus was preparing to enter Jerusalem hailed as a king, but He knew what would happen to Him afterwards. He'd be beaten, tried, and ultimately killed as a criminal, taking the punishment for the world's sins. He was at a crossroads. Once He entered Jerusalem, there would be no escaping the horrors ahead.

A crossroad is a point where an important decision must be made: your choice will determine the future. Jesus didn't hesitate to follow His Father's will. Because He was obedient, Jesus defeated death, and you and I can enjoy forgiveness, abundant life, and the promise of heaven.

When you come to a crossroad—like when your parents want to move to a new town and you don't want to go—look to the cross. Remember that God is all-powerful, all-wise, and all-good. You can trust Him. He doesn't promise the easiest route; He even says that "the road is difficult" (Matthew 7:14 NLT). But as you keep following Jesus' ways, living in obedience, you'll find that He'll use the crossroad moments of your life in ways you never imagined.

What's something good Jesus brought out of a crossroad moment in your life?

Out of the Saltshaker

You are the salt of the earth.
But what good is salt if it has lost its flavor?
MATTHEW 5:13 NLT

Salt is a seasoning that tends to make people thirsty. The substance not only adds flavor, but prevents the growth of harmful bacteria, making food last longer. As Christians, God has blessed those of us who follow Him with a tremendous responsibility and opportunity. Because we take the flavor of Christ ("salt") with us wherever we go, we can help make those who don't know Him thirsty. For what? For a relationship with Jesus. And should they accept Him, their lives, too, will be seasoned and preserved for all eternity.

The next time you open your lunch box, remember that you are "salt." As you choose to honor the Lord through your attitude and show respect for Him by bowing your head over your meal, you have a chance to make people thirsty for Jesus, to show them that their lives are incomplete without Him. Jesus wants us to show others how important His love is in our lives so they'll desire to know Him too.

How might you make someone thirsty for Jesus today?

Trading My Wants for His Will

"Seek first the kingdom of God and His righteousness, and all these things will be provided for you."

MATTHEW 6:33 HCSB

Do you ever get caught up in "I wants" and even the "I needs"? God desires that we seek Him above all else. In Matthew 6, Jesus addresses an audience concerned over what they'll eat, drink, and wear. He tells them not to worry over such things: God knows their needs and will provide. Instead, Jesus tells them, they should focus on seeking a relationship with Him.

King Solomon had that focus. God invited Solomon to request anything he wanted; Solomon asked for the Lord's wisdom. He knew the Lord could give him the wisdom he'd need to make right choices that were pleasing to God and helpful to his people. The Bible says, "It pleased the Lord that Solomon had asked this" (1 Kings 3:10 NLV).

It's fine to ask God to help you make friends, do well on a test, or make the team, but God wants to get each of us to the point where we are more interested in what He wants—in His perfect plan to help us grow and learn to trust Him—than He is in hearing our wish lists. "Seeking the kingdom of God" means surrendering our selfish motives to His will, trading our wants for a trust that believes God's ways are best, and exchanging worry and anxiety for the knowledge that God is our Provider.

When you pray, are you usually more concerned with "seeking the kingdom of God" or with listing your wants? Why?

Remember His Raisin'

"He is not here; he has risen!"

LUKE 24:6

Each time I left the house to go to school or meet up with friends, my father would say, "I love you, honey. Remember your raisin'!" He wanted me to remember that the godly way I was brought up should influence my decisions. But even more important for me to remember was the raising of Jesus—not the way Mary and Joseph parented Him, but the way God raised Him from the dead.

When Jesus, God in human flesh, died a real death on a criminal's cross, He paid the death penalty our sins deserve. But because three days later He rose from the dead, you and I can know that we too will rise to a life in heaven with the Lord. That's what Jesus meant when He said, "I am the resurrection and the life. He who believes in me will live, even though he dies" (John 11:25).

The empty tomb is a reminder there is nothing our God cannot do. Death is dead. Jesus' resurrection is what sets Christianity apart from every other religion. Jesus is alive! His promises are true and so is His power. Doesn't it encourage you to know there is nothing Jesus cannot do, including conquering death? Because His tomb is empty, your heart should be full of hope.

What difference does Jesus' resurrection make in how you live?

APRIL

He Speaks

Long ago, at many times and in many ways,
God spoke to our fathers by the prophets,
but in these last days he has spoken to us by His Son.
HEBREWS 1:1–2 ESV

Throughout the Old Testament, people mainly heard from God through His prophets. These messengers were chosen by God to speak to the people as His megaphone. One common theme among the writings of Moses, Isaiah, Jeremiah, Zechariah, and others was the people's need to turn from sin and await the Messiah—the one we now know as Jesus.

Jesus perfectly fulfilled everything God promised through His prophets. He was the sacrifice for our sin, as Isaiah said: "The Lord has laid on him the iniquity of us all" (Isaiah 53:6). Jesus was betrayed for thirty pieces of silver, as Zechariah said: "So they paid me thirty pieces of silver" (Zechariah 11:12). Jesus even fulfilled prophecies about the darkness that fell over the earth when He died. "'And on that day,' declares the Lord God, 'I will make the sun go down at noon and darken the earth in broad daylight'" (Amos 8:9 ESV). These were all written thousands of years before they happened.

Today, when you want to hear from God, you can look to the words of the prophets, but you have an added blessing. By reading the New Testament Gospels, you can read the very words of Jesus! If a friend wants you to do something you're not sure about, Christ's words can help you decide whether it's a good idea. If your grandparent asks how a person can be sure of heaven, you can share what Jesus said.

Would you rather have only the words of the Old Testament prophets or also the words of Jesus? Why?

An Eye for Truth

I want you to be wise about what is good,
and innocent about what is evil.

ROMANS 16:19

Bankers can tell if money is real or fake, because their training involves touching and studying only real money. That way, when a fake bill is passed into their hands, they're so familiar with how the real thing looks and feels that they can quickly spot a counterfeit and alert the authorities.

Similarly, we should train ourselves in only the truth and "be wise about what is good." That means we study God's Word every day and choose to spend time with friends who do likewise. We listen to music that has a message that is praiseworthy and pure. We choose entertainment we wouldn't be embarrassed to watch if Jesus were watching beside us. We practice being "innocent about what is evil," when all our friends sneak into the movie our parents said to avoid or by refusing to look at a website a buddy wants to show us that has inappropriate images. It's a refusal to do anything which goes against the example set by God's truth.

We should be so familiar with what our heavenly Father wants that we'll recognize and avoid anything bad that tries to masquerade as something that's okay.

What shows you that God is real?

Love in Action

They couldn't get to Jesus through the crowd,
so they dug through the clay roof above his head
and lowered the sick man on his stretcher,
right down in front of Jesus.

MARK 2:4 TLB

The Bible records the tenderheartedness of four men who felt so much love for their paralyzed friend that they cut a hole in the roof above the room where Jesus was teaching and lowered him down in front of the only One they knew could help. The Bible says, "When Jesus saw their faith, he said to the paralyzed man, 'Son, your sins are forgiven'" (Mark 2:5). Jesus recognized in these five friends a faith in His ability; no crowd or construction was going to stop them! Because they were so dedicated to taking their friend to Jesus, their friend not only found physical healing, but was healed of what was most broken—his relationship with God.

You and I are around people every day who need Jesus. Some of them may look completely healthy on the outside—popular, attractive, smart—but, they are paralyzed spiritually on the inside, because of sin. In fact, the Bible says we are dead because of our sins (Colossians 2:13). Often people don't recognize their sad situation, however, until a true friend does what it takes to introduce them to Jesus.

When you recognize somebody's need, how do you act?

Traveling Light

Give all your worries to him, because he cares for you.
1 PETER 5:7 ICB

As I crammed my suitcase full of clothes, my daughter Caroline commented, "Mommy, it's a good thing you are packing so much, in case we decide to stay longer than five days." Hours later, I was standing with my bulging bag at the airline ticket counter when an agent directed me to place my luggage on the scale. It was over the weight limit. I'd have to pay excess baggage costs. So I began to transfer some of my stuff into my husband's suitcase. He wasn't happy.

The Lord used that incident to remind me how often we carry fears and worries and stress over struggles in our life. All of that is excess emotional weight He never intended us to carry. Often, it comes with a high cost—making us lose sleep or react with a grumpy attitude.

When the lights are turned out at night, there's no need to carry a heavy bag of fear and worry to bed. The Bible says, "The Lord is your protection" (Psalm 91:9 ICB). And why tote that panic of failure you insist on dragging to school? Let Jesus, who can "deliver [us] from all [our] troubles" (Psalm 34:17), carry it for you.

Jesus wants to lighten your load. There is no burden too heavy for Him. After all, if we are trusting Jesus with our life, we can certainly trust Him with our luggage.

What worries are you carrying that Jesus wants you to give to Him?

Prayer Works

If we ask anything according to His will,
He hears us.

1 JOHN 5:14 NKJV

My five-year-old sister Christa protested how often our family spoke of Jesus. But Mom just kept pointing us toward Him in every circumstance, asking the Lord in prayer to help my sister understand how good He is.

One morning, Christa woke up feeling really sick. Mother put us in the station wagon and headed to the hospital. As we traveled, she asked, "Tara, would you please say a prayer for your little sister?" Before I could close my eyes, Christa shouted, "Tabba, don't you pway for me!" But, I did as Mother asked. Christa accepted it, but pouted through it.

"Dear Lord, please make my sister well so we can play together," I prayed. "In Jesus' name, amen." Five minutes later, no exaggeration, Christa's angelic face was beaming. "Tabba!" she exclaimed. "You know that pwayer you pwayed? It worked! It really worked!" Indeed, Christa felt so much better, we returned home.

Just as Mother asked Him to do, Jesus showed Christa that prayer really works. He *is* worthy. Today, Christa loves Jesus and is raising her children to love him too. She's a great prayer warrior. If you know someone who doesn't understand your love for Jesus, ask the Lord to soften that person's heart as Mother did for our Christa, to show her how wonderful He really is. Jesus will hear, and He may even work a miracle.

Talk about some ways Jesus has specifically answered your prayers.

Jesus, Friend of Sinners

"Go now and leave your life of sin."
JOHN 8:11

Jesus came to be friends with sinners, to offer them forgiveness and show them a better way to live. The Bible says, "For the Son of Man [Jesus] came to seek and to save the lost" (Luke 19:10). Jesus was in no way approving what sinful people were doing. He was accepting people in spite of what they did.

There's a big difference between "approval" and "acceptance." Approving sin is watching TV shows that criticize or make fun of God's values. It includes those times when we fail to change the subject—or walk away—when our friends are gossiping or telling dirty jokes.

Acceptance is what the Bible calls us to do to others: "Accept one another, then, just as Christ accepted you, in order to bring praise to God" (Romans 15:7). This means we're willing to love and listen, treating others with respect, just as they are. However, it doesn't mean we have to agree with what they're doing or saying if it goes against God's standards.

When Jesus made friends with the woman who hadn't kept her marriage promises to her husband, He told her to "leave your life of sin." Jesus accepts you and me in whatever condition we are in, but knowing Him doesn't leave us unchanged. When we confess and turn away from the things we do that aren't in line with His holiness, He makes us whole. He makes us His. He approves of us.

In your own words, explain the difference between "approval" and "acceptance." Talk about a friend who has made a difference in your life.

From Rags to Riches

*We praise God, the Father of our Lord Jesus Christ,
who has blessed us with every blessing in heaven
because we belong to Christ.*

EPHESIANS 1:3 TLB

Ira and Ann Yates were ranchers in West Texas during the Great Depression. Because of tough financial times in the United States, they had a difficult time making ends meet. They couldn't pay their bills. One day, Mr. Yates invited the Transcontinental Oil Company to explore his land. Drilling a well not far below the surface, a "gusher" changed the Yates' lives forever, making their land one of the most valuable oilfields in history.

For years the Yates lived like they were poor when they were actually rich. We too are rich in many blessings, thanks to Jesus' payment for our sins on the cross. But many of us live as if our sins aren't forgiven, as if we weren't adopted as children of the King. Had Mr. and Mrs. Yates realized their riches earlier, they might have lived a completely different life.

Have you ever stopped to think what we miss out on when we fail to realize God's blessings in our lives? God promises that when we give up trying to live the way the rest of the world does, and instead trust His instructions, He'll bless us in ways we cannot even imagine (2 Peter 1:4). When we say yes to Jesus, we're given the Holy Spirit who blesses us with a "gusher" of love, joy, peace, patience, kindness, goodness, faith, gentleness, and self-control that never runs dry (Galatians 5:22).

How would you live differently if you fully accepted God's blessings?

The Bright Side of Things

Have the same attitude that Christ Jesus had.

PHILIPPIANS 2:5 GW

If you've ever watched the play or movie *Annie*, you've heard Little Orphan Annie sing at the top of her lungs about the sun coming out tomorrow. Given the many challenging circumstances she's facing at that moment, her optimism is contagious. While I have never known anyone to go blind looking on the bright side of things, I do know we need to make certain our gaze is fixed on the Son.

Jesus' outlook was always based on faith in His Father and not upon His feelings. The night before He was to be crucified, Jesus prayed about His "tomorrow." He remained committed to go to the cross, praying: "Father, if you are willing, take this cup from me; yet not my will, but yours be done" (Luke 22:42). Jesus never demanded His own way. Instead, He prayed about everything. He always put His trust in God's perfect plan.

When a storm front moves into our lives, like Annie, we can sing too. However, our hope is not in the sunrise, but in the risen Son who has not left us orphans, but has adopted us as His own, putting a new song—and new attitude—in our hearts.

What can you do today to make your attitude like Jesus'?

Strength for the Asking

*I work and struggle so hard, depending on Christ's
mighty power that works within me.*

COLOSSIANS 1:29 NLT

Edward was playing outside with his father when he
decided to pick up a small boulder. When he couldn't
lift it, he grunted and said, "Daddy, I can't! It's too heavy."
His father encouraged him, "Son, I know you can do it." The
little guy strained again and huffed. "It's impossible! I can't
do it!" Still, his father insisted he could. Finally, Edward was
exhausted and slumped to the ground in defeat.

"Don't give up Edward," his father said. "Tap into your
full strength. You aren't using all your resources." When
Edward looked up, discouragement showing on his face, his
father explained, "I know you aren't using all your strength,
because you haven't asked me to help yet. My strength is
yours for the asking, son."[1]

Like Edward, do you sometimes fail to ask for help when
you're struggling? Our earthly dads aren't around all the time.
But Jesus is always with us all. He promises, "You can be sure
that I will be with you always" (Matthew 28:20 ICB). And we can
be sure that no muscles are stronger than His: "With men this is
impossible, but with God all things are possible" (19:26 HCSB).

Perhaps it's hard for you to sit still in class. Ask Jesus to
give you more patience. Maybe you lash out in anger when
things don't go your way. Pray for God's help to control
your temper. When we put our trust in Jesus, we have God's
power to help us overcome every problem.

How have you seen God's help in your life?

---

1 *Tony Evans' Book of Illustrations*, 124–25.

"Maid" for a Mission

Declare his glory among the nations,
his marvelous works among all the peoples!
PSALM 96:3 ESV

We don't know her name, but the "young girl" of 2 Kings 5:2 had been taken prisoner by the Syrians. Over 300 miles from home, she was forced to work in the house of Naaman. The girl noticed that every night Syria's top military leader came home sad and sick. Naaman had a terrible skin disease no doctor could cure. But the young maid knew God could help her master. So she told Captain Naaman and his wife about Him.

God used the faith and wisdom of the young maid, who trusted in and taught about her God, even though she'd been kidnapped, to soften the military giant's proud heart. Naaman listened to her advice—an amazing thing since she was both a little girl and a foreign slave. He humbled himself and came to trust in God's power. Then, the Lord chose to cleanse Naaman's skin *and* his sin.

Naaman was brought to faith by the witness of one of God's littlest servants, who knew she was made for a mission. Just think what you might accomplish as you let the love of Jesus shine through your life.

God has placed you where He wants you. How are you being faithful in your assignment to share His love?

Buyer Beware

"The thief comes only to steal and kill and destroy.
I came that they may have life and have it abundantly."
JOHN 10:10 ESV

Max Lucado tells of two vandals who broke into a toy store. Undetected, they stayed the night, swapping price tags for fun. The $5 sticker on a puzzle was replaced with one for $100. A $300 bicycle went down to $10. The $300 tag that had been hanging on the bike was stuck on a plastic and rhinestone tiara. All merchandise was repriced. Sadly, the store operated almost an entire day before anyone realized what had happened.[2]

The devil plays similar tricks, working to confuse us about what matters most. Jesus calls the devil a "thief" and the "father of lies" (John 10:10; 8:44 ESV). He deceives people on purpose. He tricks them into thinking that what they need is the complete opposite of what Jesus, who is truth, offers. Jesus calls our lives priceless, but the devil tells us cheap toys are the only things of value. The devil says we'll never be good enough for God. Jesus reminds us that He has paid with His life to save us and that we can rest in what He's done.

The devil wants to rob you of the great things that come along with being God's child. But our personal relationship with Jesus constantly reminds us of our true worth: we're loved and treasured children of God.

What should you remember the next time you feel sad or unloved?

---

2 Max Lucado, *No Wonder They Call Him the Savior* (Portland, OR: Multnomah Press, 1986).

Habit Forming

After his death, he … proved in many ways that he was alive.
The apostles saw Jesus during the 40 days after he was raised
from death. He spoke to them about the kingdom of God.

ACTS 1:3 ICB

One scientist said it takes twenty-one days for choices to become habits. Another showed that it takes about sixty-six days.[3] Let's give both of them a bit of credit by adding twenty-one and sixty-six, the number of days their experiments suggested it would take to form a habit, and then dividing that number by two. This brings us to an average of forty-three and a half days. To make it easier, let's round that number to forty. This happens to be a very important number in the Bible.

In Genesis 7:12, while Noah was in the ark, rain fell upon the earth for forty days. While receiving the Ten Commandments, Moses stayed on the mountain for forty days (Exodus 24:18). Joshua and Caleb explored the land of Canaan for forty days (Numbers 13:25). For forty days, the Israelites heard Goliath shout insults (1 Samuel 17:16). And the disciples had forty days after Jesus' resurrection to walk alongside Him once more (Acts 1:3).

Each of these forty days has something in common. Every one of those instances was just long enough to give God's followers the opportunity to make trusting Him a habit.

You might think reading your Bible every day is something you could never do. But grab a calendar and mark off forty days. Each day, read one chapter. By the time you get to day forty, spending time with God will be a habit.

Why is it important to make godly habits?

---

3   "How Long to Form a Habit?," PSYBLOG, accessed March 30, 2016, http://www.spring.org.uk/2009/09/how-long-to-form-a-habit.php.

Hearing and Heeding

Whoever knows the right thing to do
and fails to do it, for him it is sin.

JAMES 4:17 ESV

My twins were tossing a lacrosse ball outside the area in the front yard where I'd told them they could play. Almost immediately, Caroline and Daniel got to see—and hear—the impact of their bad decision. As I examined the broken glass from our front door, I couldn't avoid giving the "I told you so" lesson, highlighting how the damage could have been prevented if the twins had just obeyed my rule not to throw anything in the direction of the house.

In Caroline's words, "Mommy, I just didn't think something like this would happen." However, expensive damage was exactly what their father and I had warned them about. But knowing and doing are two different things. Hearing "Children, obey your parents" (Colossians 3:20 ESV) so many times, I am certain our twins can recite this verse. However, there's a big difference between hearing and heeding. And when we don't do what God tells us, we sin.

God's Word is true and His principles are for our protection. He tells us to honor, respect, and obey our parents (Ephesians 6:1–2), and He expects us to do it. Shattered glass and shattered trust can be avoided when we choose to obey God's rules.

What right thing do you sometimes fail to do? Why?

Grasshopper Faith

*Faith should not be in the wisdom of men
but in the power of God.*

1 CORINTHIANS 2:5 NKJV

On the edge of Canaan, the Israelites failed to believe God was about to give them the land He had promised as their own (Numbers 13:2). Trouble began when spies went to check on the local bad guys, then reported, "We seemed like grasshoppers in our own eyes, and we looked the same to them" (Numbers 13:33). In other words, they thought the Canaanites were too big to fight.

Sadly, people put more trust in bad reports than in the Lord. In the Israelites' case, weak faith kept them wandering in the wilderness for forty years! But when God gave them a new opportunity to enter the land He'd promised, He also helped them understand what the Canaanites really thought about the people of Israel gathering at their borders. A woman from Canaan explained, "Our hearts melted in fear and everyone's courage failed because of you, for the Lord your God is God in heaven above and on the earth below" (Joshua 2:10–11). All those years ago, while the Israelites felt tiny, they were really towering! It wasn't because they were impressive in size or ability. It was because God was on their side.

Do you have grasshopper faith—a halfhearted belief in God that questions whether or not He can really do as He promises? Remember that Jesus is far bigger than your fears. Choose to trust Him.

What is something big you think God might want you to trust Him with this week?

Rock the Boat

*He said, "Come." So Peter got out of the boat and
walked on the water and came to Jesus.*

MATTHEW 14:29 ESV

In Jesus' day, a boat wasn't powered by a motor but by
oars or sails. If you've been in a rowboat, you know they
feel tippy when you get in or out of them.

The disciples were already shaken by a fierce storm
when Jesus started walking toward them on the water. When
Peter jumped up to take a lake walk with the Lord, the other
disciples fought for stability. I can imagine Judas yelling,
Pete! We're going to flip over!

Because Peter wanted to be with Jesus so much, his
friends were able to see Jesus like never before. They saw He
was able to give them abilities they'd never imagined. More
importantly, they saw that He was deeply worthy of worship.
"You really are the Son of God!" the disciples confessed
after seeing Jesus conquer the water with Peter alongside
Him (Matthew 14:33 NLT).

Every day, we have opportunities to be so bold in our
belief in Jesus that we get out of the boat, shake things up,
and help direct our friends' eyes to the Savior. Jesus has
power over everything. But will we be courageous enough
to rock the boat so that others might understand?

Would you say you are sitting or standing in the boat of
"faith"? If you're sitting, how might you stand up and show
others Jesus this week?

Fix Your Eyes

Jesus immediately reached out and grabbed [Peter].
"You have so little faith," Jesus said. "Why did you doubt me?"
MATTHEW 14:31 NLT

Peter was the only disciple who asked to walk out onto the water with Jesus. Yet, when he failed to keep his eyes on the Lord and sank, Jesus said, "Peter, your faith isn't big enough. You didn't trust Me." If I were Peter, I might have replied, *But Lord, John didn't come. Neither did Andrew, James, Philip, or the others. I was the only one. My faith is bigger than theirs! Shouldn't that make up for my moment of distraction?*

But Jesus never weighs our faith against anyone else's. Instead, He watches us constantly to see whether we will keep Him the center of our focus. To settle for anything less than that, even for a moment, sets us up to sink. And it shows our faith is weak.

Sometimes, a coach may threaten to cut us from the team for missing soccer practice on a Sunday, so we tell ourselves it won't matter to skip out on church. Or when friends snicker and whisper when they see us bow in prayer at lunchtime, we decide we'll pray later when no one's watching. But every time we focus on fear like that, we lose sight of Jesus. We show that our faith is weak, that we doubt He's worth the attention He truly deserves.

When was the last time you took your eyes off Jesus and felt as if you were sinking?

Heavenly Nicknames

*"I will also give that person a white stone
with a new name written on it."*

REVELATION 2:17

Princess. Bear. Mayor. Boo. Mule. Ladybug. Sunshine. Mullet. These are just a few of the nicknames we use in my family. We give nicknames to people we love and know very well. Often, they describe some quality of a person's character or personality. For example, my daddy is very stubborn. Since mules are headstrong too, Daddy earned the nickname Mule. Mom makes a room brighter when she's in it. We affectionately call her Sunshine.

Jesus had many names too, given to Him by His Father: Alpha and Omega. Bread of Life. Chosen One. Good Shepherd. Immanuel. I Am. Light of the world. In fact, over two hundred nicknames for Jesus are given in the Bible. Each one is a description of His perfect nature.

Jesus assigned a few nicknames too. He renamed His disciple Simon, "Peter," meaning "rock" in Greek (John 1:42). And James and John were such a powerful pair that Jesus dubbed them "Sons of Thunder" (Mark 3:17 ESV).

Did you know Jesus is going to give you a special nickname one day? The book of Revelation tells us He will give each of us a white stone with our new name written on it. No doubt your heavenly nickname will perfectly reflect what Jesus thinks of you.

What nickname do you imagine Jesus giving you that best reflects your relationship with Him?

Trust Jesus for Plenty

*Then he said, "Throw out your net on the right-hand
side of the boat, and you'll get plenty of them!"
So we did, and couldn't draw in the net because
of the weight of the fish, there were so many!*

JOHN 21:6 TLB

The disciples were frustrated and tired after fishing all night and catching absolutely nothing. But Jesus, the living Word of God, showed up and said, "Throw your net on the right side of the boat and you will find some" (John 21:6). The risen Savior promised a blessing, if only they would obey.

When the disciples shifted their nets from one side of the boat to the other as He told them, they could hardly hoist the huge catch. The Bible records that they pulled in 153 fish. And they weren't tiny ones, either. They were "large" (v. 11).

This true "fish tale" teaches us three important life lessons: (1) When we are upset about the way something in life is going, we can trust God's Word for advice and encouragement; (2) Obedience results in blessings; and (3) Blessings are meant to be counted.

Maybe you feel anxious about going back to school or doing well in a competition. Remember that in His Word Jesus tells us that when we bring all of our concerns to Him, He hears us (1 John 5:15); honors our obedience to do what He says (Luke 11:28); and heaps on us a boat load of "blessings" (John 1:16 ICB).

Based on John 21:6, what has Jesus promised you?

The Blessing of "No"

"Your Father knows what you need before you ask Him."

MATTHEW 6:8 NLV

Jack's mom was helping him with schoolwork when he asked, "Mommy, may I ask God to help me find my favorite toy car?" She nodded and they kneeled together, taking the matter to the Lord before Jack went back to his math lesson. The next day, Jack's mother asked if he'd found his toy. "No, ma'am," he answered happily, "but God has made me not want to." God didn't answer Jack's prayer the way he wanted. Instead, God answered Jack's prayer by changing Jack's desires. That set him up for what he really needed: a hard lesson in responsibility.

Have you ever felt disappointed because God didn't answer your prayer the way you wanted? Could it be that by answering your prayer with what felt like a no, God was really showing His love for you? When you go to God in prayer, remember that He desires what's best for you. He wants your trust.

God knows everything we really need. But sometimes we require help knowing what's best for us. The best way to receive that help is to stay in constant communication with God through prayer. That's one of the many reasons we pray—even though the Lord already knows what's happening in our lives and can act without it.

Think about a time God said no to your request. What do you think He might have been teaching you instead?

Swim Buddy

I know the LORD is always with me.
I will not be shaken, for he is right beside me.
PSALM 16:8 NLT

My daughter Harrison loved swim lessons, until her instructor took away her "swimmies," the devices she depended on to stay afloat. She doesn't like the feeling of being out there without help—even though her instructor is always close.

God understands this feeling. That's why He promised in His Word, "When you go through deep waters, I will be with you" (Isaiah 43:2 NLT). In my Bible, I have circled the word *when*. God doesn't say "if" tough times come; He says "when." He reassures us with these words because sad and frustrating circumstances beyond our control are bound to happen. But as Christians, we never swim life's challenges alone. From the moment we place our faith in Jesus, we have His power and presence to depend on at all times. He's an instructor who will always stay close, keeping us afloat, even if all else fails.

Maybe you are in the middle of some deep water in your life. Maybe you've moved and don't know anyone. Maybe you're struggling at school. Whatever is scaring you, let it remind you how much you need Jesus and that He's always there for you. Remember, Jesus swims alongside you in life; you can always trust in His protection and perfect love.

When times are tough in your life, who do you reach out to first?

Let It Go

Set your minds on things above,
not on earthly things.

COLOSSIANS 3:2

One day, when Caroline was a year old, she screamed so loudly I immediately dropped the clothes I was hanging in her closet and sprinted to help. Caroline had reached her tiny hand between the slats in her crib to grab her stuffed lion. When she tried to pull her favorite toy to her side, it was too big to fit. Though simply letting go of the toy would have freed Caroline, she persisted to hold on and ended up in a panic. Not until I pried the toy from her fingers could she move freely.

We naturally want to hold onto things we love—our toys, our time, our food, our own way. But sometimes our determination to have those things gets us stuck. Maybe we like games so much that we feel lonely, because we don't take time for friends. Maybe we consume so many unhealthy snacks that we don't have the energy to play.

The Bible tells us to think about heavenly things, instead of earthly stuff. That means that instead of holding onto possessions and habits as if they were the most important things in the world, you should be thinking about Jesus—who really is of top importance. Your life, like the things you're tempted to cling tightly to—even your toy lion—should be held in open hands. That sets you free to run after the Lord.

Why does thinking on heavenly things lead to freedom?

Hard Knock Life Lessons

My troubles turned out all for the best—
they forced me to learn from your textbook.
PSALM 119:71 MSG

A Haitian teen had never slept in a bed with sheets or used an indoor bathroom. He counted himself blessed to eat daily. But all those hardships kept him thankful—and dependent on Jesus as his Provider.

Missionary friends who desired to treat him to comfort and good food flew the teen to America. They heaped abundance on him. At the end of his stay in America, the young Haitian expressed his thanks to those who had funded his trip to the United States. "But … I cannot wait to head home," he admitted sheepishly. "I have enjoyed my time in America with you where you have so much, but in Haiti, I have to depend on Jesus for everything. I miss that feeling of hanging onto Him every hour."[4]

Imagine what it would be like to have to trust Jesus for your next meal and for clothes to cover your body. Don't forget the One who has provided all of your "plenty." The next time you need something, don't think of it as an inconvenience, but as a chance to exercise dependence on Him. The Lord is our Provider. Life's discomforts help us remember that fact.

How can being uncomfortable become a blessing and help us grow our relationship with Jesus?

---

4 Patrick M. Morley, *I Surrender* (Brentwood, TN: Wolgemuth & Hyatt Publishers, 1990).

Freedom to Approach

*We have confidence to enter the Most Holy Place
by the blood of Jesus, by a new and living way
opened for us through the curtain, that is, his body.*

HEBREWS 10:19–20

The day Jesus died on the cross, He took the punishment for all the bad things you and I do wrong so we could be free. Through Jesus we are free to live without guilt, to look forward to heaven, to approach God with confidence.

Before that time, people repeatedly made animal sacrifices to try to earn God's acceptance. In fact, as Jesus died and experienced separation from His Father because of our sins, priests in the temple were slaughtering lambs for the Passover celebration. This tradition dated back to the time of Moses. Passover was in remembrance of the night when lambs' blood was wiped on the Hebrews' doorposts to protect them from the curse of death during the plagues on Egypt.

When Jesus died, the thick curtain that separated the Holy of Holies from the rest of the building ripped from top to bottom (Mark 15:37-38). That miracle was a sign that the final lamb, Jesus, had been sacrificed. This enabled anyone to come to God by placing their faith in God's Son instead of making further sacrifices.

Jesus ripped down the obstacle that separated us from God. Through faith in Him, you can draw close to God, knowing that in you He doesn't see an unholy sinner, but a child who's forgiven and acceptable in His sight.

How free do you feel to talk to God about everything going on in your life?

Trust the Engineer

"Father, I place my life in your hands!"
LUKE 23:46 MSG

Writer Corrie ten Boom said, "When a train goes through a tunnel and it gets dark, you don't throw away the ticket and jump off. You sit and trust the engineer."[5] In my midtwenties, I was ready to jump off the singleness train. But then I remembered Corrie's words. If God, Engineer over my life story, loved me enough to send Jesus to die for me, then He loved me enough to guide me to just the person He intended as my husband. First, however, I needed to learn to be satisfied in Him.

Years passed. Some days I got really frustrated waiting for my prince charming, but I kept obeying God's Word and asking Him to guide me. I kept Jesus first in my heart and talked through my feelings with my parents as I waited. Sure enough, Lee Reeves stepped into my life just when God intended.

You may have moments when you grow frustrated with your own life story. Whether you are hoping to make the varsity tennis team or want that certain someone at school to look your way, remember that all our cares can be turned into prayers. Trust Jesus as the capable Engineer of your life. Though the unknown may seem dark and the wait may feel like you're stuck in a long tunnel, your future is safest when you commit it to His hands.

How might you show Jesus that you trust Him with your future?

---

5 Corrie ten Boom, *Tramp for the Lord* (Old Tappan, NY: Fleming H. Revell, 1974).

My Thanks for Giving

*[Jesus] bore our sins in his body on the tree,
that we might die to sin and live to righteousness.*

1 PETER 2:24 ESV

The *Giving Tree* is a story about a tree and boy who love each other. The boy climbed the tree's branches daily, making crowns from her leaves, and eating her delicious fruit. But as he grew older, the boy cared less and less about spending time with the tree. He only cared about what she could give him.

Selflessly, the tree offered up all she had—apples, branches, and trunk—because she so wanted the boy to be happy. When all that remained of her was a stump, the little-boy-turned-old-man visited the tree again and rested on all she had left.[6] You and I can be like that selfish boy when we say yes to Jesus as Savior and ignore Him as Lord. Unlike the tree in the story, Jesus is not concerned about us being happy—giving us what we want with no requests in return. Instead, He wants our love for Him to be evident as we live in obedience to His commands. That's how we say thank you. It's how we show our appreciation for the forgiveness and bright future He secured for us by dying on another tree, the tree where He gave all He had for us.

In what ways do you show Jesus thanks for all He has given you?

---

6 Shel Silverstein, *The Giving Tree* (New York: HarperCollins Publishers, 1964).

The Singer

The Lord your God...will rejoice over you with gladness;
he will quiet you by his love;
he will exult over you with loud singing.

ZEPHANIAH 3:17 ESV

Every night as I tucked my babies in, I sang over them. I sang of my love and care for them, and I sang of Jesus. Worship tunes and hymns were their lullabies.

The prophet Zephaniah noted that the Lord Himself sings over His children, creating lullabies of a sort that tell of His love and care for us. And He doesn't just mumble the words. The Bible says the Lord has the kind of voice that'll give you goosebumps as He belts out assurance of His passion. Totally unashamed, the Lord sings loudly enough that all of heaven can hear what He thinks about you.

Maybe you dread bedtime because you're feeling sad. Perhaps a boy or girl you liked no longer likes you or a good friend has moved away. Maybe your teacher is covering new material so quickly that you feel overwhelmed and on the verge of tears. When you go to sleep tonight, imagine the Lord Jesus sitting on the edge of your bed. Then, remember that He loved you so much He died and rose again so that one day you can live with Him forever. Then, listen. Deep within your heart, know He is crooning a beautiful love song just for you.

What lyrics would you write in a love song for Jesus?

Be a Barnabas

Encourage each other daily, while it is still called today,
so that none of you is hardened by sin's deception.
HEBREWS 3:13 HCSB

Barnabas, called an "encourager" in Acts 4:36, stood up for Paul when everyone else doubted him. Before he met Jesus, Paul persecuted Christians, so people were afraid to accept him. But Barnabas told the disciples how the Lord had changed Paul's heart, allowing him to boldly preach in the name of Jesus. That moment transformed Paul's ministry. Because of Barnabas' encouraging word, Paul won support from the disciples. With their backing, he became the greatest missionary the world's ever seen.

You can be an encourager too. Be on the lookout for new boys and girls at school or church who've accepted Christ, but who may really need a friend to encourage them in their walk of faith. Be someone who's willing to go to others and say, *Meet so-and-so. He's a Christian and a great guy. Let's hang out together!*

When Christians encourage one another, they share the love of Jesus. They also build unity, blocking the enemy who likes to plant weeds of discouragement that make people doubt what God is doing in their lives and tempting them to return to old bad habits. Remember, your love and attitude are a testimony telling the world who Jesus is. Who knows? God might use your life to prepare the world's next Paul.

Who is a "Paul" you can be a "Barnabas" to this week?

The Deal of a Lifetime

"I have placed before you an open door."

REVELATION 3:8

The television game show *Let's Make a Deal* offered contestants their choice of prizes. But the best prize was hidden behind one of several doors. Pick the right one, and you could win a new car. The wrong door could open to reveal a goat or an empty wheelbarrow.

God doesn't play games. That's especially important since He's the only One who can grant us the prize of heaven. In the Bible, God gave us only one door to eternal salvation, Jesus Christ. Acts 10:35 says, "If you want God and are ready to do as he says, the door [to salvation] is open" (MSG). Jesus waits with arms stretched wide open for each person, inviting us to trade in sin for His forgiveness, so we can walk away a winner of eternal life.

The devil, however, likes to tempt us to think other supposed doors to heaven are just as valid. He sets up false religions, doors to counterfeit prizes that direct our attention away from Christ. But peeking behind these "trap" doors can make us miss out on the real deal.

Maybe you like ninja cartoons and are intrigued by Buddhism. It could be you like the thought of saying magic words and mixing potions like the fairies and wizards on TV. Understand that looking into such things is to consider spiritual options that can lead you away from God.

Why do you think the Bible is so clear that Jesus, the Door, is the only way to heaven?

No Compromise

*Don't you know that a little yeast
affects the whole batch of dough?*

1 CORINTHIANS 5:6 NET

The Bible teaches us to remain on guard against "yeast," which is another word for sin. But that can require tough choices. It helps to understand why it matters. Speaker Steve Farrar's teenage sons were heading to catch a movie when Steve said they couldn't. "It's a true story," they protested. "It's about bravery and sacrifice." Steve stood firm. He'd read a review that said the movie had nude scenes and cursing.

Later that evening, Steve offered the boys brownies. "Before you take a bite, I need to tell you something," he said. "I made these using the best ingredients: organic flour and sugar, cage-free eggs, and pure cacao powder. But I added a little something: dog poop." The boys dropped the dessert immediately.

Then, he continued, "Guys, the reason you won't take a bite of that brownie is the very same reason I'm refusing to allow you to see that movie. A little dog poop in your brownie is the same as mixing a little sin into your lives. When what's in there can harm you, you should stay away from it."[7]

Think about the things you watch. A little bad language, a little inappropriate content. All of it is foul stuff that can pollute your mind and damage your relationship with Christ. Make up your mind not to compromise your purity.

What things do you think are inappropriate in God's eyes for you to see or listen to in movies and TV shows?

---

7 I am indebted to Steve Farrar, who shared this personal story at his 1998 conference on "Finishing Strong" at the Billy Graham Training Center at The Cove in Asheville, NC.

Children of the Light

For you were once darkness,
but now you are light in the Lord.
Walk as children of light.

EPHESIANS 5:8 HCSB

A. W. Milne, a Scotsman who responded to God's call to become a missionary, was a child of God's light. He spent his life shining for Jesus. Milne was part of a group that was so excited about telling the world about the Lord that they called themselves "one-way" missionaries. Buying one-way tickets for various assignments around the globe, they packed their belongings in coffins. This symbolized their decision: they were going to distant parts of the world to teach about Jesus until the day He took them to heaven.

Milne went to the New Hebrides, an island group in the South Pacific inhabited by cannibals. God allowed Milne to be accepted there. Milne taught the tribesmen about Jesus for thirty-five years. When he graduated to heaven, the tribe buried Milne in their village. On his tombstone they carved these words: "When he came there was no light. When he left there was no darkness."

Milne shined for Jesus by talking about Him, showing kindness in His name, and encouraging the tribesmen in their faith. You can shine in similar ways, telling friends about how Jesus has changed your life, treating others with kindness, and encouraging Christian friends to shine too. Because you know Jesus, you have His light residing in you. Every room should be brighter with you in it.

How can you shine for Jesus in your attitudes and actions today?

MAY

Dress Code

God made him who had no sin to be sin for us,
so that in him we might become the righteousness of God.

2 CORINTHIANS 5:21

Righteousness means moral excellence. The Chinese character for *righteousness* is made up of two parts. The upper part is the character for the word *lamb*. Under *lamb* is the character for the word *me*. Translated, *righteousness* means "the lamb over me." Only through Christ, the Lamb of God, is anyone righteous—a quality God requires if we're to enjoy His approval. Without righteousness, no one can draw close to God.

Being righteous is different than being forgiven. Think of forgiveness as Jesus washing you clean and righteousness as Him dressing you up for audience with God the almighty King, who's seated in His throne room. The Bible explains it like this: "He has clothed me with garments of salvation and arrayed me in a robe of his righteousness" (Isaiah 61:10).

On the cross, perfect Jesus took our dead works and rebellion and did for us what we could never do for ourselves. He bought us a righteous wardrobe. We are in good standing before God, acceptably righteous, only if we are clothed in Christ. Without Him, the Bible says even our best efforts to clean up our act will leave us wearing "filthy rags," unfit for the throne room.

How are you treating your new "clothes"?

Truth for the Traitor

He did not retaliate when he was insulted,
nor threaten revenge when he suffered.
He left his case in the hands of God,
who always judges fairly.
1 Peter 2:23 NLT

In Shakespeare's play, *Julius Caesar*, the emperor gasps after being stabbed by a group of attackers. Among them is his longtime friend, Marcus Brutus. Shocked by the betrayal, Caesar utters these last words: "You too, Brutus?"

It's terrible when a friend betrays us, taking advantage of our closeness to bring us harm. Even Jesus experienced betrayal when Judas, one of the Twelve, turned Him over to the Jewish leaders who wanted to kill Him. Judas was a phony friend more interested in making money off his association with the Lord than in having a relationship with Him.

Jesus, while saddened by Judas' actions, did something amazing in response to betrayal. He didn't say mean things to Judas. He didn't fight back when the Jewish leaders led Him away. Jesus allowed Judas' actions to lead Him to the cross. There Jesus not only asked God to forgive those who'd hurt Him, but laid down His life so that every betrayer—every one of us who has ever taken advantage of God's love and care by turning against Him—could find God's forgiveness.

Maybe a friend has gossiped about you. Maybe your brother or sister blamed you for something you didn't do. Choose to forgive as Jesus did. When you do, your life will show the world what Jesus' love has accomplished.

Why do you think Jesus befriended a man He knew would betray Him?

A Recipe for Success

Work happily together.
Don't try to act big. ... And don't think you know it all!
ROMANS 12:16 TLB

Pulling out my Crock-Pot®, I imagined mumbling coming from the refrigerator. It seemed to get louder as I set the veggies on the counter and sliced each item into bite-sized pieces to add to my roast. The commotion grew loudest when I combined everything together and dropped them into the pot. My imagined conversation made me think about spiritual things. It went something like this: *I don't want my feathery top tangled around the roast*, the carrots complained. *Potatoes make my skin crawl*, the onion cried. Sobbing, the celery said, *I want to sit next to the roast! I do my best work with it!* Chaos ensued and dinner plans were ruined when the items in the pot refused to cooperate. Each ingredient protested having to work with the others—and none was too confident in how my recipe would turn out, anyway.

You and I are ingredients in a recipe known only to God and fashioned by His hands. He has created all of us uniquely different, but expects us to work together wherever He places us. Insulting others and whining about our situation means we don't trust God's great plans. Only when we choose to humble ourselves and submit to Him, cooperating with others, do we truly partner with Him in achieving His grand recipe for our lives.

What is your attitude about where God has placed you right now?

Use the Brakes

"Stop sinning."
John 5:14

You've probably noticed red stop signs at street corners in your neighborhood. Did you know those signs are not there to slow down your travel time, but to protect you and others? Our lives as Christians are full of stop signs too. These rules and warnings are not intended to annoy us, but to protect us, to keep us from wrecking our lives with sin.

Near the Sheep Gate at Bethesda, Jesus comforted one of His lost lambs, a very sick man. Then, He commanded him, "Stop sinning" (John 5:14). That's because Jesus knew that if the man were to continue in his ways, he'd mess up his life again and miss out on God's plans. That's why the Bible so often commands us to stop sinning and try to keep away from sin altogether.

Maybe lately you've been using bad language. In Matthew 28:18 Jesus said, "All authority in heaven and on earth has been given to me," reminding us that when our lives have been changed by His power, our choices can be too. Ask Him to replace those dirty words with good ones, to help you stop the habit you've developed.

Before Jesus, your life was like driving a car with only a gas pedal. But once you invited Jesus into your life, the Holy Spirit became the brake system that helps you stop sinning and avoid it altogether. Whether you choose to use the brakes is up to you.

Why do we sometimes still want to stomp on the gas pedal, when Jesus has told us to stop?

Include the Life of the Party

"Do whatever He tells you,"
His mother told the servants.

JOHN 2:5 HCSB

The world likes to call Christians "party poopers," suggesting that real fun only happens when we ignore what God's Word says. But life with Jesus is anything but dull and boring. It brings blessings and excitement.

Jesus' whole ministry was about blessing people. In fact, His very first miracle occurred at a wedding party in Cana. In Jesus' day, weddings were week-long celebrations. Jesus and His disciples attended one, along with Jesus' mother, Mary.

On day three of the six-day gathering, the hosts ran into a hardship. Their party's success was threatened because they were running low on refreshments. Mary knew Jesus was God's Son and could fix anything. So she told the servants to obey Jesus. When they did, the partygoers enjoyed far better refreshments than before. Inviting Jesus to the party, and honoring His instructions, turned the whole event into a long-remembered success. Two thousand years after it happened, we're still talking about that party!

In doing what Jesus tells us, we set ourselves up for the best lives possible. And we help others understand that Jesus is the real life of the party. We help them recognize the benefits of inviting Him into every moment of their lives. Like guests at the wedding feast, they can "taste and see that the Lord is good" (Psalm 34:8) when we, His servants, obey Him faithfully.

Is Jesus welcome at your parties? Why or why not?

Say No Like Joe

*Flee the evil desires of youth and pursue righteousness,
faith, love and peace, along with those who
call on the Lord out of a pure heart.*

2 TIMOTHY 2:22

In the Old Testament, we read about Joseph, a young man who knew when to say no. Day after day, Potiphar's wife insisted on Joseph, the family slave, partying with her. But Joe knew Mrs. Potiphar's plans for him involved dishonoring his relationship with God. When Mrs. Potiphar tried to *insist* Joseph go along with her ideas, Joseph fled the scene. Though he may have been tempted to roll with what probably sounded like a desirable plan, Joseph knew escape was a better choice than compromise.

Like Joseph, you and I will be invited to participate in things that go against our relationship with God. Television shows may tempt us to be disrespectful to parents, talking to them as if we know it all. "Friends" may try to make us think their approval is more important than God's, like when they encourage us to participate in wrong choices such as bullying others or ganging up to annoy our teachers. Escaping these situations—getting away from them—is the wisest course of action, if we intend to remain faithful to God.

Don't hesitate to stop watching a show in which kids speak rudely to their parents. It's okay to turn off the television. And don't cave in to bad advice or coaxing designed to make you forget about your relationship with Christ. Flee evil like Joseph did. Whether or not the action involves leaving the room, say no to anything that would harm your relationship with Jesus.

What is a temptation you have resisted by fleeing?

Put in the Work

*I discipline my body like an athlete,
training it to do what it should.*
1 CORINTHIANS 9:27 NLT

Legendary Dallas Cowboys' head coach Tom Landry was asked to explain the hardest part of being a football coach. Coach Landry replied, "The hardest part is getting a group of men to do something they don't want to do in order to achieve what they have wanted all of their lives." Coach Landry knew his players wanted to win the Super Bowl, but he had to motivate them to do the hard work—daily work-outs and drills—to get there.

There are certain hard choices we must make every day as Christians, things we may not want to do that are essential to getting us where the Lord wants us to go. Things like reading the Bible daily, praying often, and choosing to obey God help us to stay fit so we'll be ready for the assignments and positions in which God places us.

Coach Landry's Cowboys didn't always feel like enduring every test of speed, flexibility, and strength he required, but if they wanted to make their coach happy and win as a team, they had to be well trained as individuals. They had to put in the work that prepared them for the big game.

When you make daily Bible reading and prayer a part of your life, you are showing Jesus, the Coach of your life, that you want to please Him. You're also getting prepared for whatever He may ask of you.

What kind of training are you doing to be the best you can be for Team Jesus?

Trust the Facts

It is better to trust in the Lord than to put confidence in man.

PSALM 118:8 KJV

When he received word that the *Titanic* was in trouble, P. A. S. Franklin of the White Star Line responded, "We place absolute confidence in the Titanic. We believe the boat is unsinkable."[1] Moments later, the ship was under the icy sea and over 1,500 passengers were dead.

If our beliefs aren't based on the truth of God's Word, they set us up to be just as wrong and unhelpful as P. A. S. Franklin was when he foolishly trusted an opinion over reality. For example, some people believe Jesus is only one of many ways to heaven—even though that doesn't agree with what the Bible teaches. Others feel it doesn't matter what the Bible says, thinking it's perfectly fine for each person to live out his own truth—even though if I have my "truth" and you have a different truth, at least one of us is wrong. Mr. Franklin learned the hard way that substituting wrong beliefs for facts sets people up for catastrophe.

Putting confidence in false beliefs, like "all religions lead to heaven," keeps us from telling people about Jesus, the only One who can help us navigate life safely and deliver us to heaven's harbor at our journey's end. You and I must pay attention to the warning in God's Word: Jesus said, "I am the way, the truth, and the life. No one comes to the Father except through Me" (John 14:6 HCSB). That's a truth worth sharing.

How can you tell when you're placing your confidence in other people's opinions instead of God's?

---

1 "The Titanic – Why Did People Believe the Titanic Was Unsinkable?," History OnTheNet, 2016, http://www.historyonthenet.com/titanic/unsinkable.htm.

Ark of Rescue

"I am the door.
The person who enters through me will be saved."
JOHN 10:9 ICB

Noah, the "preacher of righteousness" (2 Peter 2:5), did more than build an ark, as God instructed. With every pound of his hammer and measure of his cubit, he warned an unbelieving world that God's judgment was coming. The only way to be saved from drowning was to enter the ark. But most people just laughed at Noah.

God's instructions for the ark included only one door to the outside (Genesis 6:16). If people believed Noah's words, they could've walked through it to enter the safety of the ark and avoid the flood. That door, in fact, serves as a foreshadow—a hint—of what Jesus would do.[2] As John 10:9 states, Jesus is the door of salvation we must enter through by faith to avoid death. There's only one way to be saved from God's judgment on sin.

The Bible says eight people, Noah and his family, acted on what God said. They stepped into the ark while the door was still open. Then, God shut it behind them (Genesis 7:16). These people, and the animals with them, were safe. Everyone else perished.

When you trust Jesus as your Savior, you enter the only door to salvation. You're saved and safe. You don't ever have to worry about being thrown out. God's got you sealed in. You can wait out the storms of life in confidence that God will carry you through.

Why do you think God foreshadowed (hinted at) what Jesus would do?

2 John C. Whitcomb, "Christ and the Ark of Noah," Answers in Genesis, http://www.answersingenesis.org/noahs-ark/christ-and-ark-of-noah.

Heaven

Jesus replied [to the thief dying on a cross beside His],
"I assure you, today you will be with me in paradise."
LUKE 23:43 NLT

If you've placed your trust in Jesus for the forgiveness of your sins, you get to go to heaven. Think about the most fun place you've ever visited—maybe it's a park or a city or someone's home. Heaven, described as a paradise, will be even better.

The Bible tells us there's no sickness, pain, fighting, sadness, or crying in heaven (Revelation 21:4). That's because sin causes every bad thing, and there will be no sin there (v. 27). Heaven's huge gates are made from a single pearl and the streets are pure gold (v. 21). Imagine riding your bike down that! Or, perhaps, having your own pet lion? Even wild animals won't bite there (Isaiah 11:6).

There are also angels in the home we'll share with Jesus. Some people believe when we die we become angels, but that's not true (1 Corinthians 6:3). Instead, people likely will make friends with angels in heaven. Maybe even the ones God assigned to watch over us on earth (Hebrews 1:14).[3]

The greatest news about our future home is that our best friend, Jesus, lives there, and He has lots of surprises waiting for us. The Bible says, "No eye has seen, no ear has heard, and no mind has imagined what God has prepared for those who love him" (1 Corinthians 2:9 NLT). It will amaze you!

What do you imagine living in heaven is going to be like?

---

3 Randy Alcorn, "Will We Become Angels in Heaven?," Eternal Perspective Ministries, http://www.epm.org/blog/2014/Jan/10/become-angels-heaven.

No Such Thing as Luck

*We may throw the dice,
but the Lord determines how they fall.*
PROVERBS 16:33 NLT

Your momma's back is not going to break if you step on a crack. Friday the Thirteenth isn't different from any other day of the month. And knocking on wood is only going to make noise.

Words like *luck, chance, jinxed,* and *lucky* have no place in a Christian's vocabulary, because those terms say the opposite of what we believe. Hebrews 1:3 says God "regulates the universe by the mighty power of his command" (TLB). And Psalm 139:16 says all our days were written in His book before time's beginning. Nothing is out of God's control. God—not chance—is in charge.

After they hung Jesus on the cross, four Roman soldiers decided to roll some dice to see who would be the one to get His robe (John 19:23–24). Thousands of years before, the Lord had picked the very soldier who would win His wardrobe (Psalm 22:18). Perhaps, in His perfect power, Jesus knew having His earthly coat hanging in that Roman soldier's closet would one day remind him of his need for another robe only Jesus can provide—a righteous one He paid for with His blood, one that could even save the soldier who killed Jesus from the penalty of death. God's interest in the details of life proves we're not lucky. We're loved.

Do you say certain words or do certain things in hopes of being "lucky" or changing an outcome? What can you do to trust Jesus instead?

My Prince Will Come

"If I go and prepare a place for you,
I will come back and take you to be with me
that you also may be where I am."

JOHN 14:3

Jesus promised that one day He would return to earth and lift the curse of sin once and for all. When that happens, He'll take even living believers back to heaven with Him where we'll all live together forever. Jesus is the reason the human heart so enjoys a good "happily ever after" story.

In the movie *Snow White*, Snow White thinks about her true love and sings about him coming for her someday. As the story progresses, a wicked queen tempts Snow White to eat a poisonous apple, separating the girl from her prince. But when the hero returns, his love breaks evil's power over her. Then, the two are free to live happily in their castle home.

When Adam and Eve ate poisonous fruit offered by another wicked villain, sin entered the world. Placing faith in Jesus, truly loving Him, assures each of us a future in heaven and reminds us that good will triumph in the end. When we see Jesus with our own eyes, whether at the end of our lives or at His return, sin will never again tempt us. And we'll live with Prince Jesus forever.

How are you encouraged by knowing that Jesus promises you can live forever with Him in a sinless world?

Becoming a Party Planner

Do not be misled:
"Bad company corrupts good character."

1 Corinthians 15:33

My friend Diane is a party planner. She organizes social events. Jesus wants "party planner" to be one of your jobs too. You don't need to be the kind that coordinates entertainment, but you should be the kind of party planner who knows in advance what kind of party invitation to accept and how to act when you're away from Mom or Dad's care.

Not all parties are ones we should attend. There may be a time when you are asked to join friends at someone's home even though their parents are away. Or perhaps someone will ask you to a party where there will be alcohol or R-rated movies. Such parties should be avoided.

In Matthew 10:16 Jesus gives us great advice that applies to times when we find ourselves at parties that weren't what we expected. It applies to every situation in which we can't count on someone else's care. Jesus says, "You will be like sheep among wolves. So be as smart as snakes. But also be like doves and do nothing wrong" (ICB). He is reminding us that wolves (those who don't care about Jesus) like to take advantage of sheep (those who do). In other words, it's dangerous to keep company with people who will ask us to go against what we believe. Avoid placing yourself in bad company when you can. And be ready to stick to your faith and leave when pressured to do wrong things.

What information can help you decide whether or not to attend a party?

Stop the Misery

A miserable heart means a miserable life.
PROVERBS 15:15 MSG

Nobody remembered Eeyore's birthday. Discouraged, the gloomy donkey said, "I'll stay here and be miserable, with no presents, no cake, no candles."[4] Then he threw a celebration of his own—a pity party.

Sometimes, things don't go our way and life just seems "unfair." Familiar with the feeling, God's prophet Elijah told God he'd had enough of Queen Jezebel, the woman God called him to speak against (1 Kings 19:4). Jonah became so self-centered that he cared more about a plant than the people God had called him to preach to (Jonah 4:9–11). Both men planned their own pity parties. They were completely miserable and unwilling to get over it.

Like Eeyore, maybe you've been overlooked. Or maybe a change in your circumstances is even more serious. It's okay to feel sad, but set a stopwatch on the time you allow yourself to dwell on the negative. God wanted Elijah and Jonah to get back to work, not to sit around, gloomy and complaining. You can be sure God intends to use your life to accomplish big things. Don't be like Eeyore or the weary prophets. Refuse to wallow in self-pity. Ask God to replace your misery with joy for life's journey.

What can you do in tough times so that you don't find yourself holding a pity party?

---

4   *Winnie the Pooh and a Day for Eeyore*, directed by Rick Reinert (Burbank, CA: Walt Disney Productions, 1983), VHS.

He Sees

She gave this name to the Lord who spoke to her:
"You are the God who sees me," for she said,
"I have now seen the One who sees me."
GENESIS 16:13

A little boy was forced to escape to his rooftop when his home caught fire. The boy's father stood on the ground below with arms wide open, shouting to his son, "Jump! I'll catch you." The father knew his seven-year-old had to jump to be saved from the rapidly spreading blaze. But the little boy could only see the blackness of the smoke and feel the heat of the flames. He couldn't see his father. "Daddy, I can't jump! I cannot see you," he cried. The father replied, "But Jackson, I can see you and that's all that matters."

Sometimes, the heat of the situation we're in seems so intense we think God, our heavenly Father, doesn't see us—because our own fears and distractions keep us from seeing Him. Perhaps you've been abandoned by someone you love. Maybe you had to repeat a grade in school and are worried about what your friends will think. Take heart! You're never out of God's sight. Jesus sees you and understands what you're going through. He loves you and has promised to take care of you. It's your job to trust in His closeness.

What can you focus on during challenging times so that you don't lose sight of God in your life?

Waits Build Muscle

*Wait on the Lord; be of good courage,
and He shall strengthen your heart; wait, I say, on the Lord!*
PSALM 27:14 NKJV

People often picture Popeye the Sailor Man, a muscular cartoon character, when they think of strength. But whereas Popeye downed spinach to bulk up, the rest of us must depend on exercise.

Our hearts are the hardest working muscles in our bodies—physically and spiritually. Strength training can build muscle tissue, but we need spiritual exercise to grow hearts strong in faith. The Bible teaches that God, our heavenly Trainer, uses the waiting times of our lives to build new strength for our spiritual hearts.

I've discovered that every time I've disciplined myself to wait on the Lord and not rush ahead with my plans, I do indeed grow stronger in faith—my ability to trust in the Lord. Like flabby arms taking on new tone in response to lifting a dumbbell repeatedly, my heart begins to grow more accepting of life's frustrations and more determined to remain focused on the truths of God's Word.

Maybe you've been praying a long time for a sick parent to get well. Maybe you just want to get over the thing that makes you feel sad. Whatever it is, Jesus can use your wait time to make you stronger. He loves you too much to watch you walk around with "flabby" faith, so He'll work through your season of waiting to build your heart up in Him.

What "wait" is God using to bulk up your faith muscle today?

Train Your Eyes on the Real Deal

Examine everything carefully;
hold fast to that which is good.
1 Thessalonians 5:21–22 NASB

With his red-and-white-striped shirt, beanie hat, and glasses, Waldo is quite recognizable in a crowd. If you're good at "search and find" puzzles, you'll locate him easily. But when the artists of the *Where's Waldo?* books blend that main character into a crowd full of Waldo look-alikes—impostors wearing similar shirts or the same blue pants—the real deal is a lot harder to find.[5] Studying the image of the real Waldo is the best way to train your eyes to look past all of the fakes.

The Bible tells us Jesus is "the image of the invisible God" (Colossians 1:15 NASB). When we see Jesus, we see the Father. This means the more we know Jesus, the less likely we'll be to get fooled by other religious figures who claim to offer a path to God. Many religions—Buddhism, Hinduism, Islam—offer up key figures like Buddha and Allah, who claimed to teach the only valid path to heaven. But Scripture is clear that having a faith relationship with Jesus, the Creator's Son and perfect image, is the one and only way (John 14:6).

Don't be fooled by impostors and look-alikes. Carefully examine religious claims against the truth of God's Word. And hold fast to Jesus. He's the only real deal among a crowd of pretenders.

What would you say if a friend tells you that having faith in Allah is the same as having faith in Jesus?

5 Martin Handford, *Where's Waldo?* (Cambridge, MA: Candlewick Press, 1997).

Room for Improvement

A third time he asked him,
"Simon son of John, do you love me?"
JOHN 21:17 NLT

My paternal grandfather, Pat McClary, was known for his down-to-earth wisdom. If I brought home a failing grade on a test or paper, he would first ask if I did my best. Then, he'd say, "Well, the biggest room in all the world is the room for improvement." That meant I should take advantage of the opportunity to do better next time.

Peter needed room for improvement too. Called by Jesus from his job as a fisherman, Peter left his nets as fast as he could and followed Jesus. He was Jesus' friend. But after Jesus was arrested, Peter denied even knowing Him! Three times, just like Jesus foretold, Peter said, "I don't know that man" (Matthew 26:74 CEV)! Later Peter was really sorry he'd said that and cried. When Jesus rose from the dead, He did something amazing for Peter. Instead of giving him an F in faithfulness, Jesus forgave him. Then, He gave Peter three opportunities to prove how much he'd grown in his devotion toward Jesus. One new opportunity for every denial.

We, like Peter, fail because of sin. Maybe you feel like you've messed up too many times. But that's the beauty of a relationship with Jesus. Because of the cross, there's room for every heart to improve.

What can you do when you feel you've messed up too much for God to forgive you?

The Power Walk

"Whoever forces you to go one mile, go with him two."
MATTHEW 5:41 NASB

Imagine the government passing a law that says you have to give your dessert to the school bully. In Jesus' day, a law stated that any time a Roman soldier asked a Jewish man or boy to carry his load, he had to. No matter what the Israelite was doing, the law forced him to change his plans and walk the 5,280 feet as a slave to the soldier.

Jesus says the first mile (or milkshake) is our obligation. It's the law. But going beyond what is expected is our opportunity. It's a chance to demonstrate God's love and supernatural power. Jesus says by hauling the soldier's sack a second mile, or offering to buy the bully an afternoon snack after he swallows your brownie at lunch, you are taking positive steps toward softening a hard heart, as you display the love of Christ.

Jesus came to walk the first and second miles—and many more—for us. Matthew 20:28 clearly states, "The Son of Man did not come to be served, but to serve, and to give his life as a ransom for many." When we are willing, walking that extra mile can be a terrific witness of what Jesus has done for us. Only a heart transformed by His power can show love and kindness to those who have been unlovely.

How might you "walk the extra mile" for someone today?

I Am Potential

For we are God's handiwork,
created in Christ Jesus to do good works,
which God prepared in advance for us to do.

EPHESIANS 2:10

When I was a little girl, the Gaithers wrote a song that declares we are full of po-ten-tial-i-ty.[6]

The words remind me of Gideon, who was hiding from the vicious Midianites when God called him out of the shadows to lead the Israelites in victory against their enemy. A heavenly visitor said to Gideon, "Mighty hero, the Lord is with you!" (Judges 6:12 NLT). "Me?" Gideon responded. "I'm the runt of the litter" (v. 15 MSG). He obviously thought, *How can I have any such potential?*

But then it hit Gideon. God was with him. God saw his true potential. And if the Lord had plans for him, he must've decided, he should change how he viewed himself. The coward became courageous as Gideon realized he'd been created—and equipped—for something special God had prepared in advance for him to do.

God's got a special assignment just for you too. But like Gideon, you must realize that with the Lord, what you're capable of becoming is limitless. Your potential is mind-blowing! On the battleground or on the playground, you're a hero when you trust in His plans for you.

What difference would it make to start seeing yourself as God sees you?

---

6 "I Am A Promise," words and music by Bill and Gloria Gaither, William J. Gaither, Inc. (Admin. by Sheer Publishing (Pty) Ltd), 1975.

Guard Against False Advertisement

Don't just pretend to be good!
1 PETER 2:1 TLB

We pulled up behind a white Suburban at a stoplight and my daughter said, "Whoever drives that car is a Christian, Mom. Look at her bumper stickers." Sure enough, there were three: *Choose Life*, *Honk if you love Jesus*, and *Text & drive if you want to meet Him*.

The light turned and the rolling billboard took off, disregarding the speed limit. Moments later, we passed the stopped Suburban, where its driver was arguing angrily with the policeman who'd pulled her over. "You think that woman stole the car?" my son asked. "What she's advertising on her bumper sure doesn't match the way she's acting!"

Jesus warned against hypocrisy—telling people you're His follower while shamelessly disobeying Him. The religious leaders of Jesus' day publicly acted like they loved God, but when they didn't think anyone was watching, they'd lie, cheat, and steal.

"Everything they do is done for show," Jesus said sadly (Matthew 23:5 TLB).

Jesus knows one of the enemy's most successful strategies is to water-down our witness. That's what happens when we quote the right Bible verse in Sunday school, but disrespect the authority of our teachers in homeroom. By asking Jesus to change our conduct (2 Corinthians 3:18), we don't have to worry about being false advertisements. He makes our actions match our claims.

What can you ask Jesus to change in your heart that will make you a stronger witness for Him?

War!

The flesh desires what is contrary to the Spirit,
and the Spirit what is contrary to the flesh.
They are in conflict with each other.

GALATIANS 5:17

Tug-of-war is a contest where two teams stand on opposite sides and pull a rope, hoping to drag the weaker opponent across the line. You and I are in the middle of a spiritual tug-of-war every day. On one side is the "flesh," the pull of our old sinful nature. On the other is the Holy Spirit, our Helper which shows Christ at work in us from the moment we choose to follow Him.

Because Christ is a Christian's ultimate anchor in this tug-of-war match, we can take comfort in the fact that His influence will one day win out. That will happen on the day He takes us home to heaven. But sometimes, it can be discouraging to struggle with sin in the meantime. You and I won't be free from sin until heaven. But we can certainly pull with the power of the Spirit in our daily fight against it.

Declare war on those desires that go against the good things God has planned for you by asking Jesus to help you make godly choices. He can help you avoid thinking thoughts you shouldn't and keep your eyes on your own test paper. Choices like these are what it means to resist the devil. When we do that, our enemy's only choice is to flee, to temporarily let go of the rope in the great tug-of-war for our allegiance.

How is the fact that sin bothers you evidence that Jesus is working in your life?

Who's the Boss?

*We are not our own bosses to live or die
as we ourselves might choose.*

ROMANS 14:7 TLB

One of our family's favorite places to eat was going down-hill. The managers of the restaurant had forgotten to carry out the high standards set by the owner. In time, we stopped going. But a few months later, Caroline noticed a sign in the restaurant's window: Under New Management. We gave it another try and were delighted to find that an attentive manager had everything back up to the owner's high standards.

Ephesians 2:3 teaches that people are born with evil natures—a tendency to choose a direction that is opposite of what God wants. That sets us up to be poor managers over our lives. These natures encourage us to serve ourselves rather than Him. But because He loves us so much, God offered Jesus to forgive our sins and serve as the new man-ager in our hearts (v. 8). If you've placed your faith in Jesus, you're no longer under the old management of sin. You're under new management: the Lord's.

The name *Lord* means "boss"; that's why it's such a great name for Jesus. Whenever we sin, breaking God's rules, we tell God we want to be in charge instead of Jesus. But, just as sure as that restaurant manager had to be let go because his goals weren't in line with the owner's, we need to fire ourselves and trust the Lord as leader.

Think of an area of your life that isn't running smoothly. How might putting Jesus in charge of it improve things?

Serve Others

Do not be interested only in your own life,
but be interested in the lives of others.

PHILIPPIANS 2:4 ICB

My father wears a patch where his left eye used to be, and his left sleeve is empty. He has only two fingers that work because of all the shrapnel fragments still in his hand, but I've never heard him complain. In fact, he can do more with that one injured arm than most of us can do with two. Watching him serve a tennis ball is amazing. He plays golf, hunts doves, and gives the best hugs. But buttoning his shirt, tying his shoe laces, shuffling a deck of cards, and putting on socks—small things you and I take for granted—are big challenges for Daddy.

It's my mother, owner of a servant's heart, who makes sure Daddy's belt is buckled, his shirt is buttoned, and his shoes are tied before she even dresses herself for the day. Such loving attention taught me the importance of putting the needs of others before my own.

Mother reminds me of Jesus, who washed the dusty feet of His disciples; noticed the neglected; fed the hungry; listened to the little ones; and hung on the cross to forgive our sins. When you put the needs of others above your own, you are living as a godly servant too. You are helping others see the love of Christ in action.

How will you demonstrate a "servant's heart" this week?

Going Beyond

In all the work you are doing, work the best you can.
Work as if you were working for the Lord, not for men.
COLOSSIANS 3:23 ICB

If Rebekah used the last bit of toilet paper, she'd replace the roll. If you entered Rebekah's house, she'd offer you cookies. If you passed by Rebekah's house while walking your dog, you'd find a bowl next to her mailbox filled with water for your pet.

Rebekah, future bride of Isaac, went out of her way to think of others—and animals too. When Abraham's servant asked for a drink, Rebekah not only happily shared water she'd drawn from the spring, she also volunteered to water his camels (Genesis 24:19). Abraham's servant had ten thirsty camels. Rebekah had one jar (vv. 10, 16). No telling how many steps, and hours, this kindhearted woman invested in caring for this stranger and his caravan.

We please the Lord when we, like Rebekah, are willing to do more than what's expected of us. Through kind and generous service toward others, we show our love for Him. So introduce yourself to that new kid at school and invite him to sit with you at lunch. Pull the clothes out of the dryer, then fold and put them away without being asked. And remember, sacrifices like these don't just benefit our friends or parents. They tell Jesus that we really do want to honor Him.

How does cleaning your room for God, instead of your mom, change the way you're going to do your chores this week?

God's Greater Purpose

"You intended to harm me, but God intended it for
good to accomplish … the saving of many lives."

GENESIS 50:20

Joseph was a victim of ten jealous brothers. They sold him into slavery and told their dad he was dead. Later, Joseph was falsely accused and thrown into prison. Yet, over and over, even in terrible, unjust circumstances, Joseph trusted God's character and His calendar and was blessed. Joseph never sulked or plotted revenge against those who hurt him. Instead, Joseph kept hoping in God and serving others when he had the opportunity.

One day, the king's cupbearer and baker were thrown in the same jail with Joseph. Over time, Joseph's kindness to the pair led him to freedom and power that set him up to one day save his own brothers—the same naughty lot who had sold him—from dying of starvation. Joseph realized his incredible new job and his brothers' salvation had been God's plan all along.

Often God builds the greatest stages from which to proclaim His truth out of situations in life that are far from comfortable and cozy. (Just look at the cross.) That's why you can be confident in the fact that God knows what He's doing—even when times are tough. Don't grow discouraged as you wait. Instead, think about what wonderful things God might accomplish as a result of it.

How does knowing the end of Joseph's story change the way you think about your life?

Choosing to Forget

*"I will forget their sins and never again
remember the evil they have done."*
HEBREWS 10:17 ERV

When we confess the wrong things we've done against Him, Jesus chooses not to remember them anymore (Isaiah 43:25). By doing that, He proves to us that forgiveness is not a feeling. It's a decision of the heart. An action we too can take in spite of what's been done to us.

Clara Barton was a nurse and founder of the American Red Cross. One day, she and a friend were meeting for coffee when her friend brought up a name they both knew. Clara's friend began to gossip about how awful this person had been to Clara. Clara ended the conversation as quickly as it had begun. "I distinctly remember forgetting that," she replied.[7]

You and I will struggle when someone has done something to wound us. We may want to keep rehashing the hurt or even hold a grudge against the one who let us down. But with God's power in us, we can choose to resist being held prisoner by what's been done to hurt us. Instead of dwelling on what was done to us, we can focus on what Jesus has done for us. We can forget the sins of others as we remember how many times the Lord has extended His grace, forgiving and forgetting, to us.

How can we be like Jesus when we respond to someone who has lied to us?

---

7 William Eleazar Barton, *The Life of Clara Barton: Founder of the American Red Cross, Volume 2* (Boston and New York: Houghton Mifflin Company, 1922), 345.

Soul Food

"Blessed are those who hunger and thirst for righteousness, for they will be filled."

MATTHEW 5:6

Early one morning, I heard someone in the pantry. My little boy, Daniel, came out of there carrying OREO cookies, a bag of Swedish Fish, and a carton of Goldfish® crackers. "Don't worry about fixing my breakfast," he said. "I've got it."

Daniel wanted to satisfy his hunger with the wrong choices. I stepped in and offered him healthier options, because our bodies don't work well when fueled by junk. Jesus created us to have hunger pangs. Food is necessary. We're reminded of our need for physical nourishment when our tummies growl. However, we are not designed to survive on soda and Swedish Fish. Those things can lead to drops in energy and added pounds.

God designed our physical bodies to function best on a healthy diet of water, fruit, vegetables, whole grains, and protein. Jesus tells us that our souls can only be fully satisfied when we enter into a relationship with Him. By "hungering and thirsting for righteousness," instead of always doing as the crowd does or living in expectation of that next new toy or fun experience, we resist substituting anything "junky" in His place. At the end of the day, Jesus is the only One who can satisfy us with righteousness and help us to function at our best. Reading His Word and going to Him in prayer are our daily soul nourishment.

What are some "soul foods" you are munching on today?

Thought Control

We have the mind of Christ.

1 CORINTHIANS 2:16

Air traffic control specialists, sitting high above the runways in their control towers, provide support for pilots. They give instructions on how to take off and land safely, offering knowledge about weather and the flight patterns of other aircraft that the pilot doesn't have. When pilots listen to these instructions, they avoid a catastrophe.

Our minds are the control towers of our lives; they direct the actions we take. When we surrender to Jesus, He becomes the specialist running those control towers. When we listen to His guidance, we make wise choices that help keep us—and those counting on us—safe.

Do you sometimes wonder whether you are making good choices? Whether you are being a good friend? The best way to find out is by regularly reading God's Word and praying throughout the day. These actions help us know whether we're functioning with "the mind of Christ" that the Holy Spirit provides to Christians or are ignoring Him because we'd rather fly solo. When we remain in constant communication with Jesus, He gives us permission, perspective, and power to maneuver through life and relationships. His Word protects us from things that could take us off course. It also, ultimately, guarantees us a safe landing.

How can you be sure you are making decisions with "the mind of Christ" and not your own?

The Who

We can rejoice, too, when we run into problems and trials,
for we know that they help us develop endurance.
And endurance develops strength of character, and character
strengthens our confident hope of salvation.
And this hope will not lead to disappointment.

ROMANS 5:3–5 NLT

If you're going to see a 3D movie and fail to put on the special 3D glasses, you can't enjoy the 3D production as it was designed. Life's like that too. God's provided us with the Bible so we can see life as He intended, experiencing a new dimension of His character and love every day. We can know He's the "Who" behind the human story and that He's always with us—no matter how painful our circumstances.

Look at the life of Paul. He was run out of town, stoned, shipwrecked, starved, and imprisoned (2 Corinthians 11:23–27). But because Paul remembered God is ultimately in charge, he never demanded his own way, pouted, complained, or asked, *Why me, Lord?* He focused on the Who rather than the why. He knew God could use even the worst moments in his life to accomplish great things.

On those days when friends hurt your feelings, when you don't make an A on the test or get chosen for the team, remember Who is with you. Hard times build hope. Be on the lookout for all the blessings God will bring out of your tough days.

How does knowing we never go through suffering alone, or without an important purpose, change the way you look at hard things that happen in your life?

"At Ease" but Ready

*"Be dressed ready for service
and keep your lamps burning."*
LUKE 12:35

Military officers will often say "at ease" when they want troops to get into a more relaxed position. This means soldiers spread their feet and clasp their hands behind their backs for a momentary rest. But the resting soldiers must remain in uniform and ready to react in a moment's notice, as they've been trained to do. "At ease" doesn't mean off duty.

In Exodus 20:11 God instructs His followers to rest, essentially asking them to stand at ease, while still expecting them to act in wisdom and readiness. King David, however, forgot the importance of remaining on guard during a rest season. In the springtime, kings and their armies usually went off to war. But the Bible says, "David remained in Jerusalem" (2 Samuel 11:1). As his men fought for their lives, David munched on grapes, enjoyed the comforts of his palace, and unwisely committed the biggest moral mistake of his life. He allowed too much ease to lure him off duty.

God wants you to enjoy downtime, to see its blessings as gifts from Him. But whether you're resting in the living room or vacationing at the beach, take your relationship with Him seriously. Remain more committed to doing things which please the Lord than to entertaining yourself, being just plain lazy, or getting into trouble because you're bored and can't think of anything to do. The wise Christian rests, but remains on guard.

How might you make sure comfort and fun don't turn your attention away from devotion to Jesus?

JUNE

I've Got the Power

With God's power working in us, God can do much,
much more than anything we can ask or imagine.
EPHESIANS 3:20 NCV

Lamps, flat irons, and computers all need to be plugged into a power source to do what they were created to do. Without electricity, appliances just sit around looking interesting. With it, those chunks of metal can light a room, smooth hair, and help us learn.

Did you know God works in us much like electricity flows through a lamp? It's true: you have God's power living in you! In Matthew 5:14 Jesus refers to Christians as "the light of the world." But until we're in a relationship with Him, we are like unplugged lamps. Only when we invite Jesus into our lives is the circuit connection made and the switch flipped on to let the light of God's power flow through us. And when it does, we draw a watching world's attention to Him.

If you've plugged into Jesus, you no longer have any excuse to say, *I'm weak* or *I can't*. With His Spirit surging through you, you have power to apply what you learn from God's words in the Bible. You can refuse to complain when things don't go the way you want them to go. You can say no to those decisions you know in your heart are not right. But most importantly, you've got the power to share the love of Jesus with those who don't know Him.

What would you like to see God's power do through your life?

Strength

*I can do all things through Christ
who strengthens me.*

PHILIPPIANS 4:13 NKJV

Today's verse speaks of the apostle Paul's power to face difficulties and challenges. It didn't come from his own strength, but through the supernatural ability of Jesus at work in him. Unfortunately, many claim and recite this verse as if the very words will somehow summon personal strength and ability. It's not uncommon, in fact, to hear this passage used much like the Little Engine That Could's chant: "I think I can—I think I can—I think I can."[1] But using the verse in this way leads us to ignore the work of Christ, who is the real power source who helps us meet life's challenges.

The focus in the Philippians' passage is not on what *I* can do, but on what Christ can do. That's important because what I can motivate myself to accomplish through positive self-talk falls far short of what can happen when I invite the power of the Holy Spirit to work through me.

Accepting what Jesus did for you assures you of salvation. And as you sit down to take a big test or try and figure out how to get along with a difficult classmate, know that it's Christ *in* you that gives you the power to do your best and act with kindness. So rather than cheering your own abilities, humbly ask Jesus to let His supernatural ability strengthen your efforts.

What might you accomplish by relying on Jesus' strength rather than your own?

---

1 Watty Piper, *The Little Engine That Could* (New York: Platt & Munk Publishers, 1930).

Be Kind to Your Kin

Make sure that nobody pays back wrong for wrong,
but always strive to do what is good for each other.

1 THESSALONIANS 5:15

Because of sin, family members don't always get along. Sometimes, in fact, we fuss and fight, and our homes fail to function well. The kindness that should rule our choices gets replaced by minds set on getting our own way.

When we know Jesus and look to Him for help, however, selfish reactions are optional—even when we deal with cranky siblings. I wonder whether lessons like this were part of what Jesus had in mind when he chose two sets of brothers, James and John, and Andrew and Peter, among the Twelve. Surely, by walking alongside Jesus together, these sibling pairs learned a lot about treating one another with kindness and looking to the Lord for help in getting along.

Jesus can help you in your sibling relationships too. Thank Him for handpicking each person in your family and ask Him to teach you to respond to them in the right way. Pray for your siblings and ask Jesus to bless them, even when they make you nuts. And remember, being kind to brothers and sisters when they don't deserve it is a great way to remind them of the undeserved kindness and love Jesus shows us.

What is something kind you can do for a family member today?

Masterpiece in Progress

*Before the world was made, God … planned that
we should be holy and without blame as He sees us.*

EPHESIANS 1:4 NLV

The city of Florence, Italy, planned to put a statue of David, the shepherd turned king, in the city square. It would remind citizens of God's faithfulness to defend them, just as God had defended Israel through David. A giant slab of marble was chosen. Then, in less than five years, Michelangelo carved it into a seventeen-foot-tall statue of "David." All who saw it asked, "How'd you do it?" "Simple," the master sculptor said. "I just chipped away everything that didn't look like David."[2]

Your life is a bit like that big block of unfinished marble in Florence: you've been set apart for a specific purpose. As a Christian, you are destined to resemble the image of Jesus, God's Son, in your character and actions. But to accomplish that, you need the work of God, the Master Sculptor. Delicately, thoughtfully, God removes any junk in you that doesn't look like Jesus. He won't just spend five years accomplishing this work of art. As surely as you were on His mind before He created the world, He will work on you—His masterpiece—throughout your lifetime. He wants to make you holy so that others will see you as He does, forgiven and clean, because of Christ.

What things do you think God wants to chip away from you, so you might resemble Jesus more closely?

---

2   Jane Sutcliffe, *Stone Giant: Michelangelo's David and How He Came to Be* (Watertown, MA: Charlesbridge Publishing, 2014).

Go Pro

The things you have learned and received
and heard and seen in me, practice these things,
and the God of peace will be with you.

PHILIPPIANS 4:9 NASB

Our home sits on the ninth fairway of a golf course. Throughout the year, our children retrieve wayward balls that wind up in our pool or backyard. There is one week, however, that is different. Every September, our club hosts a PGA-sponsored event. Amateurs step aside so the professional golfers can have the course. Those pros play their game for a living, rising early to master the sport and putting in hours of practice to improve their skills. So in the week of the pros, the backyard remains ball free. Pros rarely hit shots out of bounds.

We see in today's verse that Paul encouraged believers in Jesus to live the Christian life as if we are pros, in a sense. "All those things you've seen me do as I follow Christ," he says, "practice them." In other words, Paul taught that you and I need to study the Rule Book, the Bible, and pay attention to what pros in the faith are doing, so we might imitate it. As we put time and effort into such "exercise" of our faith, we become less likely to make decisions that negatively affect others. We also slowly grow to become more like Jesus.

Remember, the difference between going "pro" and remaining an "amateur" is the disciplined time you spend practicing.

What could you do today to practice your faith in Christ?

Keep Going

Let perseverance finish its work
so that you may be mature and complete.

JAMES 1:4

In the movie *Facing the Giants,* Coach Taylor decides to show football captain, Brock, that his self-doubts are holding him back and crippling the team. Brock needs a lesson in perseverance.

Coach asks Brock how far he thinks he can carry a teammate. Brock thinks he can make the thirty yard line. But Coach Taylor knows his star player can go farther, so he blindfolds the lineman and tells his teammate Jeremy to get on Brock's back.

Brock struggles under Jeremy's weight, but responds to the coach's commands to keep going. He listens when the coach tells him he can do it and believes what he says. Then, when Coach takes Brock's blindfold off, Brock finally collapses—in the end zone.[3] The team goes wild with excitement and renewed courage.

Instead of letting his feelings convince him to quit, he learned to persevere. He saw that he could keep going long past where he thought he could. He matured.

Perseverance is pushing past discouragement to obey the voice of your Coach, Jesus. When you keep giving Him your best, even when you want to quit, you grow in maturity and confidence. You may also give your own teammates just the boost they need to do the same.

How can you show Jesus your willingness to keep going the next time you feel discouraged?

---

3 *Facing the Giants,* directed by Alex Kendrick (Culver City, CA: Sony Pictures Home Entertainment, 2010).

Honor Roll

"I will honor those who honor me."

1 SAMUEL 2:30 ICB

Track star Eric Liddell made sure everyone knew what had first place in his heart. And it wasn't running. When he qualified to race in the 1924 Paris Olympics, Eric was everyone's pick to win the 100- and 220-meter sprints. However, both events were scheduled on a day Eric Liddell had committed to God as a day of worship and rest. Refusing to compromise his choice to honor God by not running on Sunday, Eric signed up to run the 400-meter dash instead. It was scheduled for another day, but it was an event for which he hadn't trained. His fans thought he was crazy.

In the award-winning movie *Chariots of Fire*, minutes before the finals in the 400 meters, one of the American runners hands Liddell a handwritten note with the words of 1 Samuel 2:30 written on it: "He that honors Me, I will honor."[4] With that paper crumpled in his hand, and God's promise burning in His heart, Eric Liddell not only won the race, but set a new world record.[5]

You will face Liddell moments in your life. Times when people will laugh and call you names for being obedient to what God has called you to do. Never let their laughter make you miss the blessings Jesus brings to those who humbly honor Him.

What does honoring Jesus look like in your life?

---

4   *Chariots of Fire*, directed by Hugh Hudson (Burbank, CA: Warner Bros., 1981).
5   Dave and Neta Jackson, *Hero Tales, Volume II: A Family Treasury of True Stories from the Lives of Christian Heroes* (Minneapolis, MN: Bethany House Publishers, 1997).

Our White-water Guide

"When you go through deep waters, I will be with you.
When you go through rivers of difficulty, you will not drown."
Isaiah 43:2 NLT

On the first day of summer, our family traveled to Walnut, North Carolina. There we embarked on an all-day white-water rafting excursion down the French Broad River. Before boarding our raft, Caroline, Daniel, Lee, and I learned the significance of listening—and obeying—the voice of our guide. If Grier the guide shouted, "Paddle!" we paddled. When she urged, "Rest," we rested.

Grier had knowledge about what was ahead. She not only knew the names and history of each section of rapid water, but she was familiar with how strong they were and where the safest spot was to enter them. So when Grier shouted orders, we immediately did what she said. Trusting her presence, knowledge, and wisdom protected us from falling overboard or giving way to panic.

Just as sure as travelers of the French Broad River will encounter stretches of white-water rapids, there will always be some turbulence on the river of life. But once we invite Jesus into our hearts, we never run the rapids solo. Our Guide never abandons ship. Nothing catches Jesus by surprise. In fact, He can walk on water—even white water. So make up your mind to obey Jesus by following the commands in His Word. He will see you safely to shore.

What should you do when you encounter a "rapids" section of life?

Blessings in Disguise

"I have purified you by giving you troubles."
ISAIAH 48:10 ICB

In Alabama is a little town named Enterprise. In the early 1900s, cotton was king there, until the Mexican boll weevil ravaged the crop. Almost all of the cotton was destroyed. Farmers were threatened with bankruptcy and the entire town faced ruin, until one resident suggested they try growing peanuts instead.

Two years later, Enterprise was the leading producer of peanuts. Since they were making more money harvesting nuts than they ever did raising cotton, citizens decided to erect a monument downtown. The statue is of a woman raising high a trophy topped by a larger-than-life boll weevil. The inscription below reads, "In profound appreciation of the boll weevil and what it has done as the herald of prosperity."[6] In the end, the citizens of Enterprise realized the awful insect was actually a blessing in disguise.

As Christians, we can trust that Jesus can turn any circumstance into a grand demonstration of His blessing. In a way, troubles can purify us. They help us let go of what was, so that we might rely on God for the new thing He wants to do or give. Maybe you are sick. Could it be that Jesus is using this downtime to make you appreciate your health even more? Perhaps your struggles in class are turning you into a better student. Don't focus on the boll weevil of the moment. Ask God to show you how your trouble will turn into blessing.

What disguised blessings have made your life better?

---

6 "History of Enterprise," Enterprise, Alabama: City of Progress, http://www.enterpriseal.gov/#!history-of-enterprise/c6gw.

Choosing Fragrant Speech

When you talk, do not say harmful things.
But say what people need—words that will help others
become stronger. Then what you say will help
those who listen to you.

EPHESIANS 4:29 ICB

The children and I were playing a board game when Caroline rolled a question which asked, *When you "flatulate" what are you doing?* She answered confidently, "Gossiping!" After explaining the correct meaning of the word—passing gas—I still gave Caroline full credit. *Flatulate* and *gossip* might as well be synonyms. Both things leave a stinky odor in their wake.

Instead of taking part in "stinky speech," like gossiping behind someone's back, we should edify—that is, build up—those around us. We do that when we are quick to offer words of forgiveness. We do it when we affirm others, saying how wonderful a friend is, instead of joining others in tearing him or her down. Every time we are pressured to speak negatively about someone, we can choose to use our conversation to communicate things about that person for which we are grateful.

If someone is making fun of a girl in PE, point out how good she is in math. If someone tells a story about how rude a boy was, suggest that he might be hurting and is in need of our prayers. Each of these actions reject stinky speech, replacing it with fragrant words that are pleasing to God and helpful to friends under fire.

Would you say your speech is usually stinky or helpful? Explain.

No Buts

*"If any man will come after me,
let him deny himself … and follow me."*

LUKE 9:23 KJV

Moses was eighty when God called him to lead the captive Israelites to the Promised Land. Sadly, Moses didn't embrace God's confidence in him immediately. "'But Lord!' Moses objected. 'How can I expect Pharaoh to listen? I'm such a clumsy speaker'" (Exodus 6:12 NLT). Moses failed to realize that limiting God's work with the word *but* shows a lack of faith. Instead, we must leave our *but*s behind, knowing that obedience to God is part of belonging to Him. So when God says go, we can't say no.

I've often wondered what Moses missed by not taking God at His Word from the start. True, God encouraged Moses by letting his brother, Aaron, tag along during his meeting with Pharaoh. Yet, what might have happened if Moses had first dropped the *but* and said instead, *Yes sir, Lord. I'll do exactly as You say*? He certainly would have proved his willingness to follow God in all things.

Perhaps Jesus is directing you toward something that seems really hard. Don't forget that Jesus paid the price for you to be free from sin's consequences. He's worthy to be Lord of your life and to be followed in all things. Remember, a heart devoted completely to Jesus is willing to get off its "but" and obey.

How can you show Jesus your willingness to follow Him?

Difference Maker

Make the most of every opportunity.

COLOSSIANS 4:5

A huge storm stranded thousands of starfish on the shore. The next morning, a man noticed a young boy picking up one of the stranded starfish and tossing it back into the water. Approaching the lad, who'd grabbed yet another one to pitch back into the sea, he asked, "Do you really think what you're doing is making a dent in this disaster? There are just too many to help." Nodding his head in agreement, the boy sighed. "You're right, sir. There are a lot." But then he threw the creature into the ocean and laughed. "But I'm sure I just made a difference for that one."[7]

During His earthly ministry, Jesus worked in the lives of Bartimaeus, Zacchaeus, Mary Magdalene, Lazarus, Jairus, and Martha, to mention a few. Those names remind us that Jesus didn't see a mass of broken people; he saw individuals—each one in need of help. That's how Jesus wants you to think about others.

Life comes with hurts and problems. Jesus wants you to share His good news with your friends through personal conversations. He wants you to offer smiles and kind words to those you interact with. He wants you to make eye contact with homeless and hurting people. Doing things like this may not change the world, but they can certainly influence—and even change—the lives of those individuals you invest in.

How can you make a difference for Jesus today?

---

7   Charles R. Swindoll, *The Finishing Touch: Becoming God's Masterpiece* (Dallas, TX: Word, 1994).

Be Thankful

*Always give thanks for everything to our God
and Father in the name of our Lord Jesus Christ.*

EPHESIANS 5:20 TLB

Rudyard Kipling, author of *The Jungle Book*, did very well as a writer. A story is told that on one occasion a newspaper reporter approached him and said, "Mr. Kipling, I just read that somebody calculated that the money earned from your writings equals over one hundred dollars a word." Reaching into his pocket, the journalist retrieved a one-hundred-dollar bill and handed it to Kipling. "Here's one hundred dollars, Mr. Kipling. Now give me one of your hundred-dollar words." Without hesitation, the writer took the money. As he placed it in his wallet, he said, "Thanks."

Thanks is indeed a valuable word, one that we can't say to God often enough. Jesus, God's Son, made it His practice to publicly say a prayer of gratitude to God before eating His dinner (Matthew 15:36). When Lazarus walked out of the tomb, Jesus thanked His Father. John 11:41 says, "Then Jesus looked up and said, 'Father, I thank you that you have heard me.'"

Never underestimate the value of thankfulness. Tell God you are grateful for His gift of forgiveness through Jesus. Thank Him for the wonders of creation. Tell Him how much you appreciate your favorite colors, scents, and experiences. Surely God places great value on a sincere *Thank You, Lord*, in recognition of all the many gifts He gives.

For what can you express gratitude to God today?

World Record Holder

"You must forgive not seven times,
but seventy times seven."
MATTHEW 18:22 VOICE

Would you like to take part in the world's largest pillow fight? How about playing basketball against the world's tallest man? For years, the *Guinness Book of World Records* has documented the names of the world's richest, speediest, and oldest, as well as listing events and creations said to be the biggest or longest to date.

Something—perhaps his brother Andrew making fun of Peter's beard one too many times—prompted Peter to ask Jesus, "When my brother sins against me, how many times must I forgive him?" (Matthew 18:21 ICB) Jesus' answer set an impressive goal for Peter. He told Peter to keep forgiving as many times as needed. In other words, Jesus encouraged Peter to forgive others so many times that it might well break the forgiveness record.

That same advice applies to us. Just as Jesus refuses to add up all of the times we sin against Him, He doesn't want us to count all of the offenses done against us. The Bible says, "Be kind and loving to each other. Forgive each other just as God forgave you in Christ" (Ephesians 4:32 ICB). So when your friend borrows your necklace and breaks it, or your little brother pulls your hair, or Mom is running late picking you up from practice again—forgive. Remember, Jesus wants us to be record breakers, not record keepers.

How does accepting His challenge to forgive demonstrate trust in Jesus?

Here Is God

"Take courage. I am here!"
MATTHEW 14:27 NLT

The disciples are afraid. They are huddled together in a boat during a raging storm in the darkest hour of the night. Desperately fearful of drowning, they cry out for help and Jesus appears to them, walking upon the water, assuring them that everything will be okay. His presence calms them.

The disciples aren't the only ones who've known what it's like to be afraid. An old sailor's map, drawn in 1525, is on display in London's British Museum. A note is scribbled along the unexplored areas of the North American coast: *Here be dragons, Here be giants*, and *Here be fiery scorpions*. In the 1840s, British explorer Sir John Franklin acquired the map. He didn't fear the unknown, because he so fully trusted God. He rubbed out every terrifying inscription and wrote, *Here is God*.[8]

At times, we may feel like the frightened mapmaker or the disciples, tossed by turbulent waves. We look at our unfamiliar situations and want to hide under the covers, feeling fearful. *There be dragons!* we protest. Yet, we too, like the disciples, can boldly shout with confidence and exclaim like Sir John Franklin, *Here is God!*

Share your special memory of how trusting God's strength helped you when you were afraid.

---

8 "Here Is God," Bible.org, https://bible.org/illustration/here-god.

Wolf Ready

*"Anyone who listens to my teaching and follows it is wise,
like a person who builds a house on solid rock."*

MATTHEW 7:24 NLT

Three pig brothers ventured into the world. The first two piggies were more interested in playtime than work. One quickly constructed a house of straw right on the loose dirt. The second made one of sticks, propping it up against a tree. The third was a sensible swine. He'd heard about the big bad wolf who lived nearby, and he wanted to be prepared for the wolf's knock on his door. So the wise pig built a beautiful house of bricks, beginning with a level, concrete foundation.

Soon the wolf sniffed out the three pigs. Within minutes, the dwellings of the first two lazy pigs were piles of rubble. But when the third little pig heard the wolf "huffing and puffing" and trying to blow his house down, he wasn't frightened.[9] He knew his sturdy home was built on a foundation strong enough to withstand wolf storms.

Jesus wants you to be "big bad wolf" ready too. That requires that you build your life on a firm foundation of obeying the Bible. When we make the choice to build our lives on the wisdom of Jesus—the Solid Rock—we will stand no matter what our enemy, the devil, blows our way.

To prepare yourself for when your spiritual enemy knocks on your door, are you more like the first two piggies or the last? Explain.

---

9 Walt Disney Studios, *Three Little Pigs* (Blue Ribbon Books, 1933).

Act with Compassion

*"A certain Samaritan, as he journeyed,
came where he was: and when he saw him,
he had compassion on him."*

LUKE 10:33 KJV

In Jesus' parable, a priest and a temple helper were close enough to hear a dying man's pleas for help, but they were running late and felt they shouldn't risk getting their robes bloody. Besides, the poor fella probably wouldn't make it anyway. Sure, they could've comforted him and taken him to shelter, but what if the same guys who robbed him were waiting? Cautiously and quietly, they crossed to the other side of the road and left the injured man to die.

Hours later, a man from Samaria walked up the same trail traveled earlier by the two religious leaders. When he heard groaning, he allowed compassion to move him toward the injured traveler. The kind Samaritan saw him as a hurting neighbor in need.

Jesus' story about the Samaritan's care teaches us two important lessons. First, every kid the Lord brings into your life is a "neighbor" worth your time, a person in need of His love. Second, God is more concerned about you living out your faith in Christ through compassionate actions than He is in you keeping your clothes clean or making it to every activity you have planned. Taking advantage of opportunities to serve others demonstrates our commitment to Jesus' call on our lives.

Why do you think Jesus emphasized taking action to meet the needs of others?

Hot or Not?

"Because you are lukewarm …
I am going to spit you out of my mouth!"
REVELATION 3:16 GNT

Soup. Cocoa. Peach cobbler. Chocolate lava cake. Many treats are served piping hot and ready to enjoy. Did you know Jesus is concerned about your spiritual temperature? In fact, He finds lukewarm Christians as unappetizing as cold, lumpy oatmeal.

When you and I make excuses for our bad behavior or don't get excited about making decisions that please God, we are lukewarm. We're a lot like the religious leaders Jesus called out in Matthew 12:30. They were supposed to know God, but didn't love Him with their whole heart. "Whoever is not with me is against me," Jesus said of such people. That means that if we aren't really living like Jesus is Lord of our lives, we might as well be His enemies. A tepid approach to faith makes Him sick.

The Bible teaches us to choose in advance how we will respond when faced with the opportunity to compromise, to make decisions that cool down our enthusiasm for Jesus. Determine to start each day with prayer and Scripture reading. Decide now that you will bow your head and thank the Lord for your lunch tomorrow in the cafeteria. Don't be shy about standing up for what God's Word says, even when His truth is unpopular. Choices like these will keep your love for the Lord piping hot.

If Jesus were to take your spiritual temperature, how would He describe it? Explain.

Remember Christ's Walk

For I resolved to know … Jesus Christ and him crucified.

1 CORINTHIANS 2:2

Simon from Cyrene was passing through Jerusalem when Roman soldiers insisted he carry Jesus' cross up to the place where Jesus would be crucified (Mark 15:21). We know little about this man other than the fact that he had two sons, Rufus and Alexander.

Can you imagine what it must've been like for Simon as he carried that heavy cross and walked alongside a bruised and bleeding Jesus? While the crowds on both sides were pressing in and yelling, "Crucify," Jesus refused to cry out. In fact, at no time did Simon witness Jesus whimpering or complaining in face of certain death. Perhaps he could even sense His love.

I like to think Jesus' attitude gave Simon strength for the hard journey that day and ultimately prepared him for the day when he would hear the gospel message, the reason behind why Jesus died and then rose from the dead. Undoubtedly, Simon later shared about his experience with Jesus that day. In fact, scholars believe Simon's son is the same Rufus that Paul calls "a good Christian" in Romans 16:13 (NLV).

Close your eyes and imagine yourself in Simon's sandals, remembering that world-changing day. Feel the weight of what Jesus came to do for you, for all of us. Then, do as it appears Simon did. Tell others about Christ's journey up the hill and what His sacrifice ultimately accomplished.

What is a benefit of remembering Christ's sacrifice by talking about it?

Be Flexible

A person may think up plans.
But the Lord decides what he will do.

PROVERBS 16:9 ICB

Ananias was enjoying his role as a disciple of Jesus and surely had a nice, safe plan of existence all mapped out for himself. He lived comfortably until word spread about a terrorist named Saul who was persecuting Christians and headed his way. No doubt Ananias wondered if he shouldn't make plans to ditch Damascus and head to a safer location. But God had another idea.

In a vision, God told Ananias to go to a house on Straight Street and minister to the very man who had murdered so many of his fellow believers. "What?!" Ananias exclaimed. "But Lord, this guy's not good." The Lord then explained to Ananias how Saul's hard heart had been changed. And so, focused on his faith in the Lord and respecting the orders of the One he served, Ananias went to see Saul. He showed Saul God's love—making a huge stretch away from the comfortable life he'd envisioned in order to honor Jesus (Acts 9:10–19).

Because Ananias was flexible and accepted God's plans, a miracle occurred: Saul (also known as Paul) became the greatest missionary in history! So don't get upset when your plans change. Rather, ask God to give you a flexible attitude and to work through the twists and turns in your life to accomplish His great purposes.

How willing are you to let go of your ideas and trust God's? Why?

Night Light

"I am the light of the world."
JOHN 8:12

Ever been afraid of the dark? When I was little, I discovered that hearing the voice of someone I trusted gave me comfort like a night light, easing my fear.

One night Nicodemus found himself worrying whether his Pharisee friends were right to oppose Jesus. The more he thought about it, the creepier the shadows on his wall seemed. So he got up and went in search of the one voice that could calm him. He found Jesus, who assured Nicodemus that he was right to trust in Him. Jesus explained, "For God so loved the world that he gave his one and only Son, [Me,] that whoever believes in him shall not perish but have eternal life" (John 3:16). Those words confirmed what Nicodemus had suspected: Jesus really is the hope of the world.

Fear of what his Pharisee friends might think of him seemed to disappear in Nicodemus' life after He trusted the Savior. The next time Nick appears in the Bible, he's actually speaking up for Jesus among his peers (7:50–51). Then, when the other Pharisees had Jesus crucified, Nicodemus helped prepare Jesus for burial (19:39). I can only imagine how excited he was three days later to find those grave clothes folded and Jesus, the light of the world, alive again.

Jesus is always present to offer you comfort when life—or your room—seems dark and scary. Call out to Him just like Nicodemus did.

In what way is Jesus like a night light?

Tin Man Testimony

This is the testimony: God has given us eternal life, and this life is in his Son.

1 JOHN 5:11

Before we accept Christ, we have a lot in common with the Tin Man from *The Wizard of Oz*. We're stuck in sin, rusty with unrighteousness, heavily dependent on others, and suffering with a serious heart condition. But the Lord promised something special for those who come to Him in faith. "I will give you a new heart," He said in Ezekiel 36:26.

Sharing a testimony, a before-and-after-I-met-Jesus-and-He-changed-my-heart story, is one of the best ways to tell others about Jesus. In *The Wizard of Oz*, the Tin Man was given a clock heart and was helped by a wizard. But if he'd instead encountered Christ, he might have said something like this: *In the past I was a slave to what my body wanted. Oil! Oil! All the time. But then my Savior gave me a new heart, just because He loved me, rust and all. After that I went from not even being able to move sometimes, to moving and talking freely because of mercy. Today my heart beats with love for my Savior and deep care for others.*

Friendship with Jesus provides us the Holy Spirit's "oil of joy" (Psalm 45:7), generously poured out to us so we can live like Jesus lived and love others by telling them about Him.

What's your testimony?

A Clean Bill of Health

"The life of the flesh is in the blood."
LEVITICUS 17:11 ESV

Before our son, Daniel, was diagnosed with cancer, a series of tests were run on his blood. That's because while he looked healthy—he could still run and hit a ball— he showed symptoms. His intense leg pain was a signal that something was wrong deep inside. In Daniel's case, healthy cells were being attacked by rapidly dividing leukemia cells.

Without Christ, people go through life looking okay on the outside, though they are anything but healthy. God's Word teaches that all people have a deadly disease called sin. The things that go wrong in our lives, like Daniel's leg pain, are more serious than we realize. Sin runs deep in our blood, deeper than even leukemia. If we don't do something about it, it will slowly kill us.

Thankfully, we have a Master Physician whose diagnosis of our sin problem comes with a foolproof cure. A prescription for spiritual health is laid out in Romans 10:9: "If you confess with your mouth that Jesus is Lord and believe in your heart that God raised him from the dead, you will be saved" (ESV). As sure as God used cancer treatments to save Daniel's life in a physical sense, He uses the blood of Jesus to save us from the curse of sin and to provide us with eternal life. Truly, life is in the blood—in the blood of Jesus.

What can you do to make sure your sin problem gets cured?

Clutter Free

*"The seed that fell among the thorny weeds
is like those who hear God's teaching, but they let
the worries, riches, and pleasures of this life keep them
from growing and producing good fruit."*

LUKE 8:14 NCV

While cleaning out our "catch-all" drawer, I thought a lot about Jesus' parable of the planter. As I removed tins of breath mints, tubes of ChapStick®, crayons, paper clips, stamps, batteries, business cards, expired coupons, and pencils from the drawer, I considered the seed that fell among the thorns. Jesus said it was unable to grow into a mature plant, because the surrounding thorns choked it. I realized all that clutter shoved into my drawer was like the "thorns" that crowd godliness right out of our hearts.

A thorny-soil Christian, one who accepts Jesus yet fails to mature, runs into trouble. That's because stuff like worry, money, and entertainment use up all the room in his heart. Spending time focusing on things like these stunts the growth of spiritual fruits, like goodness and patience, that should be evident in the life of a Christian.

If you're more concerned with the latest styles, with texting, or with thinking about your next purchase, than in developing your relationship with Jesus, examine your heart. Has it become a cramped and crowded junk drawer with no room for anything godly to grow? If so, ask Jesus to help you clean it out, so that you may receive God's instruction and bear fruit.

What can you do to make sure your heart is spiritually fruitful rather than cluttered?

Runaway Rescue

All of us, like sheep, have strayed away.
We have left God's paths to follow our own.
Yet the Lord laid on him the sins of us all.

ISAIAH 53:6 NLT

Jesus tells a story about a hundred sheep with no need to fear raging rapids, or even lions. Their shepherd loved his flock so much that he protected each one, leading them to quiet streams and safe, green pastures. But one sheep was stubborn. Instead of being content with his master's protection and provision, he complained. Eventually he ran away, leaving his loving shepherd and ninety-nine siblings behind. Baaaaaa-d idea.

The shepherd went in search of the rebellious sheep. "Precious, I'm here," he called. He found the lamb bleeding and scared, caught in a thorn bush. Incredibly, the shepherd smiled and said, "I am so glad you're mine." Then, he bent to free the lamb and lifted him onto his shoulders. Later, to prove he meant what he said, the master saw that the returning lamb was honored at the sheep pen shindig.

Jesus told this parable to describe His great love for *you*. Though you sometimes rebel against Him, allowing a sinful heart to urge you away from God's love and protection, Jesus pursues you as if you're His only sheep. And the Bible says that when you turn away from your selfish desires to accept His love, heaven throws a party (complete with angels) for you, the rescued runaway (Luke 15:10).

How does it feel to know Jesus pursues lost lambs with such love?

He Is Faithful

"By His light I walked through darkness!"
JOB 29:3

If there were an *Uz Times*, Job's face would have made the cover. Job was the richest and most successful man in the whole region. He was honest and hardworking, a man who loved his family and his Lord. But one day, his children, flocks, servants, houses, and health disappeared. He was left with a grieving wife and a few buddies that make you think picking the wrong friends may have been Job's greatest weakness. Eliphaz, Bildad, and Zophar told Job he must've committed some serious sins to have earned the Lord's disfavor and harsh judgment. How could a man who truly loved God, they wanted to know, be left with so little?

But, Job's losses didn't mean God had turned His back on His follower. In fact, the Lord had allowed the suffering to reveal the depth of Job's faith while also paving the way for Job to experience blessing. It was Job's job to trust God— not to question the fairness of his situation or wonder where he went wrong.

Maybe you've experienced a string of bad days lately. Don't assume God is out to get you or let others make you question God's goodness. Instead, ask Jesus to grow your faith and give you courage to deal with the rough days, as you wait for the blessings to come.

What challenge have you faced in your life that you now see in a different light?

Follow Orders

The weapons of our warfare …
have divine power to destroy strongholds.

2 CORINTHIANS 10:4 ESV

I magine being drafted into an army that will s fight 135,000 bad guys. You are handed your weap a trumpet and a clay jar containing a torch. *Don't y,* you're told, when you ask where the real weapon *. The Lord our God will give us success. Just obey ord* hat's exactly what happened to the three hundred m ected to fight under General Gideon.

Following Gideon's lead, the e soldiers blasted their trumpets and at the sam hey broke the clay coverings over their torches heir late night attack on Midian. The enemies we ified by the noise and lights surrounding them, t starting fighting each other (Judges 7:22)! C army won, because they trusted God's pl erything He said.

s us to "go and make disciples," telling bout Jesus, but that can seem like an overwhelming job. Our enemy, the devil, does everything he can to make us feel that's a hopeless battle to fight. But you and I can stand firm by believing and obeying the Word of God. We can share the love of Jesus successfully. By following God's directions to keep praying and keep talking about what Jesus has done, we can see victories just as impressive as the one Gideon's men enjoyed.

How might Jesus use your obedience to reach out to a friend of yours with God's message of life and love?

An Antidote

We are all infected and impure with sin.
ISAIAH 64:6 NLT

British writer G. K. Chesterton was asked by *The Times* to answer the question: "What is wrong with the world?" Mr. Chesterton's reply showed a simple yet profound understanding of the problem of sin within the whole human race: "Dear Sir, I am. Yours, G. K. Chesterton."[10]

One of Satan's most cunning schemes is to convince people that the "good" things they do make them good enough for God. If he can get us to believe that, then we think we don't need Jesus. But the prophet Jeremiah wasn't exaggerating when he wrote that our human hearts are corrupt (Jeremiah 17:9). In fact, come to my house and hang out with my toddler for two minutes. You'll notice I don't have to teach my daughter Harrison how to sin. That comes naturally to all of us. Why? Because we are all sinners in need of a Savior.

Only when you put your trust in Jesus for the forgiveness of your sins are you declared righteous. That doesn't mean you won't ever sin again. It does mean that you've accepted Christ's sacrifice as the antidote for your sin sickness. As a result, He can help you make right choices for the remainder of your life. As Romans 6:14 says, "Sin shall no longer be your master."

What is the danger in thinking of yourself as "good"?

---

10 Tanya Walker, "Is Anything 'Wrong'?," Ravi Zacharias International Ministries, http://rzim.org/just-thinking/is-anything-wrong.

Mine for Truth

Look for it as silver and search for it as hidden treasure.

PROVERBS 2:4

North Carolina is the heart of gem-mining country. A favorite summer pastime is dumping "mining rough" enriched with garnet, ruby, sapphire, topaz, and amethyst out of buckets and onto a screen. When water is washed over the dirt, the screen acts as a sieve separating the junk from the gems. My children love leaving the local flume with sacks of bling.

The Bereans loved to mine for another kind of treasure: God's truth. When Paul first went to preach to the Bereans, "They received the message with great eagerness and examined the Scriptures every day to see if what Paul said was true" (Acts 17:11). Like good miners, the Bereans diligently sifted through what Paul said, running it under the truth of the Old Testament—the only Bible they had at the time—to make sure it matched up with what God had already revealed.

You and I need to be truth miners too. Let's say you're listening to the radio and someone describes a way to get to heaven that differs with what the Bible says. Like the Bereans, take everything you hear from any preacher or teacher or friend or relative through the sieve of Scripture to make certain it doesn't contradict or devalue what God says. If it does, throw it out. If it doesn't, place it in the sack of your heart as treasure worth sharing.

When was a time you filtered something you heard through God's Word?

Trust His Track Record

"Remember how the Lord your God led you."

DEUTERONOMY 8:2

God promised to make Abraham the father of many nations and to give the land of Canaan to his family. But Abraham didn't get to see those promises fulfilled during his lifetime. Instead, God only allowed him to rent in Canaan and gave him two sons, in spite of how old he was. Still, these gifts established God's track record of faithfulness in Abraham's life; they built his trust.

This prepared Abraham for a faith test. God asked Abraham to sacrifice his son, Isaac. If Abraham obeyed Him, it seemed impossible that God's promise Abraham would be a father of many nations could come true. When Abraham set out to obey, he couldn't know that the Lord would spare Isaac's life. He didn't know the real point of the test was to put to death in Abraham's heart anything that might take the Lord's place.[11] But what Abraham did know was that God had proven Himself trustworthy in the past. So he reasoned the Lord would somehow save the day; He could even bring Isaac back from the dead (Hebrews 11:19). Abraham trusted God's record of faithfulness.

Your trust in Jesus will be tested. You might wonder, *Will He really take care of me?* The key to acing a test like this is to remember what Jesus has already done. Remind yourself of the miracles recorded in Scripture. Think about the blessings He's already given you.

What has Jesus done to make you trust Him?

---

11 Institute in Basic Youth Conflicts, *Character Sketches from the Pages of Scripture Illustrated in the World of Nature*, Volume III (Oak Brook, IL: Institute in Basic Life Principles, 1985).

JULY

Let Actions Prove Faith

Abraham's faith and the things he did worked together.

JAMES 2:22 ICB

Abraham was living in wealthy Ur when God called him to a new home—one he'd never seen. Because Abraham had faith in God, he got up and went just as he was told. His actions proved his trust in the Lord.

I'm reminded of a story about a little girl seated on an airplane next to a businessman. When the Fasten Your Seat Belt sign lit up, she buckled in and quietly read. When thunder began to roll, the schoolgirl serenely sipped her water as if at a tea party. Even when the plane jolted with turbulence and passengers panicked, Little Miss Pigtails was at peace.

Eventually, they landed. Before exiting, the businessman asked the girl, "How could you remain so calm when our trip was so crazy?" She replied, "My daddy's the pilot. He's taking me home."[1] You see, all along the girl trusted her father would get her safely from one airport to the next, so she stayed calm and collected. Her actions revealed the depth of her faith in her father's abilities as captain.

As Jesus' follower, you are promised that He is with you always, is in control, and will ultimately welcome you Home. By obeying God's Word, and refusing to let the storms of life send you into a panic, you allow your actions to prove your faith in Him.

Why is trusting Jesus not only a matter of believing, but also obeying?

---

1 *Tony Evans' Book of Illustrations* (Chicago: Moody Publishers, 2009).

Quit Babbling

If you talk a lot, you are sure to sin.
PROVERBS 10:19 ICB

*B*abbling means talking foolishly or too much, causing confusion. We tend to babble when we want to cover up our sin. In fact, talking a lot is sometimes a sign that a person is lying. Maybe your mother found out about something you did wrong. You kept trying to cover it up with a believable story, but the hole just got deeper. Or maybe you didn't feel like studying and the teacher called on you. You spoke forever about nothing, all in a foolish attempt to cover your tracks.

There's a reason the word *babbling* sounds a lot like the name of the Tower of Babel. After the flood, God told Noah's family to spread out and raise their own families. But instead of obeying, they decided to scratch God's plan and make a name for themselves (Genesis 11:4). They worked together to construct a tall tower. But God loves His creations too much to let us keep rebelling against Him, so He confused their languages to stop the work and force them to spread out. In fact, it's because of this action that you hear people speak in English, Spanish, German, and so many other languages and dialects.

Other languages, while beautiful in diversity, may sound like babbling to you. Let that remind you of what can happen when you live in disobedience to God's commands: judgment and confusion will result. In the meantime, decide not to use endless words as cover. Choose obedience.

Why is babbling bad?

Seeing through the Smoke

"I see four men loose, walking in the midst of the fire;
and they are not hurt, and the form of the fourth
is like the Son of God."

DANIEL 3:25 NKJV

Shadrach, Meshach, and Abednego were committed to God, who always wants us to obey Him—though sometimes, trouble comes when we do the right thing.

King Nebuchadnezzar insisted the three Hebrews bow to his gold statue or be put to death. They replied, "If you throw us into the hot furnace, the God we serve can save us. … We will not worship the gold idol you have set up" (Daniel 3:17-18 ERV).

This made the king so mad that he had the fire heated hotter than ever. Yet, as he watched the execution from his royal perch, Nebuchadnezzar stood in astonishment. In the flames, he saw not three men walking around freely—but four! The fourth he recognized as being "like the Son of God." Some Bible scholars believe this is an instance of Jesus Himself showing up in the Old Testament. That means that because of the Hebrew men's unwillingness to compromise, Nebuchadnezzar saw Jesus.

Trusting in Jesus may bring persecution, which means being mistreated because of your faith. You might be teased for telling others about God. The teacher might tell you not to take your Bible to school again. But God is watching your choices. It's likely someone else just might see Jesus for the first time because of your obedience.

Tell about a time when someone else's faith helped you see Jesus.

Freedom

We know that our old sinful selves were
crucified with Christ so that sin might lose
its power in our lives. We are no longer slaves to sin.
ROMANS 6:6 NLT

Harriet Tubman escaped slavery in Maryland in 1849, but didn't forget her family and friends still in bondage. She made countless trips via the "Underground Railroad," a network of trails and safe houses between the Southern and Northern states, to help free others from slavery. Tubman believed in freedom, once saying, "[God] set the North Star in the heavens; He gave me the strength in my limbs; He meant I should be free."[2]

Until people know Jesus, they are slaves to sin. Sometimes people grow so comfortable in their sins, allowing the wrong things they do to become so acceptable and familiar, that they turn down Christ's offer of freedom. They think they're fine as they are. But feeling "okay" with sin means becoming a slave to it. It's missing out on the freedom Jesus died to purchase for us. God's Word tells us, "It is for freedom that Christ has set us free" (Galatians 5:1). Harriet Tubman was so overjoyed to be free she wanted others to experience what she had received. Do you feel that same way about the freedom Jesus has given you?

What is one way you can tell a friend about God's only escape plan to freedom?

---

2 Harriet Tubman to Ednah Dow Cheney, New York City, circa 1859.

God Loves the Broken Ones

A broken and contrite heart, O God,
you will not despise.
PSALM 51:17 ESV

When my one-armed, one-eyed daddy and I walk together on the beach, he always puts a few broken shells in my bucket alongside the perfect ones. They are meant to remind me of our precious Savior, Jesus, whose body was broken for us. They also help me remember that God sees my brokenness and imperfections, and chooses to love me anyway.

Do you ever smile when you feel like crying? Act like you have it all together when, in reality, you are falling apart? Did you know that when we humble ourselves, handing over our broken pieces and hurts to Jesus, He heals our bruised hearts, crushed dreams, and chipped lives? It's true! He doesn't insist that we clean up and get perfect before we draw close to Him. He wants us just as we are. Repairs are His job.

Maybe you wonder why God didn't regrow my father's arm and eye. If you could talk to Daddy, I think you'd agree that the Lord used those flaws to mold my father into the wonderful person he is. Jesus, who loves us scars and all, can transform us into beautiful, joyful people whose lives—in all their imperfections—put God's power on display for others to see.

How does it feel to know Jesus accepts your flaws and hurts and can repair them and use them to do something good?

Garden Life

At the place where Jesus was crucified,
there was a garden.

JOHN 19:41

The Bible is full of gardens: green spaces where flowers and trees thrive. In the first one—Eden—Adam and Eve had everything they could ever need. But they wanted even more and disobeyed God to get it. The consequences of their sin included both death and having to leave Eden.

The second garden, Gethsemane, is where Jesus spent time in prayer the night before He hung on a cross to fulfill what He had promised. He'd promised He would conquer sin and death so His followers could escape the death they deserved. That scene concluded in another garden, when Christ's followers saw that His garden tomb was miraculously empty—the curse of death had been broken! The last garden mentioned in the Bible is described in Revelation. It talks about a garden in heaven where a crystal river flows down from God's throne and alongside trees that bear fruit every month!

I believe gardens appear so often in the Bible to remind us of how Jesus calls people, much like dry hard seeds, to burst into life in Him. You may have noticed that gardens look dead and dull in winter, much like our hearts do without Jesus. But with the coming of spring's sun, new life springs up from the soil and colorful flowers bloom. That's much like what happens in your life when you invite Jesus—God's Son—into your heart.

What are some good things Jesus is growing in your life?

Just Say No

If sinners lure you, do not go along.

PROVERBS 1:10 GW

Fishing lures grab the attention of their intended victim, hooking it and drawing it away from freedom. Satan is described in the Bible as "the tempter" (1 Thessalonians 3:5 GW), meaning he's a master at luring us away from God's best. Remaining alert to his schemes can help us avoid getting hooked.

In Judges, we read about a would-be hero who got reeled into sin because he failed to use good judgment and avoid temptation. Instead, Samson allowed the enemy to bait him through a beautiful date, a woman who talked him into doing what he knew was wrong.

When we belong to the Lord, we can refuse to be lured into sin (James 4:7). But Samson, rather than fleeing at the first sign of trouble, chose to fall for Delilah's flattering words four different times. As a result, he denied his faith in God and lost his freedom.

Let Samson's story remind you that friends have a big influence in your life. That's why our enemy will often pick those we consider our "buddies" to serve as bait to get us to laugh at dirty jokes, look at pictures that don't honor God, or to talk about others behind their back. Beware of this common lure. If a "friend" tries to lead you into sin, do what Samson should have done. Just say no. And swim in the opposite direction!

When people you love pressure you to break God's rules, what should you do?

Walking on Sonshine

*We who are still alive will be
taken in the clouds to meet the Lord in the air.*

1 Thessalonians 4:17 GW

When the Lord takes me home to heaven, I want to go as Enoch did. While wicked people were turning their backs on God everywhere he looked, Enoch made the decision to turn toward God. He was an evangelist, telling his family, friends, and neighbors about the only way to be saved from sin (Jude 15). The Bible describes him as a man who "walked with God" (Genesis 5:24 GW), meaning Enoch did not choose the easy path, doing what his friends did so they'd accept him. No, Enoch's best friend was the Lord, and he showed God how much He was loved by the way he lived.

The Bible says that as a reward for Enoch's devotion, he was raptured, which means he was "taken up to heaven without dying" (Hebrews 11:5 NLT). That's exciting, because it mirrors what will happen at the end of time when Jesus comes back in the clouds and calls Christians to heaven. Though we don't know the day or hour, we know Jesus is coming back to take His faithful followers home.

Jesus wants you to be like Enoch, living in a way that honors Him and remaining ready to join Him at a moment's notice. Walk with God in obedience and faith. And remember, Jesus is coming soon!

What would Jesus say about your walk (how you choose to live your life) with Him?

Needing Him

"Watch yourself, that you do not forget the Lord who brought you from the land of Egypt."

DEUTERONOMY 6:12 NASB

Our hearts are prone to wander from seeking after the Lord and toward our own ability to get what we want—especially when we live in a culture where we're blessed to have plenty of food and countless toys. It's for this reason that God's Word reminds us to be on our guard against material comfort, careful to remember that stuff has no lasting value and the Lord is the source of every good thing we enjoy.

Before the Israelites crossed over from their forty years of wandering in the desert to the "dessert" of Canaan, the fruitful land promised to them by God, He gave them a warning: Don't let riches make you poor (Deuteronomy 6:10–12). He explained that we are only "rich" when we remember He is the source of everything we have. The best protection the Israelites had against spiritual poverty, then, was making sure that they continually remembered the Lord who had brought them out of so much suffering and provided blessing.

Hard times have a way of growing our faith in Jesus in a way that easy times don't. That's why it's so important to ask God to deeply root our faith, helping us remember Who it is we really need—especially when it's easy to feel we have no real needs at all.

Has there ever been a time in your life when a blessing became bigger in your eyes than God?

Jesus Saves

"Jesus is the only One who can save people.
No one else in the world is able to save us."

ACTS 4:12 ICB

Jim was trapped in rising floodwaters. Trusting God to rescue him, he climbed on his roof. A neighbor paddling by told Jim to hop into his boat before he drowned. "I'm okay," Jim said. "I've prayed. I know God will provide." Not long after, firefighters approached in their boat, demanding he climb aboard. Jim declined their offer too. "God's going to get me," he said. Hovering overhead thirty minutes later, a helicopter lowered a rope. A man with a megaphone screamed, "Grab hold or you'll drown!" Jim resisted that recovery too, saying, "The Lord is my helper." Not long after that, Jim drowned. When he asked the Lord why He didn't save him, God said, "Jim, I sent you a canoe, a boat, and a helicopter. What were you expecting?"[3]

When God promised His people He'd send a Messiah to rescue them, they had lots of ideas about what the Messiah would look like. But Jesus didn't come in a way people expected. He was born in a stable, faced temptation like everyone else, yet still lived a sinless life. He didn't call people to become rule keepers or go to war, but to turn away from their old lives and find freedom through His death on the cross.

Don't miss Jesus as God's rescue plan. He is our salvation. There is no other.

Why do you think some people ignore God's simple plan of salvation?

---

3 "I Sent You a Rowboat," *Stories for Preaching,* http://www.storiesforpreaching.com
/i-sent-you-a-rowboat.

Follow the Leader

Jesus said to His disciples, "… follow Me."
MATTHEW 16:24 HCSB

In the game Follow the Leader, a leader is chosen and then everyone lines up, mimicking everything the leader does. When he hops on his right foot, everyone is supposed to jump likewise. If the leader claps his hands, the whole group should begin applauding. Anyone who fails to follow the leader's actions must sit out of the game.

The Christian life is not a game, but there are aspects of this party pastime that can help us better understand the relationship Jesus desires that we have with Him.

Our Leader, Jesus, wants us to carefully pattern our lives after His example. He longs for us to live in obedience to His words and ways. He said no to temptation by quoting Scripture, so we should say no to temptation by quoting Scripture. He made choices that honored God, so we should make choices that honor God. He loved and encouraged the hurting, so we should love and encourage the hurting too. Since Christ is our leader, we should seek to do as He does.

You and I will make mistakes sometimes, but we can trust that our Leader gives us grace—not an immediate "You're out!" when we mess up. He also gives His followers the Holy Spirit, who will empower us to follow Jesus' example faithfully as we request His help.

What are three things you've done today to follow Jesus, your Leader?

Giving What It Takes

*"I was hungry and you gave me something to eat,
I was thirsty and you gave me something to drink,
I was a stranger and you invited me in, I needed clothes
and you clothed me, I was sick and you looked after me,
I was in prison and you came to visit me."*

MATTHEW 25:35–36

My father gave his left arm and one eye during his military service in Vietnam. Of all the honors he received since his injuries, one of the most meaningful was a plaque that the surviving members of his platoon presented to him in the hospital. It reads, *In this world of give and take, there are not enough people willing to give what it takes.* His men recognized the extreme sacrifice their lieutenant made for them. Daddy simply says he was fulfilling his duty.

Doing what it takes to share the love of Christ with the world is putting one's self aside and thinking of others. It's thinking *and* doing what Jesus would do.

Jesus would have made eye contact with the hungry homeless man standing at the top of the freeway exit. He would probably carry a cooler of bottled water and a bunch of bananas in the backseat of His car to give to that man and others in need. When Jesus rolled down the window to hand the man the water and fruit, He would tell him how much he's loved. And, He'd smile.

Share a way you can show Jesus' love to someone in need this week.

A Masterpiece

*"I know the plans I have for you, says the Lord.
They are … to give you a future and a hope."*

JEREMIAH 29:11 TLB

The Lord planned to use Corrie ten Boom's life as a "beautiful tapestry" to point people to Him. But when Corrie saw her home raided because she'd hidden Jews during World War II, her life seemed more like a tangle of black threads, a web that soon became a prison.[4]

However, in time Corrie understood that the bad things that happened were the very things that later gave her the opportunity to travel the world speaking about Jesus. Corrie realized that when she focused on the bad things, she saw only the messy underside of the tapestry God was weaving. From that view, all the knots and hanging threads seemed to have no purpose. But when she saw her life as a blend of important pieces of a divine design, she saw a beautiful display of vibrant colors and patterns that made perfect sense.

Every thread of experience in our lives—light and dark—is skillfully woven into place. So don't allow black threads like sickness, learning disabilities, or a friend moving away make you feel like your life is filled with purposeless tangles. Instead, remember God loves you and is weaving *all* the threads of your life into a beautiful masterpiece.

How are you exhibiting faith in God's ability to weave something wonderful with the threads in your life that you may not like or understand?

---

4 "Life is but a Weaving (The Tapestry Poem)," TRUTHFORLIFE®, http://www.truthforlife.org/blog/life-weaving-tapestry-poem.

Rejected

*People made fun of him,
and even his friends left him.*
ISAIAH 53:3 ERV

Have you ever been picked last for a game on the playground or left off a friend's guest list for a party? Jesus' friends didn't always include Him either. This happened in Nazareth, the place where Jesus grew up. The Bible tells us that the people there didn't accept Him. The wise, godly things Jesus said probably made people feel uncomfortable, so they teased or ignored Him.

Sometimes, when you stand up for what's right—by not using the crude language your friends do or by sharing about what God is doing in your life—your friends may ignore or make fun of you too. But as Jesus did, refuse to get angry or try to get even. God teaches us in His Word, "If someone does wrong to you, do not pay him back by doing wrong to him" (Romans 12:17 ICB). Instead, focus on your friendship with Jesus, knowing He's been through situations much like yours. One day, in heaven, we'll be free of all loneliness and cruel teasing. But for now, ask Jesus to give you the strength to continue to live for Him right where you are—even if it feels like you are the only one.

What should you remember when friends make fun of you for choosing to do what God wants?

More Than They Thought

Jesus is the Messiah, the Son of God,
and by believing you may have life in His name.
JOHN 20:31 HCSB

It was in the home of Joseph the carpenter where God's Son, Jesus, lived His first thirty years on earth. I like to imagine baby Jesus playing with a rattle Joseph carved from a tree God made. Then I like to picture Joseph and Jesus crafting an oxen yoke, once Jesus grew older. Perhaps as they worked, Jesus explained to His stepdad that He had come to save the world, to lift the heavy yoke of sin and its consequences from our necks. Maybe Jesus talked about how He planned to shape and mold His followers, much like the wood pieces in their hands.

Living so closely with Jesus gave Joseph the opportunity to really get to know his stepson. But the people living in Jesus' hometown, who also must have seen the Lord on a regular basis, only knew Him by the work He'd learned from Joseph. "Isn't this the carpenter?" they questioned, failing to believe that He was the long-awaited Messiah God had promised. While they knew a little about Jesus, they didn't really know Him. They didn't realize He was more than they thought He was.

Get to know Jesus better by listening to Him in His Word. You'll find that He is much more than a creative craftsman. He is your Savior, and through Him you really can have eternal life.

What is the difference between knowing Jesus and knowing about Him?

Install Guardrails

A prudent person foresees danger and takes precautions.
The simpleton goes blindly on and suffers the consequences.
PROVERBS 27:12 NLT

Guardrails keep drivers from straying off the road and into danger zones, like drop–offs or rivers. These safety precautions often appear in-between lanes or alongside curves. While they can slow down a car that's headed toward disaster, just seeing them along the road reminds drivers to remain alert to possible danger.

Did you know God's Word is intended as a guardrail? God gave us the Bible both to provide protection against straying off the right path and remind us that there's danger in drifting out of bounds. When we read and remember Scripture, we choose to use the safety measures the Lord installed alongside life's road. Obeying it can prevent us from swerving deeply into sin.

For instance, when God's Word says, "Bad company corrupts good morals" (1 Corinthians 15:33 NASB), you're reminded how choosing friends who often rebel against the rules can set you up for a crash. When God's Word talks about being loyal in marriage, it provides you with solid advice for the day when you may have a family of your own. But it also encourages you to decide right now to be loyal and pure in the ways you act toward those of the opposite sex. In all things, pay attention to the guardrail God's provided for you. Read His Word and obey it.

How has something you read in the Bible acted like a guardrail to protect you?

Multiplied Blessings

"He will love you, bless you, and multiply you."
DEUTERONOMY 7:13 ESV

God promised blessings to the Israelites if they were faithful. And when they lived in obedience, the Lord multiplied their crops, herds, and families. While serving God certainly isn't a recipe for wealth, following Jesus often comes with real physical benefits. Often we won't enjoy those until heaven, and sometimes the gifts are things like peace and joy, but occasionally, the Lord chooses to send material blessings too.

God delights in giving good gifts. We see that illustrated in both the Bible accounts of the faithful Israelites, as well as in Job's story. Job started with 7,000 sheep, 3,000 camels, and seven sons and three daughters before calamity hit (Job 1:2–3). Then, by the end of his life, Job had acquired 14,000 sheep, 6,000 camels, seven more sons and three more daughters (42:12–13). So not only did God double his livestock, but He also doubled the number of Job's children. Ten lived alongside him; the other ten, I believe, Job would see again when he got to heaven. Stories like this remind us that we serve a God who can provide for us beyond our wildest dreams.

We should never view God as a genie who will grant our desires for stuff. But we should remember He is faithful to provide for those who follow Him. Sometimes, in fact, He will completely "wow" us with what He can do. Our job is to live in obedience and thanksgiving.

What blessings have you enjoyed since following Jesus?

Cowboy Christianity

Then Jesus said to him, "Away with you, Satan!
For it is written, 'You shall worship the Lord your God,
and Him only you shall serve.'"
MATTHEW 4:10 NKJV

I'll never forget visiting Frontier Days with my family. Held annually in Cheyenne, Wyoming, it's one of the oldest and largest rodeos in the world. When I was there, I saw bull riding and barrel racing. But what sticks out in my mind the most is the time I saw a cowboy take down an angry steer using only his lasso.

When I read Matthew 4:10, I picture Jesus conquering the lies the devil told Him like that cowboy lassoing that raging steer. Satan had just tried to talk the Lord into worshiping him instead of God, but Christ responded by boldly proclaiming that only God is worthy of worship.

I think the Lord is making a good cowgirl out of me as He continuously provides opportunities for me to "lasso" my wayward thoughts, to send bad attitudes and ugly words packing before they do damage. Second Corinthians 10:5 says, "We demolish arguments and every pretension that sets itself up against the knowledge of God, and we take captive every thought to make it obedient to Christ." Jesus commands us to deal with our thoughts and temptations the way He did. We've got to know and stick with what the Bible says, refusing to allow the enemy to "steer" us in the wrong direction.

What thoughts do you need to lasso today?

Hope in the Storm

We who … take hold of the hope set before us
may be greatly encouraged. We have this hope
as an anchor for the soul, firm and secure.

HEBREWS 6:18–19

No sailor leaves the harbor's safety without an anchor. Dropped anchors dig into the sea floor to hold a boat in place, so it won't drift away. When the captain of Paul's ship sailed toward Rome, he had at least four anchors (Acts 27:29). He ordered them thrown into the water when it seemed his vessel would be dashed against the rocks.

Paul knew the men needed to trust in something more dependable than those anchors. After all, they'd already endured weeks of storms. There was only one reason for their survival: God's mercy. So Paul encouraged the 275 men not to put their hope in human forms of security but rather in God. Paul told them not to lose courage, because the Lord promised to get them through and he had faith in God that it would happen just as God told him (Acts 27:25). Sure enough, everyone on that damaged ship survived. Even though the boat broke apart, they made it to safety.

Maybe you've endured a lengthy season of storms and you're doing everything you can to deal with discouragement and to hold things together. Remember your true source of hope and take courage. Anchor yourself in the truth of God's Word. The Lord is in charge, and He *can* see you safely to shore.

What can you do to anchor yourself to Jesus?

Do Your Part

God put every different part in the body just as he wanted it.
1 CORINTHIANS 12:18 GNT

President Kennedy was visiting NASA and noticed a man going about his job, sweeping with joyful focus. When asked what he was doing, this janitor replied, "Mr. President, I'm helping put a man on the moon." Even though he wasn't an astronaut or engineer, the fellow realized he played an important role in helping the US reach its space-race goal.

Christians—people who make up what the Bible calls the "body of Christ"—have important parts to play in the goal of making Jesus known. Some jobs may seem insignificant, but they're not. Just imagine what would happen if the custodial staff stopped cleaning the church building or teachers stopped showing up! What would happen if no one tended the babies?

The Lord has a purpose for everything He creates—especially His children. And as sure as your eyes and toes have different functions, yet are equally valuable, God has gifted you in unique ways that can support the work of your church. So if you can sing about Jesus, sing. If you can pick up bulletins after services, help that way. If you can say an encouraging word to your pastor, do so. Because whatever our abilities, the Bible tells us to "be sure to use them to help each other" (1 Peter 4:10 TLB). Through your service, you will do something better than helping put a man on the moon. You get to help people develop a relationship with the *Maker* of the moon.

What work do you think Jesus has assigned you?

Don't Cheat

"Do not steal. Do not deceive or cheat one another."
LEVITICUS 19:11 NLT

The Bible tells us Judas was in charge of the disciples' moneybag—and helped himself to it (John 12:6). In other words, Judas was a thieving cheat. Jesus, being God, knew Judas was stealing. But I like to think that one of the reasons Jesus kept him around was so you and I could see a clear picture of what happens to a person who makes money, instead of Jesus, his master (Luke 16:13). In the long run, rather than confessing and asking forgiveness from Jesus and the friends he cheated, Judas traded their trust for enough silver to buy a field. It was there he was buried, forever remembered for his sins.

Judas' story being included in the Scriptures reminds us that cheaters never win—not even when they hang out with Jesus' followers and put on a good face. So whether you're tempted to bend the rules while playing a game, to keep money that isn't yours, or to copy someone's homework, don't give in. Jesus sees everything and knows that the boy or girl who will steal answers, money, or a victory cannot be trusted. If you don't want to miss out on the blessings that come from being obedient to Jesus, ask Him to forgive you for any dishonest thoughts or actions. Ask Him to make you trustworthy. He is always here to help.

If you have cheated, what would Jesus want you to do?

Committed in All Things

Do everything for the glory of God.
1 CORINTHIANS 10:31 ICB

Our family frequently eats at a nearby restaurant. There are numerous reasons we enjoy it—their delicious chicken being one. We like that they are only open six days a week, closing on Sundays, in obedience to God's command to take time to rest and honor Him with worship. And their customer service, the way they treat us every time we order, is beyond compare. If we ask for sauce, they reply with a smile, "My pleasure," and normally give us extra. Everything they do, from food preparation to keeping their building clean, is meant to honor Jesus.

Their attitude, in fact, reminds me of something Daddy taught me. "Tara, if you're going to work, work hard," he said. "If you're going to play, play hard. If you're going to pray, pray hard. Anything worth doing is worth doing well." He said that because he knows that our actions should always glorify the Lord, because He always deserves our best.

Whether the task before you is picking up your toys, unloading the dishwasher, practicing sports, or studying, give your best in all things. Jesus Christ gave His life, His very best, to set you free from sin. Living with a cheerful, hard-working attitude shows Him honor. And it just might lead to opportunities to tell curious onlookers about Him.

How can something as simple as eating broccoli be done for the glory of God?

The Bread of Life

Jesus said to them, "I am the bread of life;
he who comes to Me will not hunger."
JOHN 6:35 NASB

Jesus was born in a manger, a feed trough. Through this detail, God was telling the world that He created us to need physical food, like macaroni and meatloaf, but also placed within us a greater appetite: a spiritual hunger that can only be satisfied by Jesus.

We cannot live long without eating. That's why it's important that we munch on protein, vegetables, grains, fruit, and dairy each day. But even if we eat three healthful meals in twenty-four hours, our stomachs still make noise between time. We get hungry again, because our bodies burn up our food. Because He loves us so much, God sent Jesus: spiritual food to fill up our spiritual emptiness. And there's no burning up the spiritual fuel He provides. Jesus helps us through each day and will still be with us when we get to heaven.

When Jesus describes Himself as the "Bread of Life," He means that by inviting Him into your life, you'll find that He will satisfy your cravings for feeling secure and feeling at peace, knowing everything will be all right. Being filled up with Jesus, in fact, leaves no room for loneliness, anger, unrest, or fear. When you find your satisfaction in the Bread of Life, your spiritual tummy will have a lot less room for those things.

How is Jesus food for your soul?

Happy Homecoming

"The father ran to him, and hugged and kissed him."
LUKE 15:20 ICB

Jesus tells of a selfish son who left home to waste the riches his father gave him. Soon all of his money ran out, and his "friends" ran away too. The son became really hungry. So starved, in fact, he was willing to eat pig slop (Luke 15:16). When he compared the lifestyle of plenty he once enjoyed with his dad to the life of loneliness and loss he now led, he felt sad. "All because I wanted to live life my way," he cried. "If only I had chosen to please my dad."

God used the son's growling tummy to turn him toward home. The Bible says when the father saw his son, he ran to meet him. As they embraced, the son told his dad how sorry he was for leaving. Instead of scolding and rejecting him, his father welcomed him back warmly.

Because of sin, fleeing from our generous and loving heavenly Father is what we do. And it leads to trouble. But as the boy discovered, it only takes a few inches to move our feet from going in the wrong direction to the right one. When we do, we'll find that Jesus—much like the father in the story—is running toward us with arms wide open, ready to forgive and rebuild our relationship with Him.

How do you feel when you think of Jesus running to meet you when you mess up?

Focus in the Fog

*Suddenly the cloud covered it
and the glory of the Lord appeared.*

NUMBERS 16:42

Highway 1 in California is famous for its beauty. It winds around picturesque coastlines. My father had seen it before and could hardly wait to share the drive with me. My expectations were high as I imagined looking out the car window at the waves of the Pacific Ocean, and maybe glimpsing a seal or two, before spotting the Golden Gate Bridge. Instead, from the moment we got on it, Highway 1 was socked in completely by fog. Daddy and I couldn't see a thing—except each other. That reminded me that fog—annoying as it is—can be a blessing.

One day, Jesus took some disciples up a mountain and revealed His glory. The Bible says a cloud covered them and God's voice said, "This is my dearly loved Son. Listen to him" (Mark 9:7 NLT). Whatever other grand sights surrounded them at that height, the fog helped them focus on Jesus and the wonderful message about Him.

Foggy days may be disappointing. But in times when you are hemmed in by clouds and can't see the view outside, remember that the One who is so worthy of your attention is right there with you. Let your cloudy days turn your focus to Jesus.

What cloudy days in your life has God used to let you see Jesus more clearly?

Jesus Never Changes

Jesus Christ is the same yesterday, today, and forever.
HEBREWS 13:8 HCSB

Nothing's going the way Alexander wanted. There's chewing gum stuck in his hair when he wakes up. Alexander's best friend "unfriends" him during first period at school. At lunch, his mother forgets to pack his dessert. Lima beans, Alexander's least favorite vegetable, are on the dinner menu that night. By bath time, the water is too hot, soap gets in his eyes, and his favorite toy falls down the drain. Alexander wants to run away to Australia, where he imagines things are better. For him, today has been "a terrible, horrible, no good, very bad day."[5]

Alexander isn't the only one who experiences bad days. They happen to all of us—even those in Australia. Circumstances change. But isn't it nice to know the promise of Hebrews 13:8 holds true: our God never changes.

We live in a world where weather is unpredictable. Parents are moody. Friends can love us one day and leave us the next. There are shifting seasons and we're assigned temperamental teachers. But there's one thing we can know for sure: Jesus' love is reliable. Jesus, the Master of the Storm, is still calming the whitewater in your world. When everything around us is swirling, Jesus is our anchor. We can always count on Him.

How does it feel that in the same way Jesus is with you today, He'll be with you in the future?

---

5   Judith Viorst. *Alexander and the Terrible, Horrible, No Good, Very Bad Day*. (New York: Atheneum Books, 1972).

The Living Lighthouse

The whole Bible … is useful to teach us what is true
and to make us realize what is wrong in our lives;
it straightens us out.

2 TIMOTHY 3:16 TLB

One night, a sea captain noticed a light in the distance. He decided it was that of another ship. Fearful the vessels would collide, he shouted orders to the other ship through the radio: "This is Captain Burke. Alter your course ten degrees to the south!" Moments later came a reply: "Recommend you change your course twenty degrees to the south. Over." At this Captain Burke, known for insisting on his own way, was outraged. He responded, "Negative. My boat is staying our course. Move or we will collide." A grave reply crackled back: "Captain Burke, prepare your boat for impact. I am a lighthouse."[6]

Burke couldn't order away the fixed beacon meant to keep sailors from danger. But like him, many people try to insist that God's Word, His light and fixed source of truth for our lives, get out of their way, so they can do what they think's best. They don't realize the Bible was given for our protection; it's a help for a people easily shipwrecked by poor choices.

When you need to make a decision about what to do, don't assume you have all the answers. Instead, see what pointers God's Word offers. Then, like Captain Burke, who finally admitted he needed to change course, wisely accept that you don't always know best.

Talk about a time when you had to change course in life because the direction you were insisting on going was against God's Word.

---

6 Paul Aiello Jr., "Lighthouse," Bible.org, http://www.bible.org/illustration/lighthouse.

In His Grip

If God is for us, who can be against us?

ROMANS 8:31 ESV

In the book of Esther, we read about Mordecai, Queen Esther's cousin, who was hated by an evil man named Haman. In fact, Haman wanted to hang Mordecai! But God was about to interfere with Haman's plans. One night, King Xerxes, ruler over both men, is unable to sleep. Xerxes asks his servants to read him a bedtime story, a true tale about the goings-on in his kingdom. When they do, the king discovers that Mordecai had foiled an attempt to kill king Xerxes—and Mordecai never even received a thank you.

Immediately, the king decides to honor Mordecai, and Haman is asked to plan the party. In the end, all Haman's evil schemes against Mordecai backfire; and the would-be hangman, Haman, is himself hung on the gallows he'd built for Mordecai (Esther 7:10). This unexpected turn of events shows God's hand was at work in Mordecai's life—even though to Mordecai it probably seemed that Haman, the bully, would win.

Have you ever worried about what rotten trick or mean words a bully might want to use on you? Mordecai knew the feeling. But God reminded His servant Mordecai that he was safely under His protection. The bully's plans would come to nothing.

If you, like Mordecai, are dealing with a bully, trust that Jesus is for you. You are in the grip of His protection. He has the power to move even the heart of a king on your behalf.

Describe a time when you felt the comfort of being close to the Lord.

It's All Good in God

*We know that all things work together
for the good of those who love God.*
ROMANS 8:28 GW

One night Daniel and I prayed his leg pains would get better. He finally looked up at me and said, "Mommy, we've been praying for an hour that Jesus would take my pain away. Why hasn't He done it yet?"

"God is making you into a champion," I replied. "And He takes His time building His champions."

Nobody makes the Olympics on skill alone. Each athlete must first endure training. Intense exercise and discipline, though painful, are the very things that transform men and women into champions. A similar principle is at work in the life of a Christ-follower. We all like smooth, painless sailing in life. We pray for it. But instead, sometimes God sends us challenges. And yes, He even allows pain, because He knows those are exactly what we need to become the spiritual champions He desires.

Remember Joseph's story? All of the pain Joseph endured as a result of his brothers' cruelty, and being falsely accused, proved worthwhile in time. Every hard time made him more fit for the position of power God planned for him. Those difficulties, those pains, provided strength conditioning for his soul. They helped prepare him to save many lives from famine.

Don't grow discouraged when Jesus doesn't answer your prayers exactly the way you want. Remember, He's preparing you for things you can't imagine. His Word promises that He's working all things out for your good—even when it hurts.

How does it make you feel to know Jesus has a purpose even when things don't seem to make sense?

Singing in the Pain

My heart is fixed, O God, my heart is fixed:
I will sing and give praise.
PSALM 57:7 KJV

Paul and Silas were thrown into a dungeon because they wouldn't stop preaching about Jesus. But rather than whimper about their mistreatment, the two gave a prison concert (Acts 16:25). As they sang to God and prayed, the other inmates listened. Then, God caused an earthquake that opened the cell doors and loosened the convicts' chains!

In this case, the praises Paul and Silas sang to God led to physical freedom for those held captive. But the dropping chains also hinted at the emotional and mental freedom that comes when hearts trust in Jesus. Remarkably, as soon as the earth's trembling stopped, the jailer realized that he was a prisoner, a man bound by sin instead of chains. "What must I do to be saved?" he asked Paul and Silas. "Believe in the Lord Jesus," they said (v. 31). And that very night, the jailer became a Christian. He repented of his sins, turned away from them, and asked Jesus into his heart.

Imagine what might happen if you choose to respond to discipline or to being mistreated with cheerfulness, as Paul and Silas did. When you focus on Jesus rather than your troubles, the Holy Spirit can do more than give you the power to sing through the pain. He just might use your song to open hearts to His truth.

Discuss a time Jesus used your good attitude to show others what God is like.

He's in the Inches

The Lord will guard you.
PSALM 121:8 ICB

It's a miracle I made it!" my husband, Lee, remarked as he walked through the door. "I heard brakes screech as three cars behind me collided in a chain reaction. The impact missed me by this much." Lee held up his thumb and pointer finger with a tiny gap between them. With only an inch to spare, the Lord prevented his involvement in the crash.

The Bible says angels are "ministering [helpful] spirits" sent to serve those who follow Jesus (Hebrews 1:14). Psalm 91:11 says God commands his angels to guard us. When I hear a near-miss story like Lee's, I like to think that the "gap" was made by an angel—a heavenly servant whose efforts remind us that we're loved by a God who is closely involved in our lives. Nothing can touch us without His permission.

Consider the story of God's prophet Elisha and his servant. They were surrounded by trouble. Yet, Elisha was confident the Lord would deliver them. His servant wasn't so sure. "Lord," Elisha prayed, "please open my friend's eyes so he can see how you save" (2 Kings 6:17). Sure enough, the Lord let the servant glimpse the angelic security guards spread out around them. Every inch of the mountain was covered with horses and chariots of fire!

If you belong to Jesus, you too are under angelic guard. Look with eyes of faith to see how God protects you.

How have you witnessed the power of Jesus' protection?

AUGUST

Use Time Wisely

*Be very careful how you live. Do not live like those
who are not wise. Live wisely.*

EPHESIANS 5:15 ICB

The White Rabbit in *Alice in Wonderland* dilly-dallies until he realizes he's running late. His peace turns to panic: "I'm late, I'm late. For a very important date. No time to say, 'Hello.' Good-bye. I'm late!"[1] And off he scurries.

Perhaps you, like the rabbit, fail to be a good manager of your minutes. Maybe you talked too long on the phone, then flushed a whole hour by watching some silly show. Now, Mom is saying, "Lights out!" But you still have homework.

Waiting until the last minute is an unwise use of your time. Jesus desires us to be responsible in our work. While you are a student, school is your job and schoolwork deserves your focus. Similarly, the Lord wants you to remember that people are important. It's unfriendly, and a poor witness, if we're like the Rabbit, too rushed to even say hello to one another because of misplaced priorities. So ask God to help you be more effective in the use of your time, seeking His help in forming and following a schedule that helps you get homework done and leaves room for relationship building with your family, friends, and most importantly—with Him.

What do you need to change to make better use of your time?

---

1 *Alice in Wonderland*, directed by Clyde Geronimi, Wilfred Jackson, and Hamilton Luske (Burbank, CA: Walt Disney Productions, 1951).

Sweet-Sounding Harmony

*How good and pleasant it is when brothers
and sisters live together in harmony!*

PSALM 133:1 GW

Two sisters lived in a nursing home. Each one had suffered a stroke. Evelyn's stroke left her right side paralyzed. Margaret's prevented movement on her left. Both ladies had been talented pianists and, because of their paralysis, assumed they'd never play the piano again. One day, the nursing home director encouraged them to sit side-by-side at the piano and play. They did. Evelyn took the left-hand part and Margaret the right, and the resulting music was beautiful to everyone's ears.

How would the hallways of your home sound if you chose to work with—and not against—your brothers and sisters? If you did the chores expected of you, never pushing them off onto your sister's shoulders? If you spoke kindly to your brother, instead of trying to order him around? I think you would find—and your parents would too—that harmony (pleasing sounds that work together and bring pleasure to those who listen) would result.

Jesus made siblings diverse, because He knows the beauty of harmony. He didn't want everyone to be the same. So don't criticize your sibling or make comparisons. Instead, try to appreciate the ways the Lord's designed each of you to play a unique part in the song of your home life. Then, be willing to sit down beside your sister or brother, and play.

Talk about a specific way you can show Jesus' love when you disagree with a sibling.

Never Forget

Be careful that you don't forget the Lord your God.
DEUTERONOMY 8:11 GW

For years, I received an annual card from the doorman of Exeter College in the heart of Oxford. The good-humored remembrance of my visit memorialized the time I flew to England to see a friend enrolled there. We made lots of memories, but the most memorable was my attempt to dry my hair.

When I plugged my hairdryer into the outlet of that renovated seventeenth-century dormitory room, the wattage from my appliance was too much for that foreign electrical wall outlet to take. The circuits blew, and it took two full days to get the lights on and things back to normal. The doorman said he'd never forget me, and he didn't.

I was remembered for my blooper, but God wants to be regularly remembered for all the positive, remarkable things He does for His people. Scripture is filled with reminders of how He made the world, saved those who were mistreated, and sent Jesus so that we could be forgiven and live with Him forever. Each of these things is something worthy of remembering, and thanking Him for, daily.

Every day, make time to acknowledge at least a few of the ways God has shown His love to you. It'll blow your mind, as sure as I blew Exeter's power grid.

What would you say in a letter to God about your memories of Him?

The Gift of Joy

Be joyful always.
1 THESSALONIANS 5:16 GNT

Paul exhibited joy in the worst of conditions, accepting each day as a gift and using every opportunity to share the love of Christ with a watching world. I like to imagine Paul, the tentmaker, stepping into each new morning with a confident smile on his face. In spite of all the trials he endured—beatings, shipwrecks, hunger—Paul was like a pleasant guy who routinely visits a corner coffee shop, knowing and using the name of each barista, remembering birthdays, and making everyone feel valued. You see, all the bad days Paul dealt with did nothing to dim his view on life. He could rejoice—at all times—because he knew Jesus. And that joy spilled over onto those he met.

Even when chained to a Roman soldier, Paul penned a joy-filled letter to his friends at Philippi. In it, he urged them—and us—to follow his example: "Rejoice in the Lord always; again I will say, rejoice!" (Philippians 4:4 NASB).

With Jesus' joy in your heart, each day brings an opportunity to bear witness to His love. So let His joy overflow from your heart through your attitude and actions, reaching those in your home, school, church, and community. Your rejoicing may give you the opportunity to tell someone about Jesus' love.

How will others be able to see you are rejoicing in the Lord today?

Casting Crowns

They cast their crowns before the throne,
saying, "Worthy are you, our Lord and God,
to receive glory and honor and power."
REVELATION 4:10–11 ESV

Queen Victoria's chaplain had been preaching about Jesus' returning to earth someday, often referred to as His "second coming." With tears, the queen confessed, "Oh, how I would love it if the Lord would come back during my lifetime!"

"Your majesty," the chaplain asked, "why such urgency?"

The queen answered, "I should so love to lay my crown at His feet."[2]

Victoria's words remind us of how we should feel about any recognition we receive: the credit really belongs to Jesus. Our enemy, however, tempts us to think life is all about us. He wants us to focus on *our* accomplishments. *Our* awards. *Our* trophies. King Nebuchadnezzar, whose attitude was long the opposite of Victoria's, let his crown go to his head. Buying into the devil's lies, he said, "*I* built this great place by *my* power to show how great *I* am" (Daniel 4:30 ICB). That pride led God to punish him, until Neb acknowledged that only one King, God, is worthy of worship.

Beware of taking credit for what God is doing in your life. If it weren't for Him, you wouldn't be here. So if you're good at football, let every touchdown glorify Jesus. Maybe you're an artist. Let your pictures draw applause for Him. The purpose of our talents—and tiaras—is to bring the Lord praise.

How can you use your abilities to honor Jesus?

---

2 A. J. Pollock, *The Journey and Its End*. (London: Central Bible Truth Depot, 1951).

Gathering What He Gives

"Give us this day our daily bread."
MATTHEW 6:11 ESV

The children in the orphanage George Müller ran took their seats around the dining tables. They were led in a prayer of thanksgiving for their breakfast—even though the cooks had nothing to serve.

Mr. Müller, however, had long ago learned to trust in the Lord's provision, to ask for and expect to receive what they needed each day. After all, the Bible promises that God will answer prayers that line up with His will (1 John 5:14–15). Sure enough, right after Müller said amen, the village baker knocked on the door. He wanted to share some of his warm croissants and muffins with the children. Moments later, the milkman made an unscheduled delivery, because his truck had broken down near the orphanage. He wanted to give the fresh milk and butter away before they turned sour.[3] As the last-minute gifts were brought in, Mr. Müller recognized that if the pantry had been packed, the children would have missed seeing the miracle. They wouldn't have witnessed this proof of how their loving, heavenly Father provides daily.

Jesus wants you to acknowledge Him as the source for everything you need too. He delights in taking care of His children. So ask Him to meet your *daily* needs. Then gather what He gives and be grateful.

Why is it important that we ask God to meet our basic daily needs?

---

3 Roger Steer, *George Müller: Delighted in God* (Tain, Rosshire: Christian Focus, 1997).

See Peace

Jesus came and stood among them and said,
"Peace be with you!"
JOHN 20:26

A stockbroker planned to purchase artwork for his apartment. He wanted everyone who saw it to walk away saying, *I've seen peace.* Unable to find what he was looking for, the man hosted a contest. Competing artists submitted what they considered tranquil, peaceful scenes—most of which were serene nature scenes in bright colors. But the winner was a painter whose canvas was splashed with dull gray hues. In the picture, a storm swirled around a tree swaying in the wind beside a waterfall. On one of the tree's branches was a thin limb, where a little bird rested in her nest, unbothered by the swirling commotion.[4] The picture symbolized what peace is all about: being able to rest in the assurance that everything will be okay—even when circumstances suggest otherwise.

This definition of peace is especially important when we think of Jesus. When Jesus told the disciples, "Peace be with you!" He was announcing that peace itself was right there with them (John 20:21). Jesus is not just a picture of peace. The Bible says He *is* Peace (Ephesians 2:14).

Strong winds may blow in your life right now, but don't worry. If you belong to Jesus, He's got you covered. And as you rely on Him right in the middle of the chaos, you too will help others to see "Peace." Not a painting, but the real deal.

Talk about a time you hung out with Peace (Jesus) in the middle of a stormy, troubled time.

---

4 Berit Kjos, *A Wardrobe from the King* (Victor Books, 1988), 45–46, referenced in "Perfect Picture of Peace," Bible.org, http://www.bible.org/illustration/perfect-picture-peace.

My Precious

*"You are precious in My sight and honored,
and I love you."*

ISAIAH 43:4 HCSB

One of the first songs many of us learned in Sunday school was "Jesus Loves the Little Children." It reminds us that we are all "precious in His sight" because "Jesus loves the little children of the world."[5] The word *precious* means we are greatly valued and loved. We are worth so much to our Creator that "He laid down His life for us" (1 John 3:16 HCSB). Everything about us has been perfectly planned by God. Our gifts, talents, abilities, features, and quirks are all blessings from Him.

When something is precious to you, you want to hold onto it. My twins, for instance, used to each have a special "lovey" toy they had to have when they traveled anywhere. In a sense, you are a "lovey" to Jesus. He wants you by His side and eventually home with Him too. All the things that make you *you* make you precious to Him.

Jesus knew the only way you could go to heaven to live with Him forever was for Him to die on the cross to defeat sin and to rise again to defeat death. Out of respect for His love and sacrifices for us, choose to live in such a way that shows Jesus He is precious to you too.

How can you show Jesus He is precious in your sight?

---

5 "Jesus Loves the Little Children," by Clare Herbert Woolston and George Frederick Root, Public Domain.

A Way Out

*He commanded the Red Sea to divide,
and a dry path appeared.*
PSALM 106:9 NLT

The Israelites received the okay to leave their lives of slavery in Egypt. But the Lord directed them to go to a spot that looked like a dead end. There, staring at the wide water of the Red Sea ahead of them and hearing the wheels of enemy chariots closing in behind them, the Israelites trembled in fear. They chose, however, to trust in God stepping in to save them. And in the next hours, God showed that He is not just a protector. He's a provider.

With the Egyptians fast approaching, the whites of their eyeballs nearly in view, the Israelites did as instructed. They zipped their lips and stood firm in their faith, as God positioned His cloud pillar of protection between them and their foes. Then, opening a mind-blowing avenue of escape, the Lord allowed them to walk on ground that was usually hidden under the sea. God made a path right through the middle of that sea, so the Israelites could cross to safety. Not even one of the more than two million Israelites stumbled on a starfish. They all crossed between the walls of water, thanks to the great love and power of their Savior.

Maybe you can't imagine a way out of a mess you're in. Remember that the Lord specializes in making a way when it seems one doesn't exist. Ask Him for rescue.

What are some benefits of waiting for Jesus to deliver you?

Say Nothing at All

Weep with those who weep.
ROMANS 12:15 ESV

It's hard to know what to say—or what not to say—to hurting people. But we can get ideas from Job's story. Eliphaz, Bildad, and Zophar, after they learned of the deaths of Job's ten children and his serious disease, journeyed to be with their friend. Job 2:13 says they considerately sat with Job "for seven days and seven nights. No one said a word to him, for they saw that his suffering was very bad" (NLV). They would have been compassionate comrades had they stopped there. However, two chapters later, the harsh words of their opinions wounded Job deeply.

When our son was admitted into the hospital, I received a call from friends asking me to meet with them. My husband, Lee, led me to the cafeteria, where I sat at a table crying while my friends surrounded me. What I remember most is being warmed by their gift of silence. My friends didn't try to fix anything. They were simply present with me in my pain. Before we parted, I was hugged and handed a gift basket of books for Daniel, magazines for me, a coffee card, lotion, and Kleenex®.

Silence, shared tears, and thoughtful words of encouragement are often the most effective ways to show support. So if your grandparent or classmate is hurting, be willing to listen, to offer a hug, or to simply cry with her. It's often through considerate gifts like these that we best share Jesus' love with those who grieve.

How have you helped show Jesus' love with someone who's hurting?

Beware of Anger Danger

Do not let the sun go down while you are still angry, and do not give the devil a foothold.

EPHESIANS 4:26–27

The phrase "stranger danger" reminds us of the possible risks there are in talking with people unfamiliar to us. God's Word alerts us to a bigger threat: anger danger. As Christians, if we don't obey God's command to control our tempers, we become weapons the enemy can use to create conflict and division in our homes, schools, and churches.

That's what happened to Euodia and Syntyche, who lived in Philippi (Philippians 4:2–3). Things got so bad between them that today, two thousand years later, we're still talking about it! Nursing a grudge against one another, these two women watched countless sunsets and sunrises until the roots of their bitterness grew so deep that their preacher had to call them out publicly for it. The women were Christians and the enemy had no right to have control over them anymore. But the pair were giving him permission to tear down Christ's work in their lives, as they continued to wallow in their anger, instead of forgiving and moving on.

Bickering with a friend, or someone in your family, is like welcoming in the devil to create conflict in your life. So beware anger danger. Pay attention to Scripture's warning not to let the sun set on your anger. Be quick to forgive and even quicker to apologize.

What anger dangers do you see in your life that we should pray about before turning the lights out tonight?

Chain Breaker

He broke their chains.
PSALM 107:14 ICB

Jesus came to set the captives free, to break their chains. That means through faith in Him, we have freedom from sin and death. But the idea goes deeper than that. He also wants to free us from things like fearing superstitions, tools the devil uses to shackle hearts with worry.

Maybe you received a chain letter that promised great luck if you passed it on and disaster if you didn't. Perhaps a fortune cookie predicted you'd meet the person of your dreams today, but you wonder whether you somehow missed seeing him in the crowd. If these sound familiar, the apostle Paul has wise words for you: "Be sure that no one leads you away with false ideas and words that mean nothing. Those ideas come from men. They are the worthless ideas of this world. They are not from Christ" (Colossians 2:8 ICB). We all have fears, superstitions, or things that chain our hearts with worry. Jesus came to set us free from sin's lies. Don't let anxiety tie you up in knots over nonsense.

So if your friend sends you a note saying something will happen to you if you break the chain, kindly reply to let her know you're well—doing better than you deserve, thanks to Christ's love. Then explain that your chains of fearing superstitions, thanks to Jesus, have all been broken.

How can you guard yourself against superstition?

Stop Whining

Do everything without complaining and arguing.
PHILIPPIANS 2:14 NLT

A little girl sat at a lunch counter. "Ick!" she said loudly. "Mom, this burger has cheese on it. I can't stand cheese!" A few minutes later, she was fussing about being cold. If she had any gratitude for the meal she'd received, the whiny words coming out of her mouth disguised it.

Did you know that grumbling, complaining, and whining are sure signs we're not obeying God? They suggest that we're ungrateful and disobedient toward God's will for us, including His desire that we treat others with respect. In Scripture, God commands, "Do all things without arguing and talking about how you wish you did not have to do them" (Philippians 2:14 NLV).

I'm reminded of the Israelites. After they were set free from Pharaoh's cruelty by God's miraculous help, they started grumbling as soon as their road trip got hard (Exodus 16:2). As a result, what could have been an eleven-day outback adventure turned into a forty-year wilderness wandering. Their experience teaches us that failing to obey God's instruction—even in something that may seem as unimportant as holding in a few grumpy words—always carries consequences.

Don't be like the ungrateful girl at the lunch counter. When your mom serves you something that may not be your favorite, take as many bites as she asks. You'll honor Jesus by honoring her with your good attitude. You'll also make sure that mealtime gripes don't lead to bad consequences.

Why is it wrong to complain?

There's No Outgiving God

God is able to give you more than you need.
2 CORINTHIANS 9:8 GNT

Anthony Rossi immigrated to the US from Italy in 1921 with nothing but the clothes on his back. God used a Christian couple's kindness to show Anthony the love of Jesus. He soon became a Christian and asked the Lord for an idea on how he could be a blessing for God's kingdom. Soon after, God gave Anthony the notion of making chilled, fresh-squeezed juice. That led Anthony to found Tropicana, one of the world's largest producers of orange and grapefruit juice.

In the years ahead, Anthony prayed over where each dollar earned would be most useful for God's work.[6] He wanted to thank the Lord for all He'd done for him. So instead of giving a tithe—10 percent of his income to the Lord as Malachi 3:10 instructs—he gave Him 50 percent of everything he earned every year until he died.[7] Though the man donated millions, the Lord saw that Anthony was always provided for. In the 1970s, the company sold for $500 million!

Anthony Rossi's life is a testimony to the fact you can never outgive God. He loves a "cheerful giver" (2 Corinthians 9:7) and delights in providing generously for us—meeting our daily needs—as we share with others and bless them in His name and for His glory.

Talk about a time you gave gladly to the Lord and experienced blessings.

---

6 "Anthony Rossi – Tropicana," Giants for God, http://www.giantsforgod.com/anthony-rossi-tropicana.
7 "Story: Prayer That Your Income Will Equal What You're Willing to Tithe," MAXIMUM Generosity, accessed March 31, 2016, http://www.kluth.org/church/illustrations.htm.

Live Up to Your Name

*Praise God for the privilege of being in Christ's family
and being called by his wonderful name!*

1 PETER 4:16 TLB

Alexander the Great was a mighty warrior who never lost a battle. When he wasn't on the battlefront, Alexander was home ruling the kingdom. One day, a young boy caught stealing was brought before King Alexander. "What's your name, young man?" Alexander asked as the frightened lad stood shaking before him. "My mother named me after you, sir," the thief replied. "My name is Alexander." The king got up from his throne and knelt before the boy. "Son," he said, looking into his eyes, "change your conduct or change your name."

When we put our trust in Jesus, we become "Christians." That title identifies us as followers of "Christ," which is another name for Jesus. So how we behave should be a reflection of His character. In other words, our words and actions should be in line with His.

Being a "Christian" is more than a label. It means we "live the kind of life that honors and pleases the Lord in every way" (Colossians 1:10 ICB). Jesus knows our hearts and He takes His reputation—and our sin—seriously. So ask Jesus to help you truly live up to the title "Christian." You share Christ's name. Choose to share His loving, just ways as well.

How are you making sure what you do matches up to what you're called?

Right-Side Up

A wise man's heart leads him in the right way.
But the heart of a foolish person leads him in the wrong way.
ECCLESIASTES 10:2 ICB

The box arrived with a red This Side Up label attached. So the fragile contents inside wouldn't be upended and broken, I followed the label's direction. God has a right orientation—a right-side up—for our lives too. Wise people search God's Word for directions on how to live and follow that advice. But the foolish don't care what Scripture says. They ignore God's directions and make choices that lead the wrong way. That way inevitably ends in destruction.

In Acts 17:6 Paul, Jason, and other believers were accused of turning the world upside down with their teaching about asking Jesus for forgiveness. That message, even though it was true and meant to assist everyone who heard it, clashed with the way the townspeople wanted to live. So the townspeople labeled the believers as troublemakers who were messing up the world. They refused to acknowledge that there really is only one way to live life right-side up, and it's the way that honors Jesus as Lord.

Jesus wants to help you avoid living the wrong way. His Word gives great warnings on how to avoid breakage. So choose to follow the Bible's leading. To ignore what it says is as foolish as ignoring a label intended for your good.

How can you know whether you're living life right-side up?

I'm Loved beyond Measure

*Comprehend … what is the length and width,
height and depth of God's love.*

EPHESIANS 3:18 HCSB

At our favorite ice cream stop, a sign with a painted ruler reads, "All kids under 40 inches tall get a free baby cone!" That thrills our toddler. That measure helps Harrison understand how much she's growing. For now, it's a standard that encourages her.

Our world relies heavily on measurements. Rulers accurately check length. Report cards track academics. Scales register weight. Cups calculate the exact amount of chocolate, sugar, and flour needed to make Mom's chewy, gooey brownies turn out just right. All of these standards help us to see whether our growth, or recipes, are on track. They help us comprehend things.

Jesus' cross, two wooden beams nailed together in the shape of a T, was the only instrument that could accurately track the extent of God's love for us; it was the only measure that could help us comprehend the truth that He really does love us to death. God's love is so long, so wide, so high, and so deep that He was willing to pay the penalty our sins deserve. All so we could be free to live in joy and peace. By stretching out His arms on the cross, Jesus "loved [you] and gave Himself for [you]" (Galatians 2:20 HCSB). That's a love that is off our usual scales. It's a standard that reminds us that in Jesus' eyes we are deeply, totally treasured.

How would you describe how much Jesus loves you?

Caution: Fake Fruit

*"Just as you can identify a tree by its fruit,
so you can identify people by their actions."*
MATTHEW 7:20 NLT

A fake green pear on my table is marred by teeth marks. Two-year-old Caroline bit into it one day, expecting a fruity flavor. Instead, she got a mouthful of tasteless wax. She didn't know enough to inspect it to make sure it was real before taking a bite.

Jesus warns us about being tricked by the "fake fruit" of teachers who claim to know God but really don't. Rather than telling people what they need to hear, they tell them what they want to hear. They fill their listeners' ears with lies that leave them dissatisfied.

That's why Christians must be "fruit inspectors." We should carefully look at the example and instruction of so-called Christian teachers to see whether their lives are filled with God's Spirit or with pride and false ideas. Fruit from the Father is defined by love, joy, peace, patience, kindness, goodness, faithfulness, gentleness, and self-control (Galatians 5:22–23). Someone who produces fake fruit is more likely to paste on a smile before loftily insisting that Jesus is just one of many ways to heaven—a teaching that disagrees with Scripture.

Carefully consider who you allow to influence you spiritually. Are they producing the good fruit Jesus desires? Are they upholding the truth of God's Word? Remember, the fruit produced in the lives of God's true followers tastes sweet, not just the first bite, but all the way down to the core.

What attitudes and actions can you think of that are "good fruit"?

He Catches My Tears

You have collected all my tears in your bottle.
You have recorded each one in your book.
PSALM 56:8 NLT

I keep a book for each of our children in which I tape pictures and fun memories and where I record the countless times I comforted them during shots, stitches, and even cancer. One day I'll give Caroline, Daniel, and Harrison these treasured memories in the hope that they will better understand my love.

The Bible says God keeps records of His children too. What most speaks to my heart is the fact that Jesus captures our every tear. That means there's never a time in our lives when He fails to see our grief, to bottle it as a memorial of our sometimes difficult journeys through life. Journeys that He is pleased to love us through. For this reason, I like to think that in heaven there will be a museum we can visit: one that houses God's collection of our tears.

Revelation 21:4 tells us there won't be any more crying in heaven, because our eternal home with Jesus is a place full of joy. But just as in heaven Jesus will still have the nail scars gained on the cross, so you won't forget the price He paid for you to get there, the treasury room of your tears will likely stand as a reminder of how very involved God is in your life.

Why do you think God collects and records our tears?

It's Okay to Ask

"Ask and you will receive."
JOHN 16:24

Do you like to ask lots of questions—especially when scary things make you feel anxious? Habakkuk did! In fact, in the Bible book bearing his name, Habakkuk talked to God about things that bothered him; he wanted to know why the bad guys of the world sometimes win.

God, who has generously provided an entire book full of answers for those with hard questions, didn't criticize Habakkuk for questioning. Instead, the Lord essentially said, *I know things look bad, but trust Me. I am always in control. And those bad guys you think are winning? Hang on, Habakkuk. Their day of punishment is coming!*

In the long run, Habakkuk's Q & A session with the Lord led him to deeper faith. Because he took the time to take his tough questions to God, he learned to say, despite the circumstances around him, "Though the olive crop fails and the fields produce no food, though there are no sheep in the pen … I will be joyful in God my Savior" (3:17–18). In other words, Habakkuk decided to let God's answers comfort his heart and help him trust that all things—even scary things— are under God's control.

The Lord welcomes your questions too. And He's given you the Bible as an answer book. As Habakkuk experienced, and as John 16:24 promises, we will receive when we respectfully ask of God.

What would you like to ask God, and how can you find His answers?

Clay in the Potter's Hands

We are the clay, and You are our potter;
we all are the work of Your hands.

ISAIAH 64:8 HCSB

The children and I watched as the potter's wheel went round and round. Pinched, pulled, and stretched, the clay yielded under the pressure of the craftsman's hands until it began to take the shape of a cup. When it finally yielded to the desired design, the clay was placed into a kiln—a fiery furnace. There, its softness gave way and it was transformed into a solid vessel of service.

God, our heavenly Potter, wants to shape you, His clay, too. His desire is for you to become a vessel that reflects and carries the love of Jesus to others. As you submit to His will for your life—with all its twists and turns, and even fiery difficulties—you'll be prepared to carry love, joy, kindness, and goodness to everyone you meet.

Realize, though, that rough days and disappointments are part of the shaping process God uses to make us what He wants us to be. But the good news is that because you and I are in the hands of a loving and capable Master Potter, no pressure, pull, twist, or yank on our lives is without purpose. God knows exactly what is needed to transform us into the image of Christ. So, dear clay, yield freely to the work of God's hands. He is working for your good!

Why do you think the Lord needs to "shape" you?

Faithful Travel Companion

"I will never leave you."
HEBREWS 13:5 ICB

Mary Stevenson wrote a poem in 1936, which she shared with friends who needed encouragement. In it, she told the story of a man who looked back at the end of his life as if it were one long walk on the beach with Jesus. At times, the man in the poem noticed, there were two sets of footprints pressed into the sand along the shore. But the man was bothered by the places where he saw only one set—especially when he realized that the other set, the one He assumed belonged to Christ, was missing during the most difficult days of his journey. "Lord," he protested, "you promised You would never leave me. Why, when I needed you most, did you desert me?" In the poem, Jesus replies, "My child, that one set of footprints you see in the sand is Mine. I was carrying you."[8]

When days seem like one long struggle, know that Jesus isn't just present. He is there to carry you through. In those times when you think you've done too much for Him to forgive, remember that His arms of love are wide open to pull you into His embrace. When people you thought were friends have turned their backs on you and you're afraid, His grip hasn't loosened. When you belong to Jesus, you are always in the company of a faithful and capable travel companion.

Describe a time in your life when you knew Jesus was carrying you.

---

8 Paraphrased. Mary Stevenson, "Footprints in the Sand," Official Website for Footprints in the Sand operated by the estate of Mary Stevenson, http://www.foot-prints-inthe-sand.com/Poem.php.

Arsenic and God's Grace

For the wages of sin is death; but the gift of God
is eternal life through Jesus Christ our Lord.
ROMANS 6:23 KJV

Victims of arsenic rarely recognize they are being contaminated by odorless, tasteless poison. So if I saw a scoundrel mix drops of arsenic into the glass on your nightstand, you'd desperately need me to warn you of the danger.

When they rebelled against God, Adam and Eve took a big gulp of sin, which is even more dangerous than arsenic. As a result, life's glass is poisoned: each of us sips sin! But because of His extraordinary love, God provided an antidote. Jesus, appropriately called Living Water in John 4:10–13, died on the cross so that everyone who places their faith in Him could be set free—cured—of sin's deadly effects.

If you've accepted Jesus, you've taken the antidote to sin's eternal consequences. Now, you must warn others. This week, share with a friend about the seriousness of sin. Explain how Adam and Eve's actions invited sin into the world. Then turn to Romans 3:23: "For all have sinned and fall short of the glory of God" (HCSB). Then, read Romans 6:23, "For the wages of sin is death" (KJV), which explains sin's seriousness. From there, point to the next half of that verse, the prescription that heals us: "but the gift of God is eternal life through Jesus Christ our Lord."

Open your Bible and read Romans 5:8 and 10:9. What difference does this message make in your life?

I'm Designed by God

Know that the Lord, he is God! It is he who made us.
PSALM 100:3 ESV

In the movie *The Little Mermaid*, Ariel and Flounder explore a sunken ship where they discover human treasures. Ariel is most fond of a shiny three-pronged object. Consulting Scuttle, a seagull who prides himself as being an "expert" on life above the sea, Ariel is told her valuable object is a "dinglehopper," a tool humans use to comb their hair.[9] Until the little mermaid befriends someone who knows the truth about the object's design, she and Flounder believe Scuttle's silly story. What was really fashioned as a utensil for eating food—a fork—she mistakenly uses to fix her hair.

Because some people don't first consult the Bible, the only real authority on where things come from and what they're for, they decide that they simply arrived here by chance and that the function they serve in life is whatever they—or someone else—decides it should be. But as sure as Scuttle misidentified that utensil, God's Word is clear. You and I are created in His image. We are the highlight of His creation (Genesis 1:27), His beautiful workmanship (Ephesians 2:10). We humans have been given hearts to love Him, hands and feet to serve Him, and minds to obey Him. So let's get our information on what we are—and what we are designed to do—from the Creator who made us.

Share what you are most excited about in God's design for your life.

---

9 *The Little Mermaid,* directed by Ron Clements and John Musker (Burbank, CA: Walt Disney Pictures, 1989).

Right Perspective

Everything else is worthless when compared with the infinite value of knowing Christ Jesus my Lord.

PHILIPPIANS 3:8 NLT

When Olympic gold medalist Dan Jansen was nine, he was skating in a speed skating championship in Minnesota. As he was heading into the final turn, his skate hit a lane marker and he fell. Dan lost the championship by one point and cried the entire six-hour drive home. Dan's father remained silent until he pulled into their driveway and parked the car. Mr. Jansen turned to look at his young son and said, "You know, Dan, there's more to life than skating around in a circle."[10] With those words, Dan's father took time to put defeat—and life—into perspective.

Many people zoom through life, constantly trying to out-skate, out-work, out-sprint, out-throw, out-shop, or out-own the next guy. But this super-competitive approach to life ignores the right perspective the Bible teaches. Our lives have been uniquely designed by God for His glory. We are here for a reason: to reflect God's character and build a relationship with Him through Jesus. Paul had it right when he wrote, "I have fought the good fight, I have finished the race, I have kept the faith," (2 Timothy 4:7). Life is not about finishing first. It's about finishing faithful. Remembering that helps us to always keep life—and our competitions—in the right perspective.

What is the most important thing in life?

---

10 Dan Jansen, *Full Circle* (New York: Random House, 1994).

A Ready Help

God is … always ready to help in times of trouble.
PSALM 46:1 NLT

I remember an ad on television that showed a stressed-out housewife in her fluffy pink robe, walking through her chaotic, messy home. The dog had tracked mud on the carpet. Dinner was burning. The baby was crying and the phone was ringing. The camera zoomed in as the frazzled female looked to the sky and exclaimed, "Calgon, take me away!" The next frame showed her relaxing quietly in a luxurious, scented bubble bath. The commercial suggested that Calgon bath beads would help a person escape all her troubles.

In truth, bubble baths—while they may feel nice—can't cure our cares. Problems will still be there when we dry off. That's why it's so important that we learn not to outrun or ignore our problems, instead taking them to Jesus. Jesus whispers that He will be with us in hard times and will rescue us (Psalm 91:15). With that promise, we have assurance that with Him at our side, we really can deal with our messes and stresses, instead of escaping them.

When a class assignment seems way over your head or making a new friend makes you nervous, don't run away. Instead, run in prayer to the One who's bigger than any challenge you face. While God never promised His followers a comfortable life, He will be our comfort and rescue in life's craziness.

Give an example of how you experienced Jesus' comfort or rescue.

Game Face

*The Lord God helps me … I have set my face
like flint to do his will, and I know that I will triumph.*

ISAIAH 50:7 TLB

In 1981, the year his father became the youngest head coach in the NFL, my husband was interviewed. The reporter asked how Dan Reeves was as a father versus how he was as coach of the Denver Broncos. Lee answered, "Well, really the only difference is on Sundays. That's when Dad puts on his 'game face.'" Lee was explaining that on the big game day, his dad's usual facial expression changed to show he was determined to lead his team to victory.

After learning the nation of Judah was facing fast approaching disaster, King Jehoshaphat got his game face on too. He fully expected God's help in triumphing over his opponent. Immediately, Jehoshaphat called for the nation to fast and pray. Then, he wisely admitted to the Lord that he was powerless against the vast armies marching toward them. The king said, "We do not know what to do, but we look to You" (2 Chronicles 20:12 HCSB). You see, Jehoshaphat knew the Lord was the only One who could save them and he was trusting that He would. Rather than allowing his expression to crumple in fear, the king displayed how sure he was that the Lord could deliver Judah from her enemies.

As sure as my father-in-law and King Jehoshaphat experienced victory, you too will find help as you put on your game face in anticipation of God's help.

How can your expression show if you are trusting in God or not?

Pure-Eyed

"I have made a covenant with my eyes."
JOB 31:1 ESV

Jason and Taylor were working on a science project. When the brothers typed in a term their teacher had given them, inappropriate images covered the computer screen. Jason immediately covered his eyes while Taylor glanced down, logged off, and called their mom. Neither boy even peeked.

This is what Job meant when he told his friends he had "made a covenant" with his eyes. He meant that he was determined not to look at things that could hurt his relationship with God or dishonor others. Job understood that looking at inappropriate images could lead him into sin. But as Job no doubt discovered, guarding our eyes is not a part-time job. Staying innocent and pure only happens when we plan ahead to make choices we know please God.

We have to be determined to obey Christ in all circumstances. That may mean having the courage to refuse to look at a naked image on a friend's phone. Maybe you will have to turn down an invitation to see an inappropriate movie that everybody's talking about. One positive thing you can do is tape the words of Job 31:1 to the top of your computer monitor or TV screen as a reminder not to look at things that dishonor God or others. Decisions like these can keep you pure-eyed, allowing you to see God—and others—the way you should.

Discuss how making a "covenant with your eyes" can help you draw closer to Jesus.

Know What's Praiseworthy

A woman who fears the Lord is to be praised.

PROVERBS 31:30

We don't know whether Mary of Bethany had great beauty, was popular, or was good at making things, but we do know she was worthy of admiration. When we first meet Mary, she is sitting at the feet of Jesus, soaking in everything He says (Luke 10:39). In Matthew 26:7, Mary took the most expensive thing she had, an alabaster jar filled with perfume, and poured it over Jesus. He was so moved by her actions that He said she'd be remembered for what she'd done, anytime the good news about Him was preached (Mark 14:9).

Proverbs 31:30 says, "A woman who fears the Lord is to be praised." And it's clear that Mary "feared" Jesus; that is, she showed her respect and love for Him in everything she did. Today, nearly two thousand years after her death, it is for her devotion—not her wealth or her talents or her beauty—that she is still remembered and honored.

The Bible says one of the most admirable qualities in a girl—or a boy—is a deep reverence and respect for Jesus. So if you want to be worthy of admiration, remember that love for Jesus is far more important than looks or talents. If it was because of her honor for the Lord that Jesus memorialized Mary in His Word, we should demonstrate our honor of the Lord as well.

Why is someone who "fears the Lord" worthy of being admired and praised?

Loving Proof

"Love your enemies!
Do good to those who hate you."
LUKE 6:27 NLT

Time and again, Jesus preached about helping those who hurt us—even when we don't feel like it. But Peter forgot what he'd been taught the night of Jesus' arrest when he angrily cut off a servant's ear. The Lord showed mercy to that servant, Malchus, who was one of His captors by miraculously healing his ear. Both Jesus and Peter's actions show how important it is for the world to see that our actions match our words. Regardless of how many disciples tried to tell Malchus about the good news of the loving and risen Jesus in years to come, he would've had little use for Jesus if he had to go through life with the knowledge that one of Christ's closest followers—Peter—permanently deprived him of an ear.

Peter would have done the right thing if only he had followed Jesus' lead by acting in kindness toward Malchus and the men. Instead, his hot-headed response reminds us that while it is easy to be sweet to people who do nice things for us, it is far more difficult to be kind when somebody hurts our feelings or takes a project idea and claims it as his own. In instances like these, remember that while your first response may not be to ask God to help you show that person compassion, it should be. By offering grace and forgiveness to others, you become loving proof of God's love.

Talk about a time someone was mean to you and you chose to respond like Jesus.

Speak Where You Are

*Faith comes from hearing the Good News.
And people hear the Good News when
someone tells them about Christ.*

ROMANS 10:17 ICB

Paul was under house arrest. A man who was used to having the freedom to go wherever God led him was now chained to a Roman solider 24-7. But Paul knew whatever his location—whether on a beach or behind bars—that was God's chosen mission for him. So even in such a confining situation, he remained joyfully obedient to tell everyone about Jesus, just like God asked him to. Remarkably, at the conclusion of his letter to the Philippians, he mentions that the gospel spread from his prison all the way to Caesar's palace (Philippians 4:22)!

Like Paul, Joni Eareckson Tada demonstrates that freedom of movement is not necessary to share the gospel effectively. Since 1967, Joni has been paralyzed from the neck down. Yet, through speaking on radio and television programs, and writing books, she has shared with millions across the globe about her love for Jesus and what He did on the cross for her—and for them.

If God can use Paul in prison and a woman confined to a wheelchair to spread the good news of His grace and mercy, just think what He can do as you speak to your friends about Jesus. Your telling them about the good news of Christ may lead them to faith!

Which friends of yours are not Christians? Ask God to give you courage to share with them about Jesus.

SEPTEMBER

Eye Contact

Let us keep our eyes fixed on Jesus.
HEBREWS 12:2 GNT

My sister, Christa, was toddling around the kitchen. Mom was getting dinner ready and Christa kept calling for our mother to listen to her recite the ABCs. "I am listening," Mom replied as she chopped tomatoes for her homemade spaghetti sauce. Frustrated, Christa moved her little body next to Mom. She tugged on her apron, demanding, "Listen to me with your *eyes*."

Making good eye contact is one of the most important rules when it comes to good manners and effective communication. It tells the other person you are paying attention and care about what they're saying. The writer of Hebrews tells us proper eye contact is essential, not just socially but spiritually as well: "Keep [your] eyes fixed on Jesus, on whom our faith depends" (Hebrews 12:2 GNT). Jesus is deserving of our full attention.

Perhaps you worry about what your friends are going to think when you tell them you are uncomfortable with the gossip around the lunch table. You feel your face flush when nobody else bows to pray before sipping their soup. Your heart races when you watch your friends roll their eyes when you refuse to let them copy your homework. But when you realize the only audience that matters is your Maker, you focus on Him. And that's good. Because He never takes His eyes—or ears—off you.

What helps you keep your eyes fixed on Jesus?

Stick to the Sword

Take … the sword of the Spirit, which is the word of God.
EPHESIANS 6:17

God's children are in a constant war against our enemy, the devil. God provides us with spiritual armor and one very important weapon that enables us to stand strong against our enemy's attacks. In Paul's letter to the Ephesians, Scripture is called "the sword of the Spirit." Quoting it, and living it, are effective tools in defeating the devil.

Second Samuel 23 tells of one of King David's coura-geous warriors, Eleazer. The account of how he faithfully held onto his weapon reminds us of how our relationship to our own sword of the Spirit should look. While Eleazar's buddies fled in fear of Israel's enemy, the Philistines, Eleazar "stood his ground and struck down the Philistines till his hand grew tired and froze to the sword" (2 Samuel 23:10). The man was so determined not to retreat that he battled bad guys until he couldn't uncurl his fingers from his sword hilt. As a result, "the Lord brought about a great victory that day" (2 Samuel 23:10 ESV).

The next time you're tempted to give in to the enemy's plan of attack, picture Eleazar and pick up your sword of the Spirit. Ask Jesus to help you stick to the truth of God's Word. He can bring great victory in your life too.

When has God's Word helped you fight off doing or say-ing something you knew wouldn't please God?

Inspected and Treated

Search me, O God, and know my heart!
Try me and know my thoughts.
PSALM 139:23 ESV

Termites love to eat wood from the inside out. These insects sneak into houses and nibble away at structures for years. Often, it isn't until someone's foot falls through a weakened step that their presence is detected. The damage termites do is costly. That's why homeowners pay pest control companies to inspect and treat their homes.

Sin is a spiritual termite, damaging us from the inside out. King David hosted the sin of lust, allowing his gaze to linger on a sexy scene that was offensive to His Savior. Since the consequence of untreated sin is destruction, the beams of David's life began to give way. Thankfully, David admitted his sin problem and invited God, the heavenly Inspector, to investigate and repair the damage. David prays, "See if there is any bad thing in me. Lead me in the way you set long ago" (Psalm 139:24 ICB). In other words, David granted God permission to get rid of the bug and rebuild him according to His blueprint.

Maybe your walk with Jesus has been weakened by decisions you've made to allow sin to make a home in you. Ask Jesus to show you those areas of compromise that require cleansing. Then, follow His treatment plan: agree with Him that sin is present and refuse to allow it to stay. He's already covered the cost of sin extermination on the cross.

How do you think making Psalm 139:23–24 your motto this month could help keep sin from eating away at you?

Be Bold

"Who can say but that God has brought you into the palace for just such a time as this?"
ESTHER 4:14 TLB

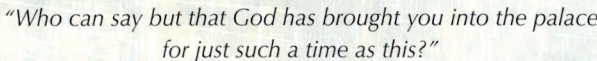

I was in a crowded grocery store when my favorite butcher, Chris, inquired loudly, "Tara, how is it you're always so joyful?" Rather than honestly replying, "My relationship to the Lord Jesus," I blushed and laughed. As I later plopped into the driver's seat of my car, I fully expected to hear a rooster crow, like Peter when he denied Christ. The Lord gave me an opportunity to share about Him, and I missed it! Rather than acting in boldness, I let shyness keep me quiet. While I later discussed Jesus with my butcher, the crowd at the counter wasn't the same as it was that day. Who knows who missed out on hearing about the Lord because my nerves got the best of me?

The Lord is looking for bold men and women, boys and girls who are willing to say aloud that God has placed us where He wants us, in order to share the only Hope available to a lost and dying world. As sure as Queen Esther was placed in the Persian palace to speak up to the king, and thus saving many lives with the Lord's help, God can reward our faithful boldness by rescuing His people through the message we share.

Seize every moment God gives you to point people to Jesus. With Him beside you, before you, behind you, and living within you, you—and I—have no excuse, but boldness.

When was the last time you told someone about Jesus?

Don't Be a Chameleon

Do not conform to the pattern of this world.
ROMANS 12:2

Designed by God on the sixth day of creation, the chameleon can blend in with his surroundings. If he decided to nibble Granny's herb garden, he would disguise himself in green to blend in with the rosemary and basil. Chameleons are also able to look in two directions at once. One eye can move one way, while the other eye turns another.

God did not design you and me to be chameleons. He made us in His image (Genesis 1:26–27) to fix our eyes on Him (Hebrews 12:2). Yet, how often do we choose to blend in with the culture around us? Instead of being faithful to live for Jesus, we become afraid of not fitting in. While friends at church may not hear us say such things on Sunday, come Monday, when the coach is cursing, we decide it's okay for us to use dirty words too. When the school's dress code policy says two inches above the knee, we try to get away with three. We fool ourselves into thinking we can look in two spiritual directions at once, one eye honoring God while the other one honors the world's ways. Chameleon Christianity, however, is unacceptable.

Jesus came so you and I can live with confidence and without camouflage. Make godly choices. Stand out for Him.

When is a time you decided to blend in to be accepted?

Be Patient and Kind

Love is patient and kind.
1 CORINTHIANS 13:4 NLT

The year was 1928. In the quarterfinals of the Olympic sculling competition, a Frenchman and an Australian rowed against each other. The Australian was in the lead when a mother duck and her ducklings paddled right into his path. Bobby Pearce lifted his oars out of the water and waited on the duck family to swim across. Though his opponent passed him by while he paused, Bobby caught up and won that race, going on to capture the gold medal in the finals.[1]

Even if Bobby had lost the race, the patience and kindness he extended toward this little duck family make him a champion in my book. Why? Because those two qualities are listed as attributes of love in 1 Corinthians 13. Bobby's actions give us a picture of how we should behave with others.

Patience, the ability to wait without growing irritated or cranky, honors the patience God has for His disobedient children. Kindness, choosing to do the thoughtful thing, whether or not we feel it is deserved, reminds us of the incredible kindness Jesus showed us in giving His life on our behalf. So if you want to show your mom, your grandpa, or a classmate that you love them, remember that patience and kindness should mark your behavior. Then you, like Bobby Pearce, will be a champion.

How do you think being patient and kind might help others see Jesus in you?

1 "Down Under Series: Australia's Rowing Icon – Bobby Pearce," World Rowing, http://www.worldrowing.com/news/down-under-series-australias-rowing-icon-bobby-pearce.

Walk Wisely

Walk with the wise and become wise,
for a companion of fools suffers harm.

PROVERBS 13:20

An African tale recounts the story of a little frog who hopped gleefully along the lily pads, until he ran smack dab into a dangerous scorpion. Frog remembered his mother had instructed him to run away whenever these known enemies were near, cautioning that scorpions were untrustworthy. But this particular creature seemed different to Frog. The scorpion spoke politely and mentioned one of his eight legs was injured. He said, "I'm crippled and cannot make it home. Would you give me a ride across the pond?"

Touched by the scorpion's problem, the frog ignored the warnings his mother had given him. Frog decided he'd make this foe his friend—at least just this once. He hoisted the scorpion on his back and took him where he wanted to go. But just before they got there, the scorpion stung the frog, wounding him terribly. "Why'd you do that?" the bewildered frog asked. "Why not?" the betrayer asked with a smirk. "You *knew* I was a scorpion when you decided to befriend me."

The Bible teaches us to be kind and loving to others, but it also tells us we must be wise in choosing friends. If your parents have told you to stay away from certain people because they don't believe those individuals have your best interest at heart, be wise and obey.

How could Frog have avoided harm?

Flourishing

*He is like a tree planted beside streams of water
that bears its fruit in season.*
PSALM 1:3 HCSB

Extreme temperatures make deserts less than ideal for life, while milder, wet climates in rain forests welcome an abundance of flowering plants, birds, and other creatures. The person who refuses to live God's way, and the one who lives as God asks, are as different as a barren desert and a bountiful rain forest. The psalmist may have had this in mind when he used the image of a fruitful tree in Psalm 1 to represent those who live for God. The main idea of the passage is that people must choose between two ways to live: we can wither or flourish.

To avoid a shriveled life, we must avoid hanging out with those who make unwise choices, insisting that keeping secrets from our parents is okay, sneaking into R-rated movies is no big deal, or taking candy from the store without paying is fun. These people, God's Word explains, actually harm others. They are like dry deserts in which only prickly cacti grow.

To thrive and grow, you and I must put into practice God's Word in every decision we make. When the Holy Spirit prompts us to say, *I'm sorry for talking to you in that tone, Mom*, we apologize. When He tells us to be patient about something we want, we wait. Then we, like the rain forest, bear fruit as we bring God glory.

What is one choice you want to make tomorrow to help your faith in Jesus flourish?

Flower Power

"I am the vine, you are the branches;
he who abides in Me and I in him, he bears much fruit,
for apart from Me you can do nothing."

JOHN 15:5 NASB

Fresh-cut flowers in a vase can brighten up any room. But in a few days the stems lose their petals because they have been detached from their main source of water and nutrients. When that happens, the arrangement must be thrown out. In contrast, a flowering plant with roots still intact will continue to thrive indefinitely. Jesus compares those who have placed their faith and trust in Him to a thriving plant—one attached to Him, the source of everlasting life and power.

Jesus is the vine and we believers are the branches. The Bible says when we "abide in" Him—when we stay connected to Jesus—He makes us mature, allowing us to bloom and be a blessing to Him and others. That means the Holy Spirit flows through us to produce love, joy, peace, patience, kindness, goodness, faithfulness, gentleness, and self-control. Fruit like this is a product of His power at work within us. But like that pretty arrangement that looks nice for a few days when it's on display, there is no spiritual fruit that can grow when we remain separate from the vine.

How are you going to stay connected to Jesus, the source of your spiritual nourishment and power?

Be a Friend Shaper

As iron sharpens iron, so one person sharpens another.
PROVERBS 27:17

Marlin and Dory. Woody and Buzz. These friends stuck by one another in good times and bad. Their friendship had a positive effect on each other. When Marlin and Buzz felt dulled by discouragement, Dory encouraged Marlin to "just keep swimming."[2] And Woody reminded Buzz, "You are a gift to the world!"[3]

God's Word tells us that "as iron sharpens iron, so a friend sharpens a friend" (Proverbs 27:17 NLT). That means friends improve each other, in much the same way that a knife sharpener run across a knife blade will improve that blade's edge. Christian friends have an added advantage as they work to encourage and affirm us. Each one of them possesses the "sword of the Spirit" (Ephesians 6:17), God's Word, the source of truth and a guidebook for life. Reminding one another of what it says can sharpen and inspire unlike anything else.

In 1 Samuel 23, David's best friend, Jonathan, came to him in the middle of his crisis. Verse 16 tells us that Jonathan helped David "find strength in God." In life, you'll find that the best way to be a friend is to do more than offer encouragement and companionship. Help others grow in their relationship with Jesus, the truest Friend of all.

How does your friendship with Jesus make you a better friend?

2 *Finding Nemo*, directed by Andrew Stanton (Burbank, CA: Buena Vista Home Entertainment, 2003).
3 Robert Velarde, *The Wisdom of Pixar: An Animated Look at Virtue* (Downers Grove, IL: IVP Books, 2010).

Be My Guest

Practice hospitality.
ROMANS 12:13

After the first wave of terrorist attacks on September 11, 2001, authorities diverted thirty-eight flights to the tiny town of Gander, Newfoundland. Within hours, the Gander community welcomed seven thousand unexpected guests. When the planes unloaded, each passenger was handed a thoughtfully packed lunch complete with lemonade and a warm cookie. Many residents invited the stranded travelers to stay in their homes. Gander's doctors and nurses donated their time and expertise to patients. Because the "plane people" couldn't leave for several days, local pharmacists didn't charge to refill prescriptions.[4] I would guess that Gander excelled at being good to their guests because they made showing kindness to others a part of what they did each day.

However, we live in a culture where people often rush everywhere they go, seldom making eye contact or offering a cheerful greeting. The Bible instructs us to "practice hospitality," meaning that we should make it a priority to reach out to others in a friendly and generous way throughout our daily routines. Extending such kindness helps people catch a glimpse of Jesus' love for, and interest in, them.

Are you making thoughtful investments in the lonely or hurting people around you? Remember: Jesus wants us reaching out to others with His love, rather than wasting time watching TV or staring down at our smartphones.

What are three ways you can practice hospitality?

---

4 Ethan Trex, "September 11th and the Hospitable People of Gander, Newfoundland," Mental Floss®, http://www.mentalfloss.com/article/31491/september-11th-and-hospitable-people-gander-newfoundland.

Stay Out of the Danger Zone

When a wise person sees danger ahead, he avoids it.
But a foolish person keeps going and gets into trouble.
PROVERBS 27:12 ICB

The royal palace interviewed possible porters for Her Majesty's portable throne. The queen asked only one question of the candidates: "If you were carrying me on a stretch of mountain road, how close to the edge would you get?" One brawny man bragged, "Queen, my strength would support you safely within twelve inches of that ledge." Another stated confidently, "Your Majesty, six inches would be all I'd need to secure you from all harm." The last man answered, "My Queen, I would stay as far away from the edge of that cliff as I can. Your life is too precious to carry you close to danger." He got the job.[5]

Just as the wise queen chose to associate with people who would keep her far from possible trouble, Jesus wants you to choose friends who care enough about you to not let you walk too close to the edge of temptation and fall into sin. Jesus yearns for you to be that kind of friend too.

Placing yourself in a compromising situation or even listening to song lyrics that cause your mind to think impure thoughts can lead you over the edge. Decide in advance to keep away from the danger zone.

What are some "danger zones" in your life? How do you plan to avoid them?

---

5 Dennis and Barbara Rainey, "'How Far Is Too Far?' Is the Wrong Question," FamilyLife Today®, http://www.oneplace.com/ministries/familylife-today/read/articles/how-far-is-too-far-is-the-wrong-question-15027.html.

Heed the Warning Signals

If you think you are standing strong, be careful not to fall.
1 Corinthians 10:12 NLT

Leaving my sister's house in Raleigh, North Carolina, with a full tank of gas, I realized our arrival in Davidson would be close to Caroline's four o'clock ballet lesson. Hours later, when the light on my dash flashed a warning, I didn't slow down or stop to refuel. I confidently put the pedal to the metal—and it wasn't long before we were stranded on the interstate, our tank empty.

As Christians, it's easy to rush through life, thinking everything is okay with us spiritually. But God has equipped us with gauges on the dashboard of life. These signs indicate when we are running on fumes and need to refuel on God's Word. So when the grumble gauge lights up, take notice. If you find yourself complaining under your breath every time Dad asks you to take out the trash, you need to fill up with a little Philippians 2:14: "Do everything without grumbling or arguing." If the indicator for anger registers red, you require a Proverbs 29:11 refuel: "A foolish person loses his temper. But a wise person controls his anger" (ICB). Every time we choose to ignore what's happening on life's dashboard, we get in trouble. But when we refuel with a proper response to God's Word, we enjoy the security of a full spiritual tank.

What warning signs might you be ignoring?

Choosing Truth, Avoiding Consequences

I have chosen the way of truth.

PSALM 119:30 KJV

Uncle Abe chose to follow God, and his nephew Lot decided to tag along. Things went well for Lot until his relative unselfishly gave him first dibs on real estate. Then, instead of seeking God's help or asking wise Uncle Abe what he should do, "Lot chose for himself" and pitched his tents near Sodom—a city known for wickedness (Genesis 13:11–12). Lot never considered the consequences of settling his family close to "Sin City." By Genesis 19, we find Lot no longer living near Sodom, but *in* it.

The Bible tells us, "When a wise person sees danger ahead, he avoids it. But a foolish person keeps going and gets into trouble" (Proverbs 27:12 ICB). Satan encourages us to make hasty decisions slyly designed to hurt our relationship with the Lord. God wants to help us choose wisely in all things and stay away from sin. He has given us His Word as our guide to lead us in the way of truth and avoid the consequences that are inevitable when we give in to temptation. (Lot, by the way, soon lost his home because of Sodom's wicked reputation.)

Every choice you make will either move you closer to the Lord or away from Him. To honor God in every situation, take time to ask questions and see what God says before rushing in and regretting it later.

What are some ways you can keep Jesus in your decision-making process?

The Myth of "Me Do It"

In the day of my trouble I sought the Lord.
PSALM 77:2 KJV

Harrison was having a hard time putting on her shoes. Eager to help, I sat down on the floor next to my two-year-old. But resisting my assistance, Harrison looked at me and said, "Me do it, Mommy!" And she did. Moments later Harrison came to me sobbing, "Boo-boo!" Her toes were hurting. She had placed her shoes on the wrong feet.

Sometimes you and I can stubbornly insist on doing things our way, instead of the right way. As Harrison's mommy, I knew what shoe was designed for which foot, but Harrison didn't care. She was focused on what she wanted, not on trusting my knowledge. All too often, we rely on our own limited understanding when the Lord is right beside us whispering, "Let Me help. I know which way is best." Only when the blisters on our heart are more than we can bear, does it dawn on us how foolish we were to ignore our loving heavenly Father's guidance.

Maybe you've bought into the myth of "me do it." And as a result of trying to do life your way, while ignoring God's help, you're now hurt and in trouble. Run to Jesus. He's here to make things right. Jesus specializes in healing broken-ness, blisters, and even self-inflicted "boo-boos."

Discuss the consequences of a time you insisted on doing things your way instead of God's.

The Peril of Pride

Pride leads to destruction. A proud attitude brings ruin.
PROVERBS 16:18 ICB

The biography of King Uzziah is not a "rags to riches" story where the pauper becomes the prince. Sadly, it's a "riches to rags" tragedy where the king loses his crown and godly reputation—all because he forgot who the real King is.

Uzziah was sixteen when he became king of Judah. The Lord blessed him with many special abilities, and "as long as he sought the Lord, God gave him success" (2 Chronicles 26:5). Some of this success revolved around inventing; in fact, Uzziah created weaponry that would be used for centuries. He was the one who invented the catapult and a machine to fire arrows (v. 15). But sadly, Uzziah's grand achievements and fame led to him having a big head, and he forgot it was the Lord who equipped him with a creative mind. In time he grew so pompous that God allowed him to be afflicted with leprosy. Kicked out of the castle, Uzziah spent his last years longing for the "glory days," when he should have been giving God the glory instead of taking it for himself.

You have been equipped with unique talents and gifts from the Lord, which He desires to use to point people to Him. Uzziah would have been wise if he had put his pride on that catapult and launched it out of his life. So will you.

What's your plan to guard against pride?

His Beloved

His banner over me is love.
SONG OF SOLOMON 2:4 ICB

Banners come in all shapes and sizes. They can be in the form of flags serving to unify a nation or they can be homemade signs wishing a loved one happy birthday! Boyfriends have even paid for personalized banners to fly behind airplanes asking their sweethearts, *Will you marry me?* There are banners awaiting passengers at the airport directing them to their ride and banners to cheer on your favorite team. Regardless of their message, one thing all banners have in common is that they aren't crafted to be hidden. They are signs to be seen.

When Moses was leading the Israelites toward the Promised Land from Egypt, the Bible mentions that every man, woman, girl, and boy camped under the flag of his family (Numbers 2:2). That way nobody could get mixed up in the two-million-man march. If anyone did wander off, she would simply search for their clan's colors. A Welcome Back banner, if you will.

Maybe you've made some poor decisions and feel a bit lost. You feel like nobody even notices—or cares. Jesus came to "save those who are lost" (Luke 19:10 NLT). Accepting His sacrifice for your sins means you are safe. No matter what you've done or how far away you've run, His banner above you is for all to see—including you. And it says, "You are mine and I love you! Welcome home."

Describe what being loved by Jesus means to you.

Handing Over Hurts

He heals the brokenhearted and binds up their wounds.
PSALM 147:3 HCSB

All the soldiers who came to arrest Jesus fell to the ground when He introduced Himself as God (John 18:6). Maybe that's when a sword dropped out of its sheath, falling within reach of Peter. The apostle was so upset by Jesus' arrest that he went on the attack. He used the sword to cut off the ear of Malchus, one of the men in the approaching mob.

Even as He handed Himself over to His accusers, Jesus healed Malchus' ear. Malchus! The servant of one of Jesus' greatest enemies! I like to think that three days later, when Malchus got the news of the empty tomb, Malchus' hearing had never been better—and that his allegiance changed, so he stopped following Caiaphas, the earthly high priest, and trusted in Jesus, his heavenly One (Hebrews 4:14). Proving that Jesus can even bring about something good through the mistakes of others, Peter's rash decision likely became a catalyst for helping Malchus recognize truth.

Maybe you feel a bit like Malchus, wounded by someone claiming to be a follower of Christ. Sadly, even "church people" like Peter or a Christian coach or a teacher can hurt us or let us down. Don't let their failures stop you from trusting Jesus, our loving healer and Savior. Instead, invite Jesus to do a surprising work in your life that turns their mistakes into blessing.

How has Jesus gotten your attention lately and what was your response?

Cross Training

Let us run with endurance the race that is set before us.
HEBREWS 12:1 NASB

The writer of Hebrews spoke about the Christian life in terms of a race. So imagine Jesus as your track coach; His instructions for your life are printed in His Word. Coach Jesus wants to strengthen you and help you grow, making you more like Him and more loving toward others you encounter on your journey toward heaven. Since He knows spiritual muscle grows best against resistance, He trains you with it. He may put a difficult person in your path, so you can practice patience. Maybe He doesn't allow you to have that specific thing you want, because He knows it will lessen your love for Him and add to your load.

When you trust Christ as your Coach, you can run through each day as if it were a lap. You can push through those painful side stitches that tempt you to slow down and stop. Because you have confidence in your Coach—you trust what He says.

Jesus promises to give you the exact measure of muscle you need for each mile marked on God's course for your life (Isaiah 40:29). When you feel out of breath and are tempted to forfeit rather than finish, remember the words of Coach Jesus, as well as His example. He faced the most difficult and challenging of times on the cross, yet didn't give up.

What is Coach Jesus asking of you right now that may be uncomfortable, but is making you stronger?

Don't Hide Your Cape

"No one after lighting a lamp covers it with a jar or puts it under a bed, but puts it on a stand, so that those who enter may see the light."

LUKE 8:16 ESV

The Incredibles are superheroes, spending their days battling bad guys and helping those in need, until they are convinced "supers" should go into hiding. Hanging up their capes, the Incredibles move to the suburbs and try to blend in. But that's hard, because they are designed to be different.[6]

The devil knows you and I, followers of Jesus, are designed to shine the light of God on a world that doesn't know Him. And so he works hard to convince us not to "stick out," to conform to culture's standards rather than pursuing God's. He is the voice telling us to effectively put our capes in the closet, constantly nagging at us to retreat. He smirks in those times when our friends question whether Jesus is real and we don't provide a ready answer. He laughs when a bad self-image day discourages us to the point that we stop seeing ourselves as unique masterpieces of God, people who are given the task not to look like we have it all together, but to point the way to Jesus.

You and I are only human, but Jesus has promised to empower us to carry out the work He has for us. Don't go into hiding. Forget about blending in. You are designed for special God-appointed missions. Keep that cape on and shine for the Lord: Jesus has plans for you.

What things can you do this week to make sure your spiritual "cape" is visible?

---

6 *The Incredibles*, directed by Brad Bird (Emeryville, CA: Pixar, 2004).

Leap of Faith

I trust Him with all my heart.
PSALM 28:7 NLT

A stretch of home movie footage shows our family at the pool on a sun-drenched day. The twins are sporting swim diapers; they are toddlers enjoying a first adventure in the big pool with Daddy. "I'm going to catch you," he says. And, happily, Caroline and Daniel take turns leaping into his arms, without a single doubt that he'll do just as he says. Caroline and Daniel don't pause at the pool's edge. They don't jump in with reckless abandon, but they plunge with purpose—toward their dad. With radiant faces, they look into their daddy's eyes, trusting his love and taking comfort in his safe embrace.

Peter wasn't in a pool, but out on a lake in a boat when he learned a similar lesson in trust. He'd been fishing all night and had caught nothing in his net. Jesus said, "Now go out where it is deeper" (Luke 5:4 NLT). Peter looked confidently into the face of His heavenly Father and did as he was told. Never before had Peter experienced such an abundant blessing.

Today, you have a similar choice. God is calling you to a deeper level of trust in Him. You can remain poolside with worry and doubt, content to swim in the shallow end. Or, you can leap into your Daddy's arms, enjoying intimate fellowship with Him in water so deep that you can't touch the bottom, but He can.

In what area of your life are you struggling to trust Jesus with all of your heart?

Trust the Loving Counselor

I will counsel you with my loving eye on you.
PSALM 32:8

Daniel's piano teacher informed me that my son had changed the piece he was going to play in the spring recital. I asked him to let me hear it. Beaming, Daniel opened his music to "A Ten Second Song" and moved his thumb and pinky between two white keys on the piano. When I asked why he'd changed songs, he replied, "Mom, this one is easier!" But when I asked Daniel which song he'd be prouder to say he accomplished, he admitted the one he'd previously chosen, composed for two hands, was the better choice.

My counsel to my son came out of my love for him. I wasn't trying to run his life or to make things more difficult for him. My words were meant to help him grow, make wise choices, value hard work, and keep him from looking silly at his recital. This is not unlike what the Lord does for us as He offers us loving counsel through His Word. Whether He prompts us to forgive those who've hurt us, to go and tell someone about Him when we'd rather stay quiet, or to select a spouse who loves Him, God's desire is to help us grow and be the best we can be.

Think of Jesus as your "Wonderful Counselor" (Isaiah 9:6). And if what He asks of you sometimes seem difficult, know that He is loving and concerned with your greatest good.

What about Jesus' counsel makes it easier to accept?

Don't Be Lazy

Hard work always pays off;
mere talk puts no bread on the table.
PROVERBS 14:23 MSG

The Little Red Hen found a grain of wheat in the field where she was pecking. Her friends, Duck, Cat, and Dog, declined when asked if they wanted to help her plant it. So Hen carefully placed the seed into the soil and it grew. Later, the resulting wheat had to be ground into flour. Once again, this was not a job Little Red Hen's friends felt like doing. When the dough was ready to be baked, Little Red Hen's friends didn't want to assist. But when the delicious loaf of bread was pulled from the oven, Duck, Cat, and Dog all wanted a piece. Rather than sharing with the lazy, selfish "friends," Hen shared the bread with her babies.[7]

Do you avoid helping your mom or dad? If so, you are choosing to be lazy. The Bible teaches that work is a gift, giving us opportunities to bless others and to serve as a means through which we can provide for ourselves. Don't be like Duck, Cat, and Dog. Remember, they went hungry because they weren't willing to help out. God's children have happy attitudes about helping others and pitch in to help, even when they aren't asked.

Talk about what you can do today to help out without being asked.

---

7 Paul Galdone, *The Little Red Hen* (New York: Scholastic Book Services, 1973).

Whispers of Hope

After the fire came a gentle whisper.
1 KINGS 19:12

No sooner did Elijah hike down the mountain where he'd witnessed God's miraculous display of power than he grew discouraged and afraid. Rather than living in confidence that God would continue to protect him from his enemies, Elijah chose to run.

Queen Jezebel was furious that God had worked a miracle on Elijah's behalf. She wanted Elijah dead. Her threats crowded out the rejoicing that should've been ringing in his head, causing Elijah's focus to turn from the Lord. But because God is "slow to anger and abounding in lovingkindness" (Nehemiah 9:17 NASB), God comforted his fearful servant in a way he least expected.

Whispering, like a good parent calming his child, the Lord asked Elijah, "Why are you here?" (1 Kings 19:13 TLB). In other words, why are you hiding in fear, instead of trusting Me? Interesting question. You see, God wanted Elijah to quit sprinting away, so he could calmly evaluate the Jezebel situation based on his faith, not his feelings.

Like Elijah, we sometimes make decisions based on our feelings, rather than allowing God's faithfulness to give us peace. Feelings are fickle. They can be influenced by how much sugar we eat or the country song we just heard. So the next time you're tempted to act based on your feelings, listen for the Lord's gentle whisper. He may ask you what He essentially asked Elijah: Why are you doing this when you should be trusting Me?

What is one way you can quiet your heart each day to listen to God's instruction?

Spiritual Treasure

Godliness with contentment is great gain.

1 TIMOTHY 6:6

First Timothy 6:6 tells us how to take hold of spiritual treasure: great gain is found when people make choices that please God and resolve to find contentment in their circumstances.

Fanny Crosby's life illustrates this principle well. When Fanny was six weeks old, she lost her sight. In the years to come, Fanny's mother and grandmother taught her about Jesus, reading to her from God's Word every day. Fanny learned that Jesus had created her for a special purpose. She accepted Him by faith, and then she began to pursue godliness—making choices that honor Him.

At age eight, Fanny wrote that she found contentment in God's plan for her. By the time she was twelve, Fanny had memorized eight books of the Bible and was inspired to write more than nine thousand hymns—many of which are still sung in churches today! For the remainder of her life, American presidents called Fanny "friend" and she traveled the world, telling everyone how delighted she was that Jesus' face would be the first she'd see.[8]

Maybe you're blinded by hard things in your life and have a crummy attitude about your current circumstances. Study your treasure map, God's Word. Live to please Him and be content in knowing He is in control.

Would the pursuit of "godliness" and "contentment" describe you? Why or why not?

---

8 "Fanny Crosby," *Christianity Today,* http://www.christianitytoday.com/ch/131christians/poets/crosby.html.

With Eyes of Faith

*We set our eyes not on what we see
but on what we cannot see.*

2 Corinthians 4:18 ICB

Thomas had missed the blessing all the remaining disciples had of seeing Jesus after His resurrection. And as he heard his friends' claims, he had a hard time believing what he hadn't seen firsthand. Sure, Jesus told them that after three days He'd come back to life, but Thomas felt he'd have to see Christ resurrected to believe that. It was because of this attitude that the disciple is remembered as Doubting Thomas.

A week later, Jesus showed up, allowing Thomas to touch His scars and to see for himself that Christ was indeed alive. At that point Thomas marveled, calling Jesus "my Lord and my God!" (John 20:28). "Because you have seen me, you have believed," Jesus said before adding, "blessed are those who have not seen and yet have believed" (v. 29).

Those words apply to every follower of Christ—including you and me—who has not had the honor of walking alongside Him as Thomas did. We are blessed when we follow Him with eyes of faith—trusting the Bible's gospel truth though we weren't there to witness Christ's resurrection firsthand.

Don't be a Doubting Thomas. Take Jesus as He is presented in His Word. Trust Him, even though you cannot see Him with your physical eyes.

What can you do to see Jesus more clearly through faith?

A Sinner Freed

Christ himself died for you. And that one death
paid for your sins. He was not guilty,
but he died for those who are guilty.

1 PETER 3:18 ICB

The two thieves and Barabbas, a murderer, trembled at the sound of the mob outside their cell. One prisoner destined for death would soon be released in honor of the Passover holiday. The three looked over at Jesus, the healer and teacher imprisoned because the religious leaders hated Him. He was so calm. Surely He was the one who would be freed. After all, He'd done nothing wrong. But the crowd didn't request freedom for Jesus.

"Let Barabbas go," the rabble roared. And as the guilty Barabbas walked unbound into daylight, and God's perfect Son was soon led to His death, something amazing happened. We were given a clear picture of what Jesus came to do: sinless Jesus gave His life so that you and I—lowdown sinners under the death penalty—could go free.

Maybe you're thinking, *Barabbas was a murderer. I'm not that bad!* Jesus taught that to commit one sin—whether it be gossip, lying, or thinking bad thoughts—is to commit them all. And the penalty of sin, just as the cross intended for Barabbas reminds us, is death. The only hope you have of escaping your death sentence is to accept that God loves you so much that He sent Jesus to die on the cross in your place.

Did Barabbas deserve freedom? Do you? Why?

Mark the Miracles

Remember the wonderful things he has done.
Remember his miracles.
PSALM 105:5 ICB

Joshua and his friends watched as the Lord miraculously parted the Jordan River at flood stage. After the nation of Israel had passed through it on solid ground, God commanded Joshua to pick twelve strong men to each retrieve a large stone from the middle of the dry riverbed to use to build a monument of remembrance on the shore. That way, they and generations after them could look at the memorial and give thanks to the Lord for how He had moved on their behalf. It reminded them that their loving heavenly Father can do anything (Joshua 4:20–24).

God is at work in your life daily. But do you take notice? Do you remember? A great way to track His involvement is to keep a memorial journal. Maybe you asked Him to heal you when you were sick. Record the date He made you better. Perhaps you were feeling low and a particular passage of Scripture encouraged you. Jot down the Bible verse and the month, day, and year in which God spoke to you so clearly through His Word. Maybe you just enjoyed a really great day. Whatever it is, track His miraculous movements. This time next year, you can look back at your list and praise God for how He has moved your faith forward.

Why is keeping a record like this a great way to grow your faith in Jesus?

Be an Ambassador of Christ

We are Christ's ambassadors.

2 CORINTHIANS 5:20 NLT

The president looked sternly at his newly appointed diplomat. "I am sending you as an ambassador to Finland, but your citizenship is here in the United States," he said. "Remember, as you live among the people there, you are representing our country."

Once in Finland, the ambassador lived on assignment. He acted and spoke in such a way that made those he encountered associate America with his respectful behavior, knowledgeable speeches, and general wisdom. In that foreign land, he taught about America and its customs through words and example—always working to paint the country in a positive light. That's what an ambassador does.

Did you know that as a follower of Jesus, you are an ambassador, a representative of heaven who temporarily occupies earth's foreign soil? This world, broken by sin, is not our true home. Instead, "our citizenship is in heaven" (Philippians 3:20). So just like that diplomat was appointed to tell the people of Finland about the United States, we are called to share with the world about Jesus. We do that not just through our words, but through our actions and attitudes. In all things, we must remember we are here as representatives of the King of Kings and our heavenly home.

Make sure the things you say and do always bring God glory. Don't neglect your duty as ambassador.

How seriously do you take your role as ambassador?

Beware of Comparisons

Don't compare yourself with others.

GALATIANS 6:4 CEV

Olaf the snowman was created for cold. But he heard that some enjoy a season called summer. He grew so obsessed with contrasting the winter he knew with the summer lifestyle he'd heard described that he sang about tanning in the heat as if it were the most glorious pastime ever. Olaf didn't realize that if he were to trade places with those in the south, he'd melt.[9]

Peter, too, compared his own situation with that of others. When the resurrected Jesus told Peter what He wanted of him, Peter immediately looked back at his friend, John. Rumor had it that Jesus had a unique set of plans for that beloved disciple. So Peter asked, "Lord, what about him?" (John 21:21 CEV). Jesus told Peter he shouldn't worry about God's plan for somebody else. Peter should focus on fulfilling his own purpose, following Jesus in his own situation, with an understanding that he was uniquely created for special things.

It's easy to hear about what someone else is doing and think, *Why don't I get to do that?* But making such comparisons is wrong. Don't be a silly snowman. Trust that you are uniquely designed to live and work for Jesus right where you are—no matter how great someone else's opportunities might seem.

How can making comparisons get us into trouble?

---

9 Kristen Bell, Idina Menzel, and Jonathan Goff, *Frozen*, directed by Chris Buck and Jennifer Lee. (Burbank, CA: Walt Disney Animation Studios, 2014).

OCTOBER

Court Mediator

There is one mediator between God and men,
the man Christ Jesus.
1 TIMOTHY 2:5 ESV

Imagine standing before Judge God. He's witnessed every rotten thing you've ever done, and He demands sin be punished by death. So for all the times you've lied, disobeyed, smarted off, or snitched cookies, you are about to pay.

All hope seems lost, until Jesus speaks up. *Your Honor,* He says to the Judge, *I want to mediate for, to speak on behalf of, the accused.* And then He comes to stand right beside you. With love in His eyes, He puts an arm around you and says, *This child has repented of his wrongs and placed faith in My death on his account. This one must go free.*

Hugely relieved, you swallow hard as the Judge reaches for a book, the Book of Life. *You are right, Counsel,* He says to Jesus. *I see this one's name right here!* The Judge then declares you not guilty, His face softening. *The penalty for your wrongs has been paid in full by my Son, your mediator, Jesus Christ,* He says. *I hereby free you and welcome you into heaven.*

No evidence you present or testimony you give could satisfy the heavenly courts in the matter of your sin. But because Jesus paid for your crimes and settles that debt on behalf of those who place their faith in Him, the Judge looks at you and doesn't see a criminal, but a dearly loved saint.

What would happen if your trial before God happened today?

Interpret His Word Correctly

Know what his Word says and means.
2 TIMOTHY 2:15 TLB

Amelia Bedelia does everything she's told, but only according to her limited understanding. When asked to dress the chicken and draw the drapes, Amelia dresses dinner in an outfit and sketches a picture of the curtains. Rather than asking questions when what was expected was unclear, Amelia jumps to conclusions and makes messes.[1]

The Pharisees had a similar tendency. They read the Old Testament's laws, rules for offerings, and holiday reminders, assuming that pleasing God was all about following laws, making sacrifices, and keeping traditions. Rather than seeing the Bible's big picture—that humanity depends on God's grace for salvation—they jumped to the conclusion that salvation is found through what they did, or didn't, do. Unfortunately, the Pharisees were quite content with their misunderstandings. By the time Jesus arrived to help them see their errors, and to clearly offer salvation in His name, they had grown so sour and judgmental that they largely rejected Jesus, the good news the whole Old Testament points to!

We can spend our lifetimes learning more about God's Word, yet never grasping all of it. But as we seek to understand Scripture better by reading it, meditating on it, and figuring out how its different stories work together and what they teach us about Jesus, we can—with the Holy Spirit's help—learn to handle it appropriately.

How can you know whether you're understanding God's Word correctly?

---

1 Peggy Parish, *Amelia Bedelia* (New York: Harper & Row, 1963).

The Passover Lamb

*"This is my body given for you;
do this in remembrance of me."*
LUKE 22:19

Throughout the Bible, God tells His people to remember His actions. And He often provided celebrations meant to help them do just that. In the Old Testament, God gave the Israelites the Passover to commemorate how He rescued them from slavery in Egypt. On the first Passover, He instructed them to put lamb's blood at the tops and sides of their doors so the angel of death would "pass over" their home and spare their firstborn sons.

For centuries, the Israelites thought Passover was *only* a remembrance. But then God used the tradition to introduce a new miracle—something that would save them from death again and give them reason to celebrate. The last time Jesus and His disciples shared a meal together was on Passover. The new Passover Lamb, Jesus, stood before His friends the night before He was going to die so spiritual death would pass over them. Sharing wine and bread was something God's people had done together for many years as a way to remember how God had delivered His people from slavery. Now, Jesus asked them to think about the perfect sacrifice He would soon make to free all of humankind from sin.

A rescue like this is worth remembering! And every time you take Communion, you remember Jesus as the Passover Lamb—God's perfect sacrifice sent to set you free. Let the bread and juice remind you that Jesus gave His life so you can one day live with Him forever.

What does taking Communion at church mean to you?

Use What God Gives You

God has given each of you some special abilities;
be sure to use them to help each other,
passing on to others God's many kinds of blessings.

1 PETER 4:10 TLB

Daniel was asked to sing a solo in church. "I cannot do it!" he cried. "All those eyes will be on me."

Whenever you're more concerned about people watching you than Jesus and what He wants to accomplish through you, you're not living as a good steward, or manager, of God's gifts. He wants you to use your talents and resources for His glory, remaining unconcerned about what anyone thinks of you personally. After all, Scripture says that in using our abilities we pass on to others God's many blessings.

Jesus gathered His friends for a special lesson on this topic, where He talked about how we should treat the gifts God gives. Jesus told a story about a man who left his estate in the care of three servants. He gave a sum of money to each one. Upon the man's return, he was pleased by the two who had invested his treasure, putting it to good use. "Well done," he said (Matthew 25:21 ESV). But one servant, perhaps fearful that he might fail, buried what he was given and made his master mad.

If God has entrusted you with a gift, whether it be your ability to sing and dance, to do math, or to help deliver pizzas, ask the Lord how you may best use those blessings to serve Him and show others His love.

How can using one of the unique gifts God's given you bless someone else?

Treasure Is His to Give

"I will give you the treasures of darkness
and hidden riches of secret places."
Isaiah 45:3 NKJV

King Cyrus didn't know God, yet the Lord said, through the prophet Isaiah, that He would "go before you [Cyrus] and make the rough places smooth; I will shatter the doors of bronze" (Isaiah 45:2 NASB). God even promised to give Cyrus treasure. Always true to His Word, God paved the way for Cyrus and his army to soundly defeat Babylon, a country that had long kept God's people, Israel, in slavery. When Cyrus surveyed his new property, the Lord led him to discover the great riches hidden away by King Belshazzar. God said He was doing all of these things so that Cyrus would know "I am the Lord, and there is no other" (v. 5).

All of the world's treasures are the Lord's. While God's people are not necessarily wealthy in a material sense, it's important we remember that everything from earth's diamond mines to the gold bars stacked in our national treasury belong to God. And He can use that wealth as He sees fit, in ways that accomplish His purposes.

Maybe your family is going through a hard time and Cyrus' treasure sounds like a blessing beyond imagination. God holds all the wealth and resources of the world in His hands. Ask Him to provide for you. And when He does, whether the blessing seems grand or small, let the treasure of His interest in your life remind you He is the Lord. There is no other.

What do you need God to provide?

King of Kindness

But when the kindness and love of God our Savior appeared,
he saved us, not because of righteous things we had done,
but because of his mercy.

TITUS 3:4–5

Forgiveness is the greatest kindness of all. As Jesus hung on the cross, He cried out to God on behalf of those killing Him, "Father, forgive them, for they don't know what they are doing." One of the criminals hanging beside Him mocked Jesus, rejecting His kindness, saying, "If You're God, then get Yourself down. And take me with You." But the other criminal, realizing Who was next to him, accepted God's kindness and placed his trust in Jesus. Jesus told the man he'd be with Him that day in heaven (Luke 23:32–43). This proves the things we do cannot save us. The thief didn't have any time left to do good things for God. Only faith in Jesus provides us with forgiveness and eternal life.

Kindness is a way of extending a gift to others which they cannot get for themselves. The Bible is clear we cannot get to heaven on our own. There's no amount of money in the world big enough to buy it and no works good enough that will get us there. The only way is to receive God's kindness by putting our faith in His Son, Jesus, who took our place of punishment.

Jesus loved you too much to come down from the cross that day. Hung over His head was a sign that read "This is the King of the Jews." However, had those Roman soldiers known any better, it should have said, "This is Jesus, the King of Kindness."

What difference does Jesus' kindness make in your life?

Doing What's Right—Regardless

Turn away from evil and do what is right!
PSALM 34:14 NET

God's battle plan for Joshua and the Israelites was rather unconventional (Joshua 6:2–5). "March your fighting men around the city once a day for six days, very quietly," the Lord said. "On the seventh day, I want y'all to march around the city seven times with the trumpets blaring. When the priests hold the last note, everyone shout loudly. Then, watch as Jericho's walls come tumbling down."

Without hesitation, Joshua did as the Lord commanded and they experienced victory. God's Word gives no indication that Joshua or any of his army personnel laughed or snickered at doing what the Lord told them to do. Maybe they remembered how much their parents' complaining had displeased the Lord. It had cost them from crossing into the Promised Land. Surely, they didn't want to repeat their relatives' rebellion. Perhaps they were still speechless from witnessing the display of God's power as He parted the Jordan River, so they could pass through. Likely, they saw in Joshua a leader who demonstrated absolute obedience to the Lord no matter what, and they were eager to do the same.

Like Joshua, when you do what God says, even if it is hard or may seem silly, you are showing that God's Word is to be trusted and obeyed. Even when His ways seem different, God knows what He is doing.

Discuss a time you were obedient to God even though it felt uncomfortable.

A Safe Supper

You prepare a table before me
in the presence of my enemies.

PSALM 23:5

David knew very well how to care for sheep. He was a shepherd. He grew up leading his lambs into green pastures and scoping out the best meadows with the greenest grass for them to graze. David would go ahead of them, making sure it was safe before they arrived. Sure enough, he would find danger lurking that his defenseless sheep couldn't deal with alone. Snakes would hide out in holes and bite the unsuspecting sheep, unless the good shepherd would take care of the problem in advance. He would take oil and coat the entrance of each snake hole. By doing this, the poisonous predators could not slither out and attack their prey with a fatal bite. Because of the lovingkindness and protection of their shepherd, the sheep could eat their supper safely, even "in the presence of [their] enemies" (Psalm 23:5).

Jesus, the Good Shepherd, specializes in guarding us against unseen danger. On the cross, He took care of the preparation. When we trust in Him, we are filled with His Holy Spirit, which protects us against the deadly traps set by Satan. Your enemy may try to strike, but his movement is limited. Don't be afraid.

Thanks to the provision and protection of the Shepherd, you can enjoy the blessings of hope, peace, and joy set before you. Swallow calmly. Jesus has prepared the way and is keeping you safe.

Describe how you feel knowing Jesus keeps you safe, even in the midst of danger.

The Lion Tamer

"He rescues and saves his people. …
He has rescued Daniel from the power of the lions."
DANIEL 6:27 NLT

Our son, Daniel, woke up fearful, tearful, and dreading what was going to happen next. His fear of the unknown was robbing him of the blessings this new day from the Lord would bring. My mother, visiting from South Carolina, wisely reminded Daniel of the man in Proverbs who was afraid to go outside because there "might" be a lion (Proverbs 22:13).

DeDah asked, "Now, Daniel, do we have lions here?" "No ma'am, they live in the zoo and in Africa," he said. "Okay, then," DeDah explained, "we have to realize that what you're worrying about right now is Satan's way of robbing you of the fun, healthy, happy life that Jesus desires for you. Instead of being scared of all the lions, I want you to think about another boy named Daniel in the Bible who was able to trust in the Lord so completely that even the lions were defeated and subdued, because of his faith in God."

Every day you choose where you put your confidence. Only Jesus knows what tomorrow holds, because He is already there. He is trustworthy and able to subdue the "lions" like fear and worry that cloud your focus and cause your mind to doubt in His good plans for your life.

What is a lion-like fear in your life that could rob you of joy—if you didn't trust Jesus?

Teach Friends
There Is More Beyond

*How can they believe in him
if they have never heard about him?*

ROMANS 10:14 NLT

In Spain, there's a memorial that commemorates the great explorer Christopher Columbus, the man who completed four voyages across the Atlantic Ocean. Prior to his first voyage, the people of Spain were sure the land they saw on their maps was all that existed. Their motto, carved in Latin at the top of the monument, was "Non Plus Ultra," which means "No More Beyond." But after Columbus' 1492 voyage and the reports he shared, Spain was forced to rethink this view. Not only were previously unknown lands out there, but they were extensive and filled with wonders! Columbus confirmed there certainly was "more beyond" what the people of Spain initially thought. For that reason, the memorial statue contains a lion tearing off the word *Non* with its paw, leaving the declaration "More Beyond."[2]

Many people mistakenly think that we cease to exist after our short lifetimes. But the Bible—the same book from which Columbus gained much of his interest in creation and knowledge of geography—insists that the human soul will live forever with God or separated from Him in hell. So learn about and share the Bible's promises of eternal life with Jesus. Help others embrace the exciting news that there really is more beyond for those who choose to follow Jesus.

What can you do to help others accept the reality of eternal life?

2 "Christopher Columbus," Bible.org, http://www.bible.org/node/10347.

The Bible Is the Box Top

Scripture is inspired by God and is useful for teaching and for showing people what is wrong in their lives. It is useful for correcting faults and teaching how to live right.

2 TIMOTHY 3:16 ICB

One of the world's largest puzzles contains 33,600 pieces! How would you begin to make those thousands of small, colorful pieces into a wildlife scene? You'd look first to the image on the puzzle box's top, and then you'd get busy sorting and connecting. But without the big picture as a reliable reference, putting that puzzle together would be hopeless.

Some days, life itself feels like a pile of pieces—a puzzle for which some say there is no box top. But God never intended for us to go through life frustrated and confused, wondering why we are here and what we should do with our lives. Instead, He gave us His very useful Word, the Bible. It was inspired by Him and tells us we are on earth to bring glory to Him. It shows us where we mess up, teaches us how to live in a way that pleases God, and reminds us that the most important piece in life's puzzle box is Jesus. Make Him the center point of life and everything else can be clicked into place.

When you trust God's Word for direction, you can make decisions with confident assurance, knowing life's pieces will eventually connect to form a divine design.

What danger do you think there is in not reading the Bible regularly?

Quit the Blame Game

You will never succeed in life if you try to hide your sins. Confess them and give them up;
then God will show mercy to you.

PROVERBS 28:13 GNT

Both Eve and Adam disobeyed God by eating fruit He'd declared off-limits. But when confronted by the Lord about these wrongs, Adam pointed his finger at God and Eve, determined to shift blame to someone besides himself (Genesis 3:12). "It's *Your* fault, Lord," he said, pouting. "I wouldn't have done it if *You* hadn't made me marry *her.*" God, an eyewitness to everything that goes on, then turned to Eve to hear what she would say. "Don't look at me," she cried. "That snake made me do it." In those moments just before humanity was banned from the garden, the world's first game was born. And we've been playing that blame game ever since.

Blaming others is a selfish attempt to hide our sins, while letting someone else bear consequences we earned. God says in His Word that we will never succeed in life if we try to hide our sins. (Adam and Eve, for example, certainly didn't earn a lighter penalty when they added blaming to their offenses!) So the next time you and a school chum get in trouble for talking during class, don't blame the teacher or your friend. Own up to your mistake. God shows mercy to those who confess. Your teacher might show you a little grace too.

Why is Jesus pleased when you take responsibility for your actions?

No Backtracking!

> *"Live by trusting in me …*
> *I will not be pleased with the one who turns back in fear."*
> HEBREWS 10:38 ERV

When Hansel noticed the forest ahead was growing darker, he gathered pebbles. "I'll drop them as we walk," he told Gretel, "so we can find our way back."[3] No matter what adventures lay ahead, Hansel wanted assurance he could make his way back to where they started. In this case, the plan was a good one, but Hansel's actions remind me of an important spiritual truth.

One day, while Elisha was plowing, God called him to step into the shadowy unknown of ministry. God said Elisha would be a great prophet for the nation of Israel, a dangerous job that would take him all over the country. Elisha didn't respond to this call by loading his pockets with markers to help him find his way back home. Instead, Elisha hosted a feast with a big bonfire made up of the very plow he would've needed if he ever wanted to return to farming (1 Kings 19:21). Then, he boldly headed out into God's future for him.

It's likely Jesus had Elisha's courageous, no-planning-for-the-possibility-that-things-might-not-work-out response to God's call in mind when He said, "No one who puts a hand to the plow and looks back is fit for service in the kingdom of God" (Luke 9:62). In other words, you and I must follow Jesus with the attitude that returning to our lives before we met Him is not an option.

Why does backtracking displease God?

---

3 Jacob and Wilhelm Grimm, "Hansel and Gretel," in *Folk and Fairy Tales*, ed. Martin Hallett and Barbara Karasek (Toronto: Broadview Press, 2002), 137–143.

Search for the Good

*The one who searches for what is good finds favor,
but if someone looks for trouble, it will come to him.*
PROVERBS 11:27 HCSB

The weather was perfect as the Georgia Tech team surveyed each hole of the golf course before their tournament's start. "Boy, that rough is thick," one in the group grumbled, pointing out the tall grass alongside the fairway. It was so tall it could easily trap a ball. "Those sand traps look impossible to avoid," another griped, scowling. "Forget all that," a third player said, pointing to a large pond. "How are any of us going to get the ball past that water hazard?"

David Duvall quietly listened to his comrades' comments, knowing that to focus on troubles was a distraction that could lead to added swings. When asked what he thought about the hole, David smiled. "Yeah, but look at the size of that green," he said. In other words, he told them the hazards need not scare us if we instead choose to focus on the good things in our grasp.

Don't go through life only focusing on what's wrong with the world. The Bible teaches that's a recipe for trouble. Instead, look for and mention the good. Then, like David Duvall, you will be a positive example to your friends. And you'll find what you're aiming for.

What should you do when the children at school speak negatively about class? Why?

Be Sincerely His

We have this treasure in jars of clay.

2 CORINTHIANS 4:7

Scripture speaks of humans as fragile clay jars. Without Jesus, we are filled with cracks caused by sin. The only way to repair them is to give our hearts to Jesus, acknowledging what we've done wrong and placing faith in Him as our help. Then, Jesus becomes the treasure carried safely within us. But many people go to church and do good things as if that outer glaze of goodness will make them whole, will make them true Christians. These people aren't sincerely devoted to God, and they can't carry Jesus in their hearts.

The English term *sincere* is made up of two Latin words, *sine* and *cera*, meaning "without wax."[4] Long ago, clay pots were handcrafted. Some dishonest merchants, not caring about defects in their merchandise, filled these cracks with wax, then covered them over with glaze before selling them. When unsuspecting buyers put new pots to use, water leaked out, proving that the cracks had not been repaired, but were only smoothed over. This became such a widespread problem that honest sellers stamped *sine cera* on their pots to distinguish their wares from the faulty pottery.

When you are honest, confessing your sins and repenting of them, the Lord will make you new. Then, you can stand "sine cera" before Him, truly carrying His Holy Spirit in your heart and serving Him faithfully.

What have you done to address your sin cracks?

---

4 N. S. Gill, "The Possible Origins of the Words Sincere and Sincerely," About.com, http://www.ancienthistory.about.com/od/etymology/f/Sincere.htm.

Care for God's Creatures

The godly care for their animals.
PROVERBS 12:10 NLT

When God created mammals, reptiles, birds, insects, and fish, He called His work "good" seven times in Genesis chapter 1. And in Genesis chapters 6–9, which record the great flood that happened as a result of humanity's sin, God did not forget His creatures: He instructed Noah to take them on the ark (6:19–20). Animals show up throughout Scripture. We can safely assume there were a few animals in the stable where Jesus was born. The Lord was "with the wild animals" during His desert temptation (Mark 1:13). And when Jesus entered Jerusalem riding a donkey's colt, He used an animal to fulfill Zechariah's five-hundred-year-old prophecy (Luke 19:35; Zechariah 9:9).

Animals reveal much about God's creative abilities, and throughout history they have helped humanity in many ways. But they are a gift that comes with responsibility. One of God's first instructions to Adam was to care for God's creation. That included dogs, kittens, rabbits, and gerbils, as well as the creatures we consider wild.

So don't kick a dog when you're mad or pull a kitty's tail when trying to be funny. Be sure not to litter, leaving trash on the beach that could cause a turtle or gull to get tangled. Remember your responsibilities of watering and feeding pets who are unable to care for themselves, and report mistreatment. Being gentle and caring toward the creatures God made is one way to demonstrate your love for Him.

What are a few ways you could care for animals that would please God?

What Goes Around Comes Around

If you set a trap for others, you will get caught in it yourself. If you roll a boulder down on others, it will crush you instead.

PROVERBS 26:27 NLT

In 1949, Warner Brothers introduced their *Looney Tunes* series with Wile E. Coyote and Road Runner. Each cartoon was characterized by Wile E. Coyote trying to catch the Road Runner for dinner. But the skinny coyote's plans always backfired. When Wile E. Coyote targeted Road Runner with a boomerang, it returned to knock the coyote out cold. If Wile E. wanted to smash Road Runner with a boulder, the big rock would come rolling back on him. In fact, as hard as he tried, Wile E.'s scheming and plotting never succeeded. They only got him into trouble.[5]

Maybe your brother makes you so frustrated that you want to get even. Perhaps you find yourself mentally creating ways to get him into trouble with Mom. Or maybe you think a girl in class thinks too highly of herself and needs someone to take her down a peg. You've thought about pulling a prank on her, embarrassing her, like she's embarrassed you. Caution! Remember the Bible's teaching and the painful truth that Wile E. Coyote discovered: setting traps for others is a good way to find yourself in deep trouble. Schemers often become victims of their own plans. Jesus wants us to pursue forgiveness instead.

When have you seen scheming backfire?

5 "The 9 Rules of Every Wile E. Coyote and Road Runner Cartoon," *Time*, http://www.time.com/3735089/wile-e-coyote-road-runner/.

It's Okay to Cry

Jesus wept.

JOHN 11:35

Throwing myself across the bed, I sobbed. Plans I'd made failed miserably. I cried so loudly, in fact, I didn't hear the door to my bedroom open and Daddy enter. Without saying a word, my father came in, sat beside me—and cried. I never doubted Daddy's love for me before, but that night I experienced it in a way I never had. Knowing his little girl was hurting saddened him, and he joined me in the grief.

Jesus' friend Mary also knew about grief. She fell at Jesus' feet crying hysterically. Her brother, Lazarus, was dead and she was a wreck. If anybody could've said, *No tears! It'll be okay*, it would be Jesus. Jesus knew He was going to raise Mary's brother Lazarus from the dead. However, the Bible doesn't tell us Jesus told Mary to cheer up and smile, masking her heartache. Instead, God's Word says that Jesus burst into tears too.

Whatever you are facing today, know that it's okay to cry. Be real with how you feel, because you have a living, loving God who is "acquainted with grief" (Isaiah 53:3 NKJV). He understands that life on a sin-broken planet is difficult and sometimes very sad. But after you've dried your eyes, remember what Jesus did when He and Mary stopped weeping over Lazarus. He broke up the funeral with a miracle and surely gave that sad family reason to cry tears of joy.

What does Jesus' example teach you about grieving?

Eat in Moderation

Do you like honey?
Don't eat too much, or it will make you sick!
PROVERBS 25:16 NLT

In *Cloudy with a Chance of Meatballs,* Flint, an inventor, builds a machine that creates food out of water. People far and wide make their way to Flint's hometown because of the countless culinary delights that fall from the sky there. But having constant access to too much of a good thing leads people to become gluttonous, their eyes and bellies growing huge, because of their lack of self-control.[6]

God made our bodies to need food and created the flavors we enjoy, but He warns us in His Word about the dangers of too much of a good thing. Sweet and salty treats, like ice cream and chips, are yummy and okay in moderation. But eating too much of them—or even too much healthy food—is called gluttony, and that's a sin that can harm us.

The moment you made Jesus your Savior, your body became the very home of the Holy Spirit (1 Corinthians 6:19–20). An important way to honor God with your body, and to show the Holy Spirit that He is welcome, is by refusing to overeat. So remember that even when a sign says a buffet is "all you can eat," you should choose to take only what you need. That's moderation.

How can you honor God with your eating?

---

6 *Cloudy with a Chance of Meatballs*, directed by Phil Lord, Chris Miller, et al. (Culver City, CA: Sony Pictures, 2009).

Laughter

"He will fill your mouth with laughter."
JOB 8:21 GW

Mary Poppins' Uncle Albert loves to laugh. In fact, his bouts of laughter have an unusual effect, causing him to float high into the air. About his laughing condition, Uncle Albert sings, "It's getting worse every year."[7] Abraham's wife, Sarah, had the opposite problem.

For decades, Sarah dreamed of adding a nursery to the tent she shared with her husband, Abraham. I can picture Sarah staring longingly at her swatches of pink and blue. After all, she had wanted a baby her whole life. God had told her husband he'd be the father of many nations (Genesis 17:5) and Sarah had planned to have a really big family by now. But the crib Abraham crafted many years ago remained empty—and Sarah began to believe God's promise was too. Thankfully, as Sarah soon discovered, God is always true to His promises. A baby boy named Isaac was born to her when she was over ninety years old and Sarah, the Bible says, was overjoyed. "God has brought me laughter," she exclaimed (21:6 GW).

God's Word tells us, "Tears may flow in the night, but joy comes in the morning" (Psalm 30:5 GNT). So no matter how hard today is, trust that when God makes a promise, He keeps it. He will "fill your mouth with laughter" in His perfect timing (Job 8:21).

When has Jesus surprised you with laughter?

---

7 *Mary Poppins*, directed by Robert Stevenson (Burbank, CA: Walt Disney Pictures, 1964).

Flee and Pursue

*Flee the evil desires of youth and pursue
righteousness, faith, love and peace.*

2 TIMOTHY 2:22

The apostle Paul mentored a young man named Timothy, training him to become a missionary for Jesus. The books of 1 and 2 Timothy are letters written from the apostle to his young protégé, and in them we find much wisdom about what we can do to live for Christ.

Timothy accepted Jesus into his heart at a young age, but, like us, he needed ongoing teaching to know how best to serve Him. In 2 Timothy 2:22 Paul tells the young man to flee evil desires—to turn away from things like lying and being disrespectful to authority. Instead, as a young man saved by Jesus and determined to live for Him, Timothy should chase after things that make Christ happy. He should work to live honorably, to grow in faith and love, and to maintain peace.

Paul's advice to Timothy applies to us too. Once we've accepted Christ, we need to turn away from—to flee from—our rebellious tendencies every time they try to pull us in the wrong direction. That means the second we're tempted to do something that would displease God, we run from the idea as if it were an angry wasp we wanted to escape. Similarly, when it comes to making choices that please God, we pursue them as if they are as necessary to our survival as water and air. These are habits we can develop.

When have you fled from an evil desire to pursue what pleases Jesus?

Own Your Sins

I confess my iniquity; I am sorry for my sin.
PSALM 38:18 ESV

When confronted with his sin, King Saul downplayed what he'd done wrong. First, he blamed others. Then, after Samuel told Saul his crown would go to someone else, he transformed into a drama king. Grabbing the prophet's robe, Saul pleaded, "I have sinned. But please honor me before the elders of my people" (1 Samuel 15:30). In other words, Saul was ready to say or do anything to avoid punishment or lose his authority and the crowd's favor. Dishonoring God didn't bother him. He felt no need to own his sins.

Can you relate? Let's say your mother catches you playing a game on your phone that she's asked you not to play. As a consequence, she takes away your phone for a week. Are you more upset about having your phone taken away than you are heartbroken over having broken God's rules about obeying your parents? If so, then like King Saul, you'll likely make excuses and cry more over the consequences your behavior earned than cry out of repentance. That's what it looks like when we choose not to own the things we do wrong. On the other hand, owning our sins means admitting we did something wrong, accepting the consequences, and resolving to not repeat that same poor choice in the future.

Don't blame your mistakes on someone else or lose your temper when you're punished. Remember, being truly sorry means owning up to what you did through confession, accepting discipline, and then repenting of displeasing God.

How can you own up to your sins?

Just Do It

Be doers of the word.

JAMES 1:22 ESV

Cameras focused on eighty-year-old Walt Stack as he jogged his daily seventeen miles across the Golden Gate Bridge. He joked that when it was cold and his teeth wanted to chatter, he just left them at home in his locker.[8] The commercial ended with three simple words in white on a black background: JUST DO IT. Nike's idea that people should just get out and do the athletic challenge they'd only been talking about—as Walt did when he actually made that long jog every morning—led to one of the most successful advertising campaigns in modern history.

Nike can't really take the credit for coining the "Just Do It" phrase. Almost two thousand years ago, Jesus' half brother, James, wrote about the importance of just doing it when he said, "Be doers of the word" (James 1:22 ESV). He meant that we shouldn't just talk about obeying God's Word: we should also "do what it says." James, in fact, was such a champion of just doing this very thing that people called him "Camel Knees." Hour after hour, he prayed and sought the Lord's direction and strength, because God's Word asked him to.

Throughout the day, whatever the situation, ask God to help you apply the wisdom in His Word: to give you the discipline to "just do it," for His glory.

What do you need to "just do" for Jesus today?

---

8 David Gianatasio, "Happy 25th Birthday to Nike's 'Just Do It,' the Last Great Advertising Slogan," Adweek, http://www.adweek.com/adfreak/happy-25th-birthday-nikes-just-do-it-last-great-advertising-slogan-150947.

All Ears

Be quick to listen, but slow to speak.
JAMES 1:19 GNT

In the Dr. Seuss book *Horton Hears a Who!* Horton the elephant pays attention to the cries of tiny voices longing for someone to take notice and listen.[9] His actions remind me that being a good friend requires us to make listening a priority. After all, we can't know what a friend needs or how we can help until we first close our mouths and pay attention to what she has to say.

Do you put your ears to good use like Horton? Scripture emphasizes that we should listen attentively. Doing so shows humility, a character quality Jesus desires in all of His children. It also demonstrates our love.

If your buddy is speaking, don't tune him out to think about what you are going to say once he pauses long enough to gather his thoughts and feelings. Instead, decide to be present and hear what's on his heart. By making this a practice in your relationships, you'll show your willingness to live in a way that pleases Jesus. And you'll have the information and time you need to form a wise response, when your opinion or help is requested.

Ask friends or members of your family to recall a time they felt respected because of your willingness to listen. Who has made you feel this way, because of how carefully they listened to you?

---

9 Dr. Seuss, *Horton Hears a Who* (New York: Random House, 1954).

Be a Good Neighbor

"Love your neighbor as yourself."
MARK 12:31

Four lepers had depended on the kindness and care of the people living inside the city for their meals. But when famine struck, everyone was starving. No one was thinking of the poor lepers outside the city gates, because no one had enough food to feed their own families.

One day, the lepers discovered the campsite of Israel's enemy, abandoned. The Lord had caused the Arameans to hear the commotion of chariots and horses, so they fled, thinking they were under attack (2 Kings 7:6–7). Immediately, the hungry lepers gobbled up some grub and gathered the supplies left behind. But their consciences bothered them. They said to each other, "What we're doing is not right. This is a day of good news and we are keeping it to ourselves" (v. 9). So off they went to tell their city neighbors, who were still starving to death, how God had sent rescue and food in one miraculous night.

How can you bless your neighbors? You can share meals with the less fortunate, as the city's inhabitants did. But like the lepers, you can also share good news, alleviating an even bigger problem. Tell those who are spiritually dying of starvation the good news you know: God loves the world so much that on one night He sent His Son Jesus, the Bread of Life, to save us. Loving your neighbor as yourself means doing for the other guy what you would want him to do for you.

How can you be a good neighbor this week?

Check Your Own Eyes

"Why do you look at the speck that is in your brother's eye,
but do not notice the log that is in your own eye?"

MATTHEW 7:3 NASB

On the classic TV show *I Love Lucy*, Lucy Ricardo is certain her husband's headaches are because his eyes are bad. But at the eye doctor's office, it turns out that Lucy is the one unable to read the eye chart while husband Ricky can see it clearly. That night Lucy is scheduled to perform a dance routine. Because of her blurry vision, she loses her dance partner and ends up dancing in the wrong direction.[10]

Jesus teaches that you and I can spin off in the wrong direction too if we remain blind to our own problems. One way we're likely to do that is by focusing on the issues of others. Unfortunately, it's incredibly easy to see minor faults in those around us, while completely missing our own shortcomings. That, in fact, is what Jesus was addressing when He said, "First take the log out of your own eye, and then you will see clearly to take the speck out of your brother's eye" (Matthew 7:5).

Don't develop a critical spirit toward siblings and friends. Instead, ask Jesus to help you see your own faults and correct them.

What should you do when you're tempted to point out someone else's shortcomings?

---

10 Lucille Ball, Desi Arnaz, Vivian Vance, and William Frawley, "Lucy Has Her Eyes Examined," *I Love Lucy*, season 3, episode 10, directed by Willam Asher (New York: CBS/Fox Video, 1989).

We Need to Turn

Jesus began to preach,
"Repent, for the kingdom of heaven has come near."
MATTHEW 4:17

Hope yelled at her mother for the fifth time in a day. "You apologize to me … now!" Mother demanded. "Okay," Hope snarled. Stomping upstairs she shouted, "I'm sorry!"

Mother's shoulders sagged. Hope's tone and the fact they'd relived the scene a hundred times before told her Hope wasn't sincere. There was no repentance in Hope's heart. While she could say apologetic words, she refused to turn away from her sin and choose the right words and actions the next time she was tempted to be disrespectful.

Jesus wants more from us than empty apologies. He taught repentance, a complete turning away from sin with the Holy Spirit's help. Repentance, in fact, is essential to salvation. Unless you are willing to turn from your sinful, self-centered way of living to follow Jesus, you will "perish" (Luke 13:3). You see, your behavior reflects what you really believe about your need for Jesus' forgiveness and grace. If you're continuing to act out, constantly apologizing only to repeat the same hurtful ways, you are not taking sin seriously. Repentance shows your willingness to do whatever is necessary to follow Jesus. So ask Him today to soften your heart and remind you of the price He paid so you could be free of sin's control. Choose to turn away from sin.

What makes repentance better than simply offering an apology?

Be a Prayer Warrior

Pray in the Spirit at all times and on every occasion.
Stay alert and be persistent in your prayers.

EPHESIANS 6:18 NLT

Going into the garden of Gethsemane on the night He was arrested, Jesus took Peter, James, and John with Him, surrounding Himself with like-minded loved ones who could encourage Him in prayer. But though Jesus told Peter, James, and John to stay awake and pray for Him, these disciples—who had just said they'd be willing to do anything for Jesus—didn't resist the enemy's temptation to fall asleep instead of supporting Jesus in prayer (Mark 14:32–41). Rather than proving they were alert, dedicated prayer warriors, they showed themselves to be weak friends.

How many times have you decided to pray after you've put your head on your pillow, only to fall asleep before getting a few minutes into your prayer? It's wonderful to go to bed thinking about Jesus and asking Him to protect your friends and family, but He wants you to pray when you are alert too. If fighting for those you love on your knees in prayer before bedtime helps you stay focused and aggressive against an enemy who's always quick to discourage prayer (because it's an effective tool against his schemes), get as uncomfortable as you can. True warriors engage in combat, not comfort.

How can you become a better prayer warrior?

A Trustworthy Source

Some trust in chariots and some in horses,
but we trust in the name of the Lord our God.
PSALM 20:7 ESV

The Philistines held a monopoly on iron weapons and the skill needed to sharpen them. They charged a pretty penny to any Israelite who needed a Philistine blacksmith to sharpen his dull ax or plow blade. Tired of the oppression by this neighboring enemy, Israel wanted to fight. But King Saul was frightened by an obvious disadvantage: they had no weapons!

Saul's son, Prince Jonathan, realized something his father did not. Israel didn't need to worry about the size of the Philistine army or their arsenal. With the God of the universe on Israel's side (1 Samuel 14:6), they could not be defeated. Jonathan put his faith in Who was carrying him and not in what he carried. He followed the Lord's lead and led the attack. Because of his obedience, God rescued Israel and defeated the entire Philistine army!

Maybe you fear what seems like a huge problem, wishing you were bigger so you could fight it better. Perhaps you're struggling to find courage to trust God for help. Remember what He did for Israel. And take courage in the truth that Jonathan's faith influenced his friends to climb out of the holes in which they were hiding. Through faith, they experienced divine victory.

When has God given you victory in spite of the odds against you?

Plant Truth

"The farmer plants the word."
MARK 4:14 GW

Two Christian businessmen became friends while traveling. God used that friendship to give birth to a ministry that continues today. Gideons International is an association that leaves free Bibles in the drawers of hotel rooms across the globe. The Gideons' hope is that in making God's Word easily accessible to travelers, they're helping plant it in people's hearts. They understand that Christians are to be like farmers who sow truth—Scripture—wherever they go.

Truth took root in Shelly's heart a few years ago. She traveled often and found herself reaching for a Bible left in her hotel room by the Gideons. Prior to that night, Shelly knew little about Jesus. But because she was curious about the green book left in a drawer, she opened God's Word. There she learned she was a sinner, but that God loved her so much that He sent Jesus to die for her. That night, the seed that had been planted went down deep in her heart. Shelly surrendered to Jesus and began living for Him.[11]

You can share God's Word too, planting it as you travel through life. Maybe you'll copy a Bible verse in a note you send to your grandparents. Maybe you'll collect money to send to missionaries who can put Bibles in the hands of those who've never seen one. Or maybe you'll purchase a Bible for a friend. Plant truth so that others can harvest it and be nourished by it.

How does Shelly's story encourage you to be a truth planter?

---

11 http://www.gideons.org/ChangedLives/ChangedLivesText.aspx.

Sweet Truth

*The grace of the Lord Jesus Christ, and the love of God,
and the fellowship of the Holy Spirit, be with you all.*

2 CORINTHIANS 13:14 NASB

Deuteronomy 6:4 says, "The Lord is one!" (NASB). But did you know He's actually three persons working together? Consider a candy corn: it's one sweet treat made up of three parts. The white, orange, and yellow colors remind me of the three distinct persons of the Trinity.

The Trinity—the three distinct persons of God who function together as one—is seen first in Genesis, the first book of the Bible. God says, "Let Us make man in our image, according to Our likeness" (Genesis 1:26 NASB). "Us" and "Our" refer to God the Father, God the Son (Jesus), and God the Holy Spirit.

All three, correctly understood as being one God, worked together to make the world. All three also cooperate in the amazing process of saving us. John 3:16 says, "For God [the Father] so loved the world, that He gave His only begotten Son [Jesus], that whoever believes in Him shall not perish, but have eternal life" (NASB). The Bible explains that the Holy Spirit helps make us aware of our sin, and once we've accepted Christ, He serves as our helper and teacher (14:26).

If that sweet truth about the Trinity seems beyond comprehension, take comfort in Isaiah 55:8, when God says, "My ways are far beyond anything you could imagine" (NLT). Then, remember the candy corn. Those three distinct parts really do function as one. And our one God, in all three persons, loves you very much.

Which person of the Trinity do you feel closest to? Why?

NOVEMBER

Don't Sit on a Wall of Pride

Before a downfall the heart is haughty.

PROVERBS 18:12

Humpty Dumpty sat confidently—until the moment he fell. Then, his injuries were so bad that "all the king's horses and all the king's men" couldn't put him back together.[1] We don't know why Humpty toppled, but his story reminds me of the messes that result when we sit on a wall of pride.

Pride, or having a "haughty" heart, is a sin that makes us think highly of ourselves. We believe we're better than anyone around us and above the rules. Left unchecked, pride will convince us that we—rather than the Lord—are in charge. Israel's prideful Queen Jezebel led a country established by the one true God, without bowing to Him. She was so confident that she thought nothing of encouraging God's people to worship an idol. But as sure as God's Word warns us to expect heartache if we try to put ourselves above Him, Jezebel—not unlike Humpty—toppled to her death (2 Kings 9:33).

A haughty heart will come to ruin. So if you find yourself thinking you are too grown up to listen to your parents or think you are doing just fine without obeying what God's Word says, watch out. It's time to climb down from the pride wall in repentance, confess your sin, and ask God to create in you a humble heart—before you find yourself in a mess.

What proud behaviors do you think might be a sign you'll soon topple into trouble?

---

1 Traditional, "Humpty Dumpty," *Nursery Rhymes and Traditional Poems*, Lit2Go Edition (1910), http://etc.usf.edu/lit2go/74/nursery-rhymes-and-traditional-poems/5181/humpty-dumpty/.

Perfect Power

"My power is made perfect in weakness."

2 CORINTHIANS 12:9

Three times, Paul asked the Lord to remove something that was bugging him—a "thorn in [his] flesh" (2 Corinthians 12:7). Maybe his vision was bad and he was tired of looking at things with blurry eyes. Maybe a particular person in the apostle's life was harassing him. Whatever it was, Paul regularly took the issue to God. While the Lord gently refused to remove the problem, He comforted Paul with the knowledge that many times pain is part of His plan. And it's in our weaknesses that God's power is perfected in our lives.

My friend Jerry Cromer broke his neck waterskiing. For three years, Jerry prayed God would enable him to use his arms and legs again. Then Jerry changed his prayer asking the Lord to heal his mind and help him make a difference from his wheelchair. God gave Jerry the inspiration for a device that enables those with no arm movement to operate electronic devices and computers independently. Jerry, now an inventor, saw his "thorn" become a blessing.[2]

Maybe you're struggling to understand a painful situation in your life. Like Paul and Jerry, take it to the Lord in prayer. Then, trust that whether or not God chooses to take away the "thorn" sticking you, He will provide you with grace. His perfect power will help you to not only endure, but to witness amazing things along the journey.

When have you seen Jesus use someone's weakness to do something great?

2 "The Need to Succeed - The Jerry E. Cromer, Jr. Story," Quadapuck™, http://www.quadpuck.com/story.html.

Get Well Soon

Jealousy will rot your bones.
PROVERBS 14:30 ICB

Jealousy, that selfish feeling that makes you hot and angry that someone else received praise or a prize when you did not, can be as destructive as a disease. The first time we see jealousy's work in the Bible, the firstborn son of Adam and Eve, Cain, offered a gift to God that was not received as well as was his brother Abel's. In truth, Abel's gift was brought to the Lord with thanksgiving and love, while Cain's was presented out of obligation. But Cain only cared that Abel had received approval, and he had not. The idea ate at him until he decided to get even—by killing his brother.

Before Cain's awful action, the Lord spoke to him, encouraging him to correct his bad attitude and to choose to do right. Doing so would've led to healing in Cain's relationship with God and with his brother. But Cain didn't want to get well. I can imagine Cain shuffling around the land of Nod on a cane in his latter years, separated from his parents and out of fellowship with God, bitterly regretting he didn't listen to the Lord.

The Bible tells us jealousy is a disease. It'll rot your bones (Proverbs 14:30). So make sure your selfish desires don't make you sick. Confess jealousy to God and ask Him for healing, and do it immediately.

What prescription do you think God would give to help you recover from jealousy?

Guard Against Loose Lips

Lord, help me control my tongue;
help me be careful about what I say.
PSALM 141:3 NCV

During World War II, the US War Office printed thousands of posters with the slogan "Loose Lips Might Sink Ships" to remind servicemen and the general public to be guarded against careless talk that the enemy could use against them.[3] Likewise, followers of Jesus need to stay alert because our enemy the devil wants to sink his enemies—all followers of Christ. And often he'll use the very words our tongues speak as torpedoes!

Loose lips gossip when their owner feels hurt. They say unkind things to get revenge. Those are just the kind of actions that lead to the ongoing battles and destruction Satan desires to see happening among Christians. But if you have a personal relationship with Jesus, His power in you makes it possible to respond in unexpected ways—ways that completely foil the enemy's schemes. First Peter 3:9 instructs, "Don't retaliate with insults when people insult you. Instead, pay them back with a blessing" (NLT). Doing so is as good as calling a ceasefire.

Ask God for words of kindness for those who mistreat you. Remember, what you say can start wars—or end them.

What is the best way to guard against loose lips?

---

3 "Loose Lips Sink Ships," EyeWitness to History, http://www.eyewitnesstohistory.com/lslips.htm (1997).

Read the Directions

If you act too quickly, you might make a mistake.
PROVERBS 19:2 ICB

Mrs. Nelson handed us a pop quiz. Everyone shifted in their seats as she said, "I want each of you to read all the questions on the test before you answer any of them. Okay? Begin." I flipped that sheet over to discover thirty questions that simply couldn't be completed in the ten minutes we'd been given. I quickly dismissed Mrs. Nelson's directions, thinking perhaps I could knock out a few more problems if I jumped right in.

With my heart pounding, I wrote quickly. Minutes later, when I saw Lisa Livingston turn her paper in, I thought to myself, *Poor thing. Lisa's a smart girl. I'm surprised she'd give up on this so quickly.* Three minutes later Mrs. Nelson commanded, "Pencils down." Without collecting our papers, she asked us to read number 30 on the worksheet. *Ignore questions 1–29,* it said. *Sign your name and turn this in to me.*

Had I done as directed, I would have earned 100 percent on that quiz and saved myself a lot of hurt. It's a lesson that applies to life. When we take the time to read God's directions for us, the truths found in Scripture, we can avoid making costly mistakes. The Lord wants us to prepare for the tests of life. So search His Word for direction. You'll spare yourself a lot of stress.

When has a hasty or uninformed decision led you into trouble?

Prevent Wildfires

*The tongue is a small thing, but what enormous damage
it can do. A great forest can be set on fire by one tiny spark.*

JAMES 3:5 TLB

The longest running public service ad campaign in American history involves a bear named Smokey. "Only you," Smokey says, "can prevent forest fires."[4] His role is to remind everyone that by taking a little extra care in how we manage campfires, we can prevent a lot of costly damage. Interestingly, one of the oldest public service announcements in world history involves a similar warning. God's Word calls our tongue "a fire" (James 3:6). If we don't control what we say, the Bible warns, the resulting blaze can sizzle harmony out of a family, burn lines of communication between friends, and scorch reputations. Our harsh words can start figurative wildfires.

So how can you avoid starting one? Just as you must be extremely cautious not to strike a literal match in the woods, where conditions are dry or hazardous, saying rude things to your brother in a moment of "drought" in your affection for one another can become a match. And you don't want to play with it! It can cause a heated fight and damage you never intended. Shouting something hateful and mean is a recipe for combustion. So instead use kind words to soak the ground of your relationships with forgiveness, patience, and love.

Talk about a time that something you said sparked an argument. How could that fire have been prevented?

---

4 "American Icon," The Advertising Council, Inc., http://www.smokeybear.com/vault/history_main.asp.

Don't Go Stealing God's Glory

*Can the ax boast greater power
than the person who uses it?*

Isaiah 10:15 NLT

Glory stealers. Turn on the news and you will hear them. The football player who credits his winning touchdown to "luck." The mom whose little girl was cured thanks to "our good doctors." The successful businessman described as a "self-made" millionaire. All such credits rob God of the glory due Him.

Paul describes human beings well in his second letter to Timothy when he says we are born "arrogant, … ungrateful, … [and] swollen with conceit" (2 Timothy 3:2, 4 ESV). "Look at how great we are!" we scream. "See what we can do!" But, God says that idea is as silly as an ax jumping up and down with excitement over the tree it just cut down—without acknowledging that its power really came from the lumberjack's strength.

You and I can do nothing without God. Our breath and existence are gifts from Him. Our successes—and those of the football player, doctors, and millionaire—are based on His goodness, blessings, provisions, and interest in our lives. Make it a point today to be a glory revealer, not a glory stealer. Credit Jesus—not chance or yourself—for your blessings. Doing so is one way you can tell others about Him.

How do you see Jesus' hand at work in today's circumstances?

Sure-Footed

The one who doubts is like a wave
of the sea that is driven and tossed by the wind.
JAMES 1:6 ESV

A boy staggered as if walking across the deck of a ship on a stormy sea. His father asked Jesus if He could do anything to help him. Aware of the doubt in this father's heart, Jesus asked, "Why did you say 'if you can'? All things are possible for the one who believes." The father replied with one of the most beautiful prayers in the Bible: "I do believe. Help me to believe more!" (Mark 9:23–24 ERV). And with that solid declaration of faith, Jesus answered the man by healing the boy. Immediately, both the son and the father found a whole new sense of stability. The boy could walk smoothly and the father stopped stumbling over doubt. They found sure footing in Jesus.

Doubt—questioning whether Jesus really is who He claims He is and can do as He promises—will cause us to wobble. It leaves us vulnerable to the winds of false teaching and discouragement. But when we trust in Him, asking Him to deepen our faith as the father in the story did, we are delivered from doubts and given new strength to stand strong in life's storms. Don't doubt God's ability to provide. Trust what you've learned in His Word and ask Him to take care of you. As you do, you will become sure-footed in your walk with Jesus too.

When was a time you needed Jesus to help you "believe more" as this father did?

Work in Partnership

Two are better than one.

ECCLESIASTES 4:9

The first time Jesus sent His disciples out to minister, He assigned each a buddy (Mark 6:7). He probably did this because He knew the rejection they would face and recognized that these teams could offer one another encouragement and support. This would help them be more effective conveying His truth together.

God made partnership a pattern for the family when He paired Adam and Eve. He also often worked through friendships and relationships, like that of Paul and Silas, to spread the gospel. But one of my favorite Bible pairings involves Aquila and Priscilla. They weren't just a married couple. They served the early church as home missionaries.

One day, Aquila and Priscilla went to hear Apollos preach a sermon in the synagogue (Acts 18:26). They noticed that while what he taught was accurate, there were things he didn't understand. So the husband and wife invited Apollos to their house for dinner, where they shared with him more about the risen Jesus. The teachings and hospitality of this duo prepared Apollos for more effective ministry.

Christians need each other. So don't try to live for Jesus without attending church, having spiritual conversations with other believers, or inviting others to partner with you in sharing the gospel. Two—or more—followers of Christ working in unity really are better than one.

When have you seen Jesus do wonderful things through your partnership with other believers?

Don't Be a People Pleaser: Please God

Am [I] trying to win human approval? No indeed! What I want is God's approval! Am I trying to be popular with people? If I were still trying to do so, I would not be a servant of Christ.

GALATIANS 1:10 GNT

People had gathered to hear Jesus speak. As they listened to Him, some people in the audience wanted to accept Him as Messiah. But the Pharisees, the ones in charge of the synagogue where everyone wanted to belong, scowled at the hope and joy on their faces. No doubt about it, Jesus' listeners realized the Pharisees would reject, and say rude things about, anyone who chose to follow Him. Many in the crowd shuddered at the thought of losing the Pharisees' goodwill. So they wouldn't openly confess their faith "for fear they would be put out of the synagogue; for they loved human praise more than praise from God" (John 12:42–43).

In Galatians, the apostle Paul spoke about how foolish it is to try to win people's approval when God's approval is all that matters. The only way we can enter a relationship with Jesus is to follow Him in faith, no matter what anyone thinks about it. Don't sacrifice the joy and peace that only friendship with Jesus can bring for acceptance by the crowd. The approval of others is fleeting, but Jesus' lasts forever.

When was a time when you chose to honor Jesus, even though you knew other people might not approve?

Free to Fly

Where the Spirit of the Lord is, there is liberty.
2 Corinthians 3:17 NASB

Veterans Day recognizes those who've demonstrated boldness and bravery by serving in our military.

In World War II, after the Japanese surprise attack on Pearl Harbor, Lieutenant Jimmy Doolittle orchestrated a heroic air raid over Tokyo. Bombardier pilot Jacob DeShazer saddled up for that mission, knowing he would use all of his fuel to reach their target. There would be no return flight to safety. The mission was a success, but he and many others were forced to parachute onto unfriendly soil. Staff Sergeant DeShazer was captured and transported to a prison camp where he spent much of the next forty months in solitary confinement.

DeShazer asked one of his guards if he could borrow a Bible. Soon he placed his trust in the Lord Jesus Christ he read about. After he was freed, DeShazer attended seminary and returned to Japan as a missionary. Two years later, Captain Mitsuo Fuchida, one of the leaders of the attack on Pearl Harbor, read a tract about Staff Sergeant DeShazer's experience. Amazingly, Fuchida prayed to ask Jesus to forgive him of his sins and soon became a missionary too.

Several times, DeShazer and Fuchida preached together, the once bitter foes now brothers in Christ's family. The love of Jesus set them free.[5] The veterans spent the rest of their lives working for Jesus, the ultimate Freedom Fighter.

What do you think it would be like to be in the military? How would knowing Jesus help you do your job?

---

5 Spivey Larkin, "Stories of Faith and Courage from World War II," http://litresp.ru /chitat/en/S/spivey-larkin/stories-of-faith-and-courage-from-world-war-ii.

Be a Home Missionary

*"Go home to your family, and tell them
how much the Lord has done for you."*

MARK 5:19 GW

Most people hear the word *missionary* and picture men and women leaving their homes and extended families to spread the gospel overseas. But did you know that some missionaries serve in their home countries? And that all followers of Jesus are missionaries in a sense—whether they serve in a different country or in their own living rooms?

When Jesus healed a man tormented by demons, the fellow was so thankful for his freedom and new identity in Christ that he longed to leave with Jesus. He wanted to become a traveling disciple, alongside Peter and John. But Jesus had another plan. He said, "Go home to your family, and tell them how much the Lord has done for you and how merciful he has been to you" (Mark 5:19 ISV). In other words, Jesus wanted him to live out his faith in the presence of his family and to tell them the good news about what he'd experienced. They were his mission field.

Taking the good news of Jesus across the globe might sound like the most exciting way to be a missionary. But your family needs to know about Jesus too! So don't forget to provide your relatives with the truth about our Savior. There's no better way to show your family love.

What do you think a home missionary should do?

Be Willing to Take Advice

Listen to advice and accept correction.
Then in the end you will be wise.
PROVERBS 19:20 ICB

Esther was in a contest in which the winner became queen. Contestants were free to use whatever they wanted as an advantage. So if one young woman thought the king would be impressed by a dress with sparkles, she got it. If another thought red lipstick was better than pink, she got her way. Most girls were certain their choices were the best ones. Few stopped to consider that a little feedback from those who knew the king best might be helpful.

But Esther knew God's Word encourages us to seek advice and to accept correction. So she gained the counsel of someone who knew what would please the king. Esther "asked for nothing other than what Hegai, the king's [servant] who was in charge of the harem, suggested. And Esther won the favor of everyone who saw her" (Esther 2:15). Because she was willing to take advice and apply it, God blessed Esther's obedience. She won the grand prize and became queen.

Perhaps you think you know best. You roll your eyes when Mom offers advice or when Dad tells you to change your behavior. Don't miss out on the chance to gain wisdom by listening to their words and accepting correction. In learning from others, you, like Esther, may find yourself crowned with blessing.

When was a time when you took someone's advice and it turned out to be a blessing?

Rest in Him

*"Come with me by yourselves to
a quiet place and get some rest."*

MARK 6:31

Busyness tempts us to think a relationship with Jesus is all about working for God. This can cause us to miss the joy and refreshment of resting in Him. In Mark 6, the disciples had been busily preaching and teaching and were excited to report to Jesus all they'd been doing. But Jesus, in a preview of Paul's later warning to the Galatians, "Let us not become weary in doing good" (Galatians 6:9), knew that getting worn out—even by doing good things—can lead to burnout. It might even make us forget the whole point of what we're doing for the Lord. So Jesus encouraged His disciples to rest, refocus, and take some time in prayer. By doing so, they'd be better prepared for the ministry adventures ahead.

Let's say you enjoy texting, even using your messages as a tool to talk about Jesus. You realize you've developed a habit of picking up your phone for feedback on things you've shared, instead of setting aside time by yourself to get into God's Word. Resting in the Lord means a lot more than taking a pause. It means setting boundaries—like only checking messages once a day and scheduling a half hour of daily prayer—to make certain you're truly pursuing the only relationship that rewards us with rest.

How do you rest in Jesus?

Don't Be a Fair-Weather Friend

A friend loves at all times.

PROVERBS 17:17

Fair-weather friends are only there for one another when things are going well. But the second one friend needs help, a fair-weather friend moves on. In contrast, Ruth proved herself a faithful friend. She didn't just love Naomi in the good times; she loved her at all times.

Naomi and Ruth had both lost their husbands and needed a way to live without their support. When Naomi announced she was traveling back to Bethlehem to build a new life, young Ruth could have cut ties with her mother-in-law and found a new husband locally to care for her. But Ruth knew her friend couldn't make it back to Bethlehem alone and would have little to live on once she got there. So Ruth decided to travel with her. In the coming months, Ruth encouraged and provided for Naomi as best as she could. Even when Naomi grew bitter, focusing more on her pain than God's plan, Ruth reminded Naomi of the Lord's love. Her gentle words were exactly what Naomi needed to hear. Ruth's willingness to work hard to care for her friend kept both her and Naomi fed and soon provided a new home and family for them.

Christians should be friends like Ruth, encouragers seeing the needs of those we love as being more important than our own. So look for ways to offer practical support and encouragement to your friends, even when they're having a bad day. Remember, a true friend loves at *all* times.

What's wrong with being a fair-weather friend?

Be a Young Hero

Don't let anyone look down on you because
you are young, but set an example for the believers
in speech, in conduct, in love, in faith and in purity.

1 TIMOTHY 4:12

In Holland, a little boy was alarmed to see a small hole forming in the dam above his village. If the hole wasn't filled, he knew that the water behind it would eventually gush out and drown the villagers below. So the boy plugged the leak with his finger and called for help. He called out all night long, refusing to give up, even when he grew tired and his throat grew sore. No one heard him until morning. When his brave action was discovered, the townspeople hailed him a hero.[6]

Another brave boy acted heroically when Paul was facing trial for teaching about Jesus. He overheard forty men planning to kill Paul the next day, so the boy raced to where Paul was being kept and informed officials of the plot (Acts 23:16). Because of that nephew's courage, Paul's life was spared. He was able to keep spreading the gospel.

The Bible is clear that kids like you can courageously set a good example, showing grown-ups what it looks like to live for Jesus. You can also save lives by sharing the truth about what He came to accomplish. So be brave. You too can be a hero.

How can you be brave for Jesus today?

---

6 Mary Mapes Dodge, *Hans Brinker or The Silver Skates: A Story of Life in Holland* (New York, NY: J. H. Sears, 1926).

Stay in Bounds

Stay true to what is right and God will bless you.
1 TIMOTHY 4:16 TLB

Suppose your mom says you can eat as many gallons of ice cream as you want and Dad announces you can stay up all night. The suggestions sound fun at first, but you'll soon find such freedoms come with a catch. Before you could finish off that first gallon of ice cream, you'd be sick. And soon after that, you'd long for bed.

Boundaries help keep us safe. That's why your parents set limits over the amount of food you eat and the number of hours you sleep. It's also why they tell you to stay on the sidewalk or in the bike lane when riding your bike, rather than encouraging you to ride down the middle of the street. They love you and want you to enjoy a long, healthy life.

Even greater than your earthly parent's love for you is that of your heavenly Father. God is the Creator of fun and joy. He wants you to experience the pleasures of life without pain. But that requires paying attention to the boundaries He's given us in His Word. God has written out His rules to show you how to stay true to what is right. When you do what God says, you show Jesus how much you love Him and set yourself up to be blessed.

When have you obeyed God's rules and seen a blessing come your way because of doing the right thing?

Grow Up!

Anyone who lives on milk is still a baby and is not able to understand much about living right. But solid food is for people who have grown up. From their experience they have learned to see the difference between good and evil.

HEBREWS 5:13–14 ERV

Brian asked Jesus into his life years ago, but he still doesn't understand much about the way God wants him to live. He's more concerned with having the biggest Bible than he is with opening it. He goes to church, but spends most of his time there comparing his snazzy outfits to everyone else's. Brian is what the writer of Hebrews called a "baby Christian," because while he sincerely gave his heart to Jesus, he hasn't matured enough to understand that God wants the rest of him too.

Believers must choose to grow up, reaching out to grasp more about Jesus, just as a baby starts reaching for table food when he decides that what's in his bottle isn't nearly as appetizing as the interesting choices on Mom's plate. As growing Christians gain understanding and apply what they're learning, they become less vulnerable to false teachers who twist the truth of God's Word—and they become far more effective in sharing it.

Don't be a baby like Brian. God desires you to grow, to be able to understand the difference between what is right and holy and what is not. So feed on the truths of God's Word every day, trusting it and putting it into practice.

What are you doing to grow in your relationship with Jesus?

Don't Lose That Lovin' Feeling

"This is what I have against you:
you do not love me now as you did at first."

REVELATION 2:4 GNT

Sitting shoulder to shoulder in their truck's cab, a young couple in the vehicle ahead of Tom and Marge were as close to one another as they could get. "Remember when we used to sit like that?" white-haired Marge asked her husband, who was in the driver's seat of their own truck. Tom looked at his wife, whose head was leaning against the passenger window. "Well," he said with a smirk, "I haven't moved. Why don't you scooch closer, so we can cuddle too?"[7]

Throughout Scripture, Jesus refers to the church as His "bride." In Revelation, He addressed a particular church congregation that was once commended for being so in love with Jesus, but had now begun to distance herself from His love. The church at Ephesus was serving the Lord out of duty, rather than devotion. They no longer cuddled up to Jesus through prayer and obedience.

If Christ is not the first thought on your mind when you awaken or go to sleep, your love for Him might be growing cold. If you find yourself making excuses for the times you mess up, breaking God's rules and calling them mistakes, you've moved. Jesus' love for you never changes. He delights in you. So scooch closer. Show that you love Him too.

How can you show Jesus He still owns your heart?

---

7   Lewis Grizzard, "Hubby: I haven't moved," The Tuscaloosa News, Friday, March 4, 1983.

A Heart Like His

*"I will remove their stubborn hearts
and give them obedient hearts."*
EZEKIEL 11:19 GW

As a child, I loved watching the TV show about fictional character Steve Austin. A former astronaut severely injured in a crash, his damaged left eye, right arm, and legs were replaced with bionic parts. These enhanced his sight, strength, and speed for government work. They called him The Six Million Dollar Man.[8]

Steve's story is make-believe, but it reminds me of what God does when we put our faith in Jesus. The Bible tells us He removes our hard, self-centered hearts and replaces them with hearts that are open, willing to serve, and led by the Holy Spirit. These are hearts like Christ's. That miraculous change enables us to have supernatural strength like David's—you can trust God, instead of your own abilities, when you stand up against the towering Goliaths in your life. It enables us to have devotion like Daniel—you can trust God's provision when your faith clashes with your culture. And it gives us moral strength like Joseph's—you really can run away from temptation and even find the courage to forgive.

Scientists who enhanced Steve Austin put a $6 million price tag on his new limbs and eye. But no amount of money can come close to the true value of having a heart like Christ's.

What evidence of a new heart have you seen in your own life?

8 Lee Majors, Richard Anderson, and Martin E. Brooks, *The Six Million Dollar Man* (New York: NBCUniversal Television Distribution, 1973–1978).

Shout Your Love through Actions

Our love should not be only words and talk. No, our love must be real. We must show our love by the things we do.

1 JOHN 3:18 ERV

Nowhere in Scripture do we find a word quoted by Mary's husband, Joseph. Instead, Joe let others know where he stood by letting his actions do the talking.

Described in Scripture as a "righteous" man (Matthew 1:19), Joseph cared about maintaining his reputation as a godly individual. So when Mary came to him saying she was pregnant, and he was concerned people might wrongly assume that he was the father, the Bible tells us Joseph's first thought was to break off their engagement. After all, God's law is clear that men and women should not come together to create children unless they are married. But when an angel of the Lord appeared to him in a dream, confirming that Mary was pregnant with God's Son, and telling Joseph to step up to name and raise the child, Joseph trusted God's wisdom. He married Mary and named the baby Jesus (vv. 20–25).

Joseph's submission to the Lord's leading and quick obedience in the years that followed make clear that his love for God wasn't something he had to convince people of. Others could see that it was real, because Joe lived it out in the decisions he made and the actions he took.

Check to make sure that your behavior matches what you say you believe about Jesus. Your actions shout.

What can you do to show your love for Jesus?

Pardon to Paradise

*"For God did not send His Son into the world
to condemn the world, but that the world
through Him might be saved."*

JOHN 3:17 NKJV

Eating turkey on Thanksgiving has been a tradition since the Pilgrims sat down with the Indians in 1621. The bird has become such a celebrated main entrée on this holiday, which commemorates our thankfulness for God's provision, that some people even refer to Thanksgiving as "Turkey Day."

A more recent tradition that has captured the imagination of the public and certainly brought relief to at least one nervous, condemned bird is the official "pardoning" of the White House turkey. This pardon is granted by the president of the United States in the days leading up to Thanksgiving. One bird is saved from certain death and is transported to a quiet Virginia farm to live out the rest of its days.

God has not created us like turkeys, but we are similar in that we both face a death sentence. The Bible says, "The payment for sin is death" (Romans 6:23 ICB). However, the good news is that God has made a way for us to be pardoned, forgiven from our offense against Him, through the blood of His only Son, Jesus. He came to this world for one purpose—so that we might be set free from being held captive by sin. And we don't end up on a farm in Virginia. We're headed to heaven.

Don't wait for Thanksgiving to receive the pardon offered through the blood of Jesus Christ. Thank God for His pardon right now. Then, share one way that God's forgiveness has changed your life for the better.

Be Honest

Lies will get any man into trouble,
but honesty is its own defense.
PROVERBS 12:13 TLB

Near the town where Willy lived, a mean and hungry wolf roamed. And Willy loved to use the wolf as an excuse for avoiding outdoor chores. He'd wander out to the trash can and seconds later cry, "Wolf!" before rushing back to his toys inside. Meanwhile, folks ran to see if they could capture or destroy the recently sighted predator. But after a week of such shenanigans, Willy's mom and the townsfolk realized Willy wasn't being truthful. So they stopped rushing to his rescue. Then, a day came when the wolf really did encounter Willy. But no matter how loudly Willy called out, nobody answered his cries.[9]

Had Willy made honesty a habit, he would've had a ready line of defense when that wolf showed up. But his lies had cost him the respect and quick response of the very people he needed to come to his aid.

The Bible says Jesus "never sinned, never told a lie" (1 Peter 2:22 TLB). Don't repeat Willy's sin, leaving yourself open to situations like his. Instead, speak with honesty. You'll steer clear of trouble and will honor Jesus by following the example He set.

What can you do to make honesty a habit?

---

9 Tony Ross, *The Boy Who Cried Wolf* (New York: Dial Books for Young Readers, 1985).

Let Your Comfort Be Contagious

Praise be to … the God of all comfort.
He comforts us every time we have trouble so that
when others have trouble, we can comfort them.

2 CORINTHIANS 1:3–4 ERV

My father suffered the amputation of his left arm and loss of an eye as a result of combat in Vietnam. But not long after, as he underwent rehabilitation, both my father and mother met Jesus. God not only helped and encouraged them through that very difficult time, He also prompted them to bless and encourage others who were facing similar circumstances. Throughout my childhood, my parents visited with amputees, athletes whose dreams of playing professionally were dashed due to injury, and couples questioning their commitment to each other after tragic accidents. My parents didn't hoard the truth of God's faithfulness in their deep suffering. They generously shared what God taught them, doing all they could to help others find His comfort too.

God equips wounded souls to be His exceptional warriors. Maybe at one time, you felt you had no friends. God could have allowed that so you'd get to know Jesus as your best Friend and would then introduce Him to that lonely person who was new to your school. Perhaps your dad was unemployed. Did God provide for your family in surprising ways? Why not share about it with a friend whose parent is out of work? The comfort God provides is a comfort worth spreading.

How will you turn the comfort Jesus provided you into something contagious?

Anger Management

Don't sin by letting anger control you.

EPHESIANS 4:26 NLT

Fictional superhero Bruce Banner was exposed to a massive dose of gamma radiation. After that, anger transformed Banner into the Hulk. It made Banner's skin turn green and his strength and speed become superhuman. The angrier the Hulk got, the mightier his muscles grew. He could leap great distances, causing earthquakes. One powerful blow with his fist could send any object flying.[10]

In contrast, the angrier you and I get, the more our spiritual muscles shrink. Though the Bible doesn't say anger is wrong, God does say that we have to let His Holy Spirit take charge of our emotions. When you put your trust in Jesus, His Holy Spirit comes to live inside you, giving you the strength of self-control. That means that when things don't go your way, you don't pout, shout, or pull hair. Instead, you confess to God how upset you are and ask Him to help you apply His wisdom to the situation.

Let's say a bully screams bad words in your face. As a hero for the Lord, you have superhuman strength. You don't need to give in to the temptation to shout back. Rather, you are given the power to walk away and tell a parent you are being bothered. Your respect for God's Word and His authority will ultimately show that bully whose muscles are really big!

How will you let God manage the situation the next time you get angry?

---

10 "Hulk," MARVEL, http://www.marvel.com/characters/25/hulk.

Glorify God with Your Grades

*Everything you say and everything you do
should all be done for Jesus your Lord.*

COLOSSIANS 3:17 ICB

I imagine Noah, who had to measure all of those cubits while constructing the ark, must have been strong in math. Surely Paul was accomplished in writing. And I bet Samson rocked physical education. But none of these Bible heroes were great at everything. Both Noah and Samson struggled with discipline, and Paul's skill with words wouldn't have helped him build an ark or take out Philistines with a donkey's jawbone.

Sometimes our report cards, peppered with various letter grades, can make us feel like failures. They make us think that everyone has to be great at everything. That doesn't line up with Scripture. People are uniquely gifted, each of us having strengths and weaknesses. That's why it's important to realize we bring God glory not when we ace every subject, but when we sincerely do our best, seeking help as we need it. Everything we do at school, in fact, should not be done just to get a good grade, but to faithfully follow the Lord to the best of our ability.

For you, certain subjects may not come easily. You may find you are great in things your teacher doesn't even grade. Don't get discouraged. Ask the Lord to provide you the help you need to accomplish your goals. And remember, we don't work hard for grades. We live to bring God glory.

How do you think Jesus would like you to respond to school grades you receive, high ones or low ones?

Resist Peer Pressure

My child, sinners will try to lead you into sin.
But do not follow them.

PROVERBS 1:10 ICB

Leanne, Hayden, and Kennedy were asked to leave the classroom. They didn't know Mrs. Werner wanted to teach the class a lesson about peer pressure. She told the students who remained in the room that when the trio reentered, she would ask them questions. Possible answers would be on cards at the front of the room. The teacher told the class to deliberately point to the wrong answer to see whether they could sway the opinions of their friends.

Sure enough, when Leanne, Hayden, and Kennedy reentered the classroom from the hall, Mrs. Werner's trap worked. She asked each of them a simple question, and all three children allowed the bad advice their classmates gave to sway them from choosing the answer they knew to be right. The three gave in to peer pressure—every time.[11]

The power of your peers is persuasive. That's why the Bible warns strongly against being led into sin. You must know what you believe and why you believe it, refusing to be dragged into wrong thinking and poor choices. As sure as the classmates in today's story misled Leanne, Hayden, and Kennedy, friends will sometimes lead us astray. Remember, God's Word is truth you can trust. Follow it.

What should you do when the group's opinion goes against God's truth? Why?

---

11 David Jeremiah, *Gifts from God* (Colorado Springs, CO: Chariot Victor Publishing, 1999).

Choose Joy

This is the day which the Lord has made;
Let us rejoice and be glad in it.

PSALM 118:24 NASB

James Franklin Miller III, affectionately known as "Jim-daddy," served with his wife, Libby, as senior directors at Camp Greystone, where I enjoyed many summers as a camper. Jimdaddy loved Christ, Ms. Libby, our heroes in the military, and life itself. Each morning, right after the bugle would blow reveille, Jimdaddy urged us campers to sit up in our beds, clap our hands, and say, "It's going to be a great day!" He treated every day as a grand adventure from God.

You too have a choice to greet the dawning of each new day as a blessing. If you are truly taking God at His Word and trusting in His promises, then you know He is good and what He has planned for your life is sure to be special. You can take joy in the fact you are here for a divine purpose.

So instead of dreading sunrise, focus on the fact that each new day brings opportunity to spend time with and serve the Creator. Knowing how much Jesus loves you and that every need you have is met in Him, should be reason enough to greet each morning with the attitude, *It's going to be a great day!*

What else might you do to demonstrate rejoicing in each today?

Gray Matters

*"Show respect to the elderly, and honor older people.
In this way you show respect for your God."*
LEVITICUS 19:32 GW

Jennie Craver Fowler's husband died after they'd been married fifty-four years. The thought made my mother, Jennie's granddaughter, sad. I was three when my parents moved great-grandmother Goggie in to live with us. The next fifteen years were filled with joy.

Goggie was my TV and radio. I'd climb into her lap and listen eagerly to her stories about growing up in the olden days before cars. Unconditioned by the immediate gratification of modern conveniences, Goggie never rushed. Whenever we'd host a gathering, she'd take the time to bake one of her delicious desserts from scratch. While the cake was still fresh from the oven, Goggie would serve my sister and me, telling us we were the "most special" company. Having Goggie under our roof was one of the greatest blessings of my life.

The Bible says we should show respect to elderly people. And when you take the time to befriend the seniors in your life, you'll likely discover the same thing I learned: older people are priceless treasure of wisdom and can teach us many wonderful things. So make time for the elderly, offering smiles and listening respectfully when they say hello. Don't be sassy. Be willing to help them. Appreciating the gray-headed folks around us matters; our respect for them shows our reverence for God.

What is one way you can show Jesus' love to an older person today?

Hope Floats

*May the God of hope fill you with all joy
and peace as you trust in him.*

ROMANS 15:13

Elisha was always doing the Lord's work, tirelessly investing in the lives of future teachers and preachers. He even helped to build a school where they could study. One day, Elisha and his students were cutting down trees to make room for their new classrooms, when one guy's iron ax head fell into a nearby river and sank. The man, who had borrowed the expensive tool, was horrified by the loss and cried out for help.

Elisha, a man of God, knew that their only hope of ever retrieving the metal tool was with God's help. In a surprising move, Elisha cut a stick and threw it into the Jordan River, right over the place where the tool sank. In that moment, God worked a miracle. The ax head, which had been resting on the river bottom, floated to the top, where it was easily retrieved!

The Lord cares about what's important to you too. Lost keys. Lost pets. Lost homework. And especially, lost hearts. None of them are beyond His reach. Just as He used Elisha's wooden stick to draw the metal to the surface and used the cross to draw our wayward hearts to His love, God can work another miracle for you. But you'll only find joy and peace as you trust in Him.

For what situation do you need to put your hope in God today?

DECEMBER

No Excuses

*"Do not say, 'I am only a youth,' for you will go to everyone
I send you to and speak whatever I tell you."*

JEREMIAH 1:7–8 HCSB

Jeremiah was picked by God to announce His judgment on Judah. It was a tough message to communicate and one that Jeremiah didn't want to preach. "I'm too young," he whined. "Nobody is going to listen to me." But God told him not to make excuses. He reminded the young prophet that his purpose was already planned. In fact, it was planned even before Jeremiah was growing in his mother's womb (Jeremiah 1:5). God reminded Jeremiah that He would be with him as he lived out God's plans for his life. After that, Jeremiah believed God. He agreed to do the tough job.

Those who place their faith in the Lord will sometimes be asked to do things that may sound overwhelming at first. Nevertheless, God will give us the strength we need to do what He asks. Maybe you feel Him prompting your heart to share His plan of salvation with a teacher. *That's silly*, you think, *I'm just a student.* But remember God's words to Jeremiah. The Lord handpicks each of us for certain missions. So whatever He commands, don't think, *I can't.* Rather, trust that He can accomplish amazing things through you.

Discuss a time you made an excuse instead of trusting Jesus. What do you want to remember the next time you're asked to do something challenging?

Steer Conversation

[Ships] are steered by a very small rudder
wherever the pilot wants to go. Likewise, the tongue.
JAMES 3:4–5

Hidden under the water behind a boat, a small rudder goes unnoticed. But its power is obvious to all watching the vessel's movement. God compares our tongues to this steering instrument. He says they are like "a small rudder [that] makes a huge ship turn wherever the pilot chooses to go" (James 3:4 NLT). Tongues are tiny but powerful, their words maneuvering our lives in directions that will either honor Jesus or not.

As a Christian, you want every word you speak to point people to Jesus. But that means you must be intentional, every day, about the things you say. You must choose a pattern of speaking that honors the Lord, one that avoids gossip, bad language, and complaints. Doing so will steer your life in a direction that makes people take notice. Then, when someone asks what's different about you, you'll have a chance to gently and respectfully tell them about Jesus—the One who died to pay the price for your sins so you might live with Him forever. The One who calls you to speak with love and kindness that reflect His heart toward boys and girls.

Don't let your mouth steer you down a wrong course. Consider each comment before you speak it.

What kinds of words take us in a direction that honors Jesus?

Fewer Toys

*"Be on guard against all greed because one's
life is not in the abundance of his possessions."*
LUKE 12:15 HCSB

Ebenezer Scrooge and the Grinch are greedy fictional characters always eager to own more things. Each foolishly thinks that more toys equals happiness. Jesus describes a similar character in a parable.

In Luke 12:13–21, we read about a farmer who enjoyed another bumper-crop year. His plants were always so heavy with fruit and vegetables that he was considered a very rich man. He already had several storage barns and decided he should reward his continued success by tearing them down and building bigger ones to store his produce. It made him feel good to peek in on his stuff throughout the day, admiring the fruit of his labor. But the farmer died suddenly—and couldn't take all of that stuff with him. While he was alive, the farmer could've used his wealth to bless others as God intended, but the foolish farmer wasted his years storing up things that don't last.

You and I can be like Scrooge, the Grinch, and that foolish farmer, when we hoard our things and constantly thirst for more. True happiness has nothing to do with how full our toy boxes are but in the knowledge that we belong to Jesus, who has great plans for us. When we share the blessings He has entrusted to us with others, we please Him and avoid becoming greedy characters.

What could you do with the things God has given you that would please Him?

Cautious within the Crowd

The wise are cautious and avoid danger;
fools plunge ahead.
PROVERBS 14:15 NLT

Buffalo feel protected when they're huddled together. Long ago, Native American hunters took advantage of the animals' herd mentality by arranging buffalo jumps. One archer targeted an animal, sneaking up behind the beast and letting out a scream. Panicked, the young bull bolted. His friends, sure that whatever was after him was best avoided by togetherness, dashed after him at full speed. The thunderous stampede was so eager to get away that they paid no attention to where they were going. Time and again, the Indians used this tactic to chase many of these creatures over cliffs where their meat could be easily harvested.[1]

The Bible warns us not to assume there's safety in doing whatever the crowd is doing. We too have an enemy, with a strategy designed to take advantage of our desire to find security in the pack. Caution is our best defense.

For instance, let's say you're at a sleepover, and everyone decides to toilet paper the neighbor's yard. Don't just plunge ahead with the plan. Consider the consequences and be the voice of reason among your group. Remember, it's often wise to say no to joining in when your friends are ready to run toward a bad idea. Not only will you avoid danger, but you just might save your herd from a bad fall.

When have you plunged ahead without caution and wound up in trouble?

---

1 *Character Sketches from the Pages of Scripture Illustrated in the World of Nature,* Volume III.

Be the Right Kind of Foolish

We are fools for Christ.

1 CORINTHIANS 4:10

An old man led a boy and donkey. The townspeople thought it was silly that no one was riding on the animal's back and told him so. As a result, the man saddled up. But when the trio entered the next neighborhood, onlookers criticized him for making the child walk. So off he got and boosted the boy to the creature's back. The next village attacked the lad for being lazy, suggesting both should ride. Things went well until they reached a fourth town. There the community cried, "Animal cruelty!" at the sight of the beast carrying such weight. And so the man and boy stepped down and carried the donkey. Their story illustrates how when you try to be a people pleaser, you can end up looking silly.[2]

We all look foolish sometimes, because there are times each one of us lives for the approval of someone. That's why the Bible says there are two kinds of "fools." We can be a fool for others—like the poor man in the story—or we can be fools for Christ as Paul the apostle was. A fool for others thinks he can please everybody and exhausts himself trying. A fool for Jesus lives to please Him alone, making all of his choices based on Jesus' desires.

Don't spend your life adjusting to the opinions of those around you. Live for the Lord.

When were you a fool for other people by being a people pleaser? How did that work out?

2 Wayne Rice, *More Hot Illustrations for Youth Talks* (Nashville, TN: Zondervan Publishing, 1996).

Skid Control

He lifted me out of the slimy pit,
out of the mud and mire; he set my feet on a rock
and gave me a firm place to stand.

PSALM 40:2

Years ago, my mom unrolled a long sheet of yellow plastic in our yard and then attached the garden hose to it. Little holes in the sheet sprayed water onto the plastic surface, making it a very slippery slide. My sister, Christa, and I would repeatedly run up to that slide, throw ourselves on it Superman-style, and skid all the way to its end.

Aside from riding the long yellow slide or enjoying a day at the skating rink, I've found that slippery situations in life are rarely fun. Tough things happen to us, allowing us to go from standing up straight and feeling at ease to making us feel knocked off our feet through tragedy or hardship. Loved ones die. Companies cut back. Moms and dads get mad at each other. In times like these, we long for skid control, a way to slow all the madness.

In Exodus 14:13, the Lord told Moses, who was caught between the muddy banks of the Red Sea and an approaching angry pharaoh, not to fear. He told him to stand and see that the Lord was about to accomplish great things on his behalf. When Moses felt things were sliding out of control in his life, he depended on God to steady and help him. We too can rejoice in knowing that God is working in our lives today. He's giving us traction so we can find our footing when hard times come.

When has God provided skid control for you?

Know What You Sow

Don't be deceived: God is not mocked.
For whatever a man sows he will also reap.

GALATIANS 6:7 HCSB

When the Israelites witnessed the walls of Jericho come tumbling down, they were careful to spare faithful Rahab and her family and to destroy everything else in the city as the Lord commanded. But while Achan took care of business in Jericho's ruins, an ornate robe and some shiny knickknacks caught his eye. Ignoring God's direction, Achan took the coveted items and buried them in his tent. *No one will ever know,* he must have thought to himself.

But Achan was wrong. The Lord is aware of everything we think, say, and do (Proverbs 15:3), and He loves us too much to let us get away with sin. So Achan was forced to reap the consequences of his actions. He soon watched his army get defeated at Ai, and eventually, his own family was destroyed (Joshua 7:19–26). Achan found that choices are like seeds that produce either gladness or sorrow. He decided to sow seeds of deceit, discontentment, and disobedience and reaped a harvest of hurt.

Making sinful choices and then telling yourself God does not see what you do is sowing bad seeds, and—as Achan's story illustrates—it sets you up for a harvest of discipline. Ask Jesus for forgiveness and help in spreading seeds of righteousness instead.

When is a time when you reaped what you sowed, for good or for bad?

Be a Super Friend

Encourage each other and build each other up.

1 THESSALONIANS 5:11 NLT

Batman, Robin, Superman, Wonder Woman, and Aquaman are five superheroes. This team of Super Friends encourages each other in their individual strengths and uses the power of their friendship to promote good and to prevent disaster.

The Bible tells us exactly how we can become real-life super friends—not the kind that fly or wear costumes, but the kind of friends who help to strengthen one another with our conversation and our company. Sometimes, it's hard to know what to say around people, but you'll never go wrong saying something nice. Just put 1 Thessalonians 5:11 into practice: *Great job during yesterday's game, Ben! Carly, your artwork should be on display in a museum! Don't get discouraged about the test grade, Kelly—you'll do better next time! I struggled on that one too.* Your willingness to encourage others can be just the lift your friend needs—a line of defense against the schemes of our shared enemy.

Super friends can be counted on to cry when there is sadness and smile during times of joy. So be sensitive to situations and the feelings of others. Most importantly, remember that as a real-life super friend, you are powerless to fix people's problems. But you can pray and direct them to Jesus, who really can do anything and everything.

Who has been a super friend in your life? How has he encouraged you to live for Jesus?

Have Faith

Without faith it is impossible to please God.
HEBREWS 11:6

Chapter 11 in the book of Hebrews lists the names of a few of God's faithful followers who were "sure" and "certain" of a Savior whose hand they couldn't always see, but in whose heart they trusted. They knew God was always working, even when they lacked visual or physical evidence. The brave actions they took proved their faith in God. Take Noah, for example. He obeyed God by building a boat in the middle of dry land, simply because God said to do it. He hammered away for almost a hundred years before ever seeing a raindrop. Noah and the saints of old trusted that God was to be obeyed for no other reason than because He is God—and that kind of faith pleases Him.

We too please God when we live in obedience to His Word; doing so reveals the sincerity of our faith. Having faith in Jesus isn't just a matter of believing He exists. The Bible says that "even the demons believe that" (James 2:19). Having faith requires honoring Jesus as our Savior and Lord. It means that we will obey His Word to demonstrate our love.

If you want to please God, you must have faith in His Son, Jesus. And if you do, you'll show it by living in a way that applies Scripture's truth.

When has your faith led you to take actions that may not have been popular, but showed obedience to God?

A Praying Life

*During the days of Jesus' life on earth, he offered up
prayers and petitions … and was heard because
of His reverent submission.*

HEBREWS 5:7

During His life on earth, Jesus was in constant communication with God. Throughout the New Testament, we see Jesus praying publicly and privately. Sometimes His prayers were short, like the one He prayed before raising Lazarus (John 11:41–42). Other times He pulled all-nighters (Luke 6:12). And we know for certain that Jesus didn't always close His eyes while praying, as if there's only one posture for prayer. He demonstrated that variety is acceptable when He took the loaves and fish and looked up to heaven and gave thanks (Matthew 14:19), and when He went to the mountain to pray—a place where He surely enjoyed the beauty of creation while He spoke to the Father (v. 23).

Jesus prayed sincerely and not for show. He worshiped the Lord (6:9), respected His will (v. 10), and trusted Him for His every need (vv. 11–13). In all of this, in every moment, Jesus lived in complete dependence on and obedience to the will of His Father.

Do you have a praying life? Are you talking to the Lord throughout your day, sharing your feelings, asking for help, thanking Him for all He does? Let Jesus' example serve as a model for how you can make an ongoing conversation with God part of your day.

In what ways is your prayer life like that of Jesus?

Keep Knocking

"Ask and it will be given to you; …
knock and the door will be opened to you."

Luke 11:9

Never grow discouraged if you don't see an immediate answer to prayer. God desires that we be persistent, approaching Him again and again for the things we need.

To help His disciples understand the power of persistence in prayer, Jesus told a story about a man—I'll call him Harry—who was surprised by a friend's late-night visit. When Harry peered into his pantry, he found he was out of food and his guest was starving. Quickly putting on his housecoat, he raced to his neighbor's house. The clock struck midnight, but he knocked anyway.

"Who's there?" a voice called out from inside. "Sorry, George," Harry said. "I know it's late, but I need to borrow food. My friend's arrived and he's desperately hungry. I need your help, please." "Go away," George griped. But Harry wouldn't give up. His guest had a real need, and so his knocks grew louder and his pleas more persistent. Finally, the neighbor gave in, opened his own fridge, and handed Harry an armload of provisions.

If Harry's persistence won the help of a grouchy neighbor, how much more can our persistence move our loving heavenly Father to action? Don't give up praying for that loved one to come to know Jesus or for that friend to be healed. By continuing to ask, seek, and knock, you show your confidence in God's ability to provide. That pleases His heart.

What prayer have you prayed for quite a while, persistently?

His Presence among the Group

*"Where two or three gather together as
my followers, I am there among them."*

MATTHEW 18:20 NLT

Moses' arms were getting tired. He was watching Israel fight her first combat mission. As long as Moses, who sat on a hilltop, kept praying and raising the staff of God high in the air, the Israelite soldiers were reminded the Lord was in charge. This made them fight courageously. But the second Moses' arms began to droop, the enemy began winning. Finally, Moses' brother, Aaron, shouted to fellow leader, Hur, "We need to help!" The pair took a rock and made a seat for Moses. Then, they stood "one on one side, one on the other" (Exodus 17:12). Each grabbed one of Moses' arms, keeping his hands high and steady until the sun set. Together, they prayed for the Lord to be victorious. The four of them—Moses, Aaron, Hur, and the Lord's obvious presence—stayed locked in what I like to picture as a group hug.

Praying together with other believers is like being wrapped in a warm group hug in which Jesus takes part. When we bring our requests to the Lord together, resting on Him as our Rock (Psalm 18:2), and lifting up His name, we find renewed strength.

When you're facing a tough time, ask godly friends to gather around you, figuratively holding up your hands and hugging you in prayer, as you trust Jesus through your trial. And remember, the Lord will join in.

Which of your friends needs you to join them in prayer?

A Happy Meal

Your words were found, and I ate them,
and your words became to me a joy and
the delight of my heart.

JEREMIAH 15:16 ESV

In 1979, McDonald's introduced America to the first Happy Meal. Inside the colorful cardboard box, designed just for children, were a hamburger, fries, cookies, and a catch. The company included a toy in every box. From that point forward kids begged for McDonald's, not always because they wanted the food, but because they were lured by clever merchandising.[3]

Unlike fast food, God's Word needs no clever marketing gimmicks. As Jeremiah the prophet knew, God's truth is a wholesome spiritual meal that brings delight. The Bible is enough to nourish us and satisfy us down to our core. But our enemy, the devil, the cleverest merchandiser ever, is constantly trying to get God's people to turn down this good nourishment in favor of the toys and empty calories he offers. Consider his lies to Eve. She could eat the fruit of any tree in the garden. But he lured her to eat the only forbidden fruit by making her believe she was somehow missing out on the best stuff.

If you're looking for joy and fulfillment, reach for a big serving of Scripture. As the prophet Jeremiah attests, a feast of God's Word really is our happiest meal.

When has God's Word brought "delight" to your heart?

---

3   Selena Maranjian, "The Stealth Toy Giant," The Motley Fool, September 3, 2004.

All In

Do not love the world nor the things in the world.
If anyone loves the world, the love of the Father is not in him.

1 John 2:15 NASB

In Paul's final letter to Timothy he wrote, "Do your best to come to me quickly, for Demas, because he loved this world, has deserted me and gone to Thessalonica" (2 Timothy 4:9–10). Paul was in chains, facing certain death at the hands of Nero in a cold, dark, lonely prison in Rome. Christians were being killed for their faith and Demas, once described by Paul as his fellow coworker (Philemon 24), did not like what he saw. Working for Jesus had been fun when he felt like his team was winning, but under the pressure of persecution, Demas decided the fun was over. So he fled.

Demas was a fair-weather fan of Jesus. He proudly wore a J on his jersey when he was in a crowd that cheered the Lord and His followers. But when the tide of opinion turned, he left that jersey home in his closet. His love of the world's approval and his personal comfort, it seems, were more important than continuing in the work God gave him.

Don't be a Demas, living for the world's approval and turning on Jesus and His people when things get tough. Go "all in" with Jesus. Ask the Father to let His love keep working through you.

What do you think being "all in" for Jesus looks like?

I Must Live Untangled

*Let us strip off anything that slows us down or holds us back,
and especially those sins that wrap themselves
so tightly around our feet and trip us up.*

HEBREWS 12:1 TLB

As a baby, Rapunzel was locked away in a high tower, where she stayed for the next eighteen years. Cruel Gothel was her captor. She didn't want Rapunzel to know she was really the daughter of royalty. Not until Rapunzel's fabulously long and tangled mass of golden hair was cut was she free to leave and run home to the place she really belonged: the palace of her father.[4]

Hair is one of God's beautiful creations, and the Bible says that God knows exactly how many hairs you have on your head (Luke 12:7). But Rapunzel's hair, as portrayed in the Disney movie, reminds me of how often we get tangled up in things this world prizes. Some of us think beauty or sports or popularity or making good grades are all that matters, and we allow our pursuit of those things to hinder us from running to the Father with full abandon. We get so tangled up in wanting to be smart, pretty, or the best at something that we live as prisoners.

Let the words of Hebrews 12:1 above remind you that Jesus wants you to pursue Him, not things or personal recognition. Take the scissors to anything that keeps you from chasing after Him with everything you've got. It's time to live an untangled life.

What entanglement keeps you from following Jesus with your whole heart?

4 *Tangled*, directed by Nathan Greno and Byron Howard (Burbank, CA: Walt Disney Animated Classics, 2010).

Seeing His Will

Your word is a lamp to my feet and a light to my path.
Psalm 119:105 NASB

Imagine having a little light to clip onto your shoes when trudging through the woods at night. Then think about how much better it would be if that little light could talk and actually tell you how to get to the nearest campfire and s'mores.

Amazingly, God's given us something better. His Word, which the psalmist calls a "lamp," doesn't just illuminate our path through life. It actually tells us which steps to take! Sadly, however, many fail to use this awesome navigation tool. Others look at it only occasionally, telling themselves God's Word is something to be applied down the road rather than today.

As you make daily decisions—Who should I befriend? How should I talk to Mom? Do I really have to study for that test?—and as you wonder about your future—Where will I go to college? How will I pay for it? Who will I marry?—go to God's Word. While it won't always give you a clear "do this or do that" answer, it will give you priceless guidance and wisdom for navigating your way through life.

So don't think you have to feel your way through life's forest in the dark. You can see God's will clearly. Just look for it in the pages of Scripture.

When have you found direction and guidance, a light for your path, in the Bible?

Salvation Certainty

"I give them eternal life. ...
No one will snatch them out of My hand."
JOHN 10:28 HCSB

Harrison looked at me with teary brown eyes and asked, "Mommy, are you coming back?" I promised her I was. Then, as I walked away, I wondered how many of God's children live with a terror much greater than my toddler's. They ask Jesus to be their Savior, but then they remain fearful that He will forget about them.

The Bible is clear. First John 5:11–13 tells us that "God has given us eternal life, and this life is in His Son. The one who has the Son has life" (HCSB). These things were written for those of us "who believe in the name of the Son of God, so that [we] may know that [we] have eternal life." But to rest secure in this fact, we have to take our heavenly Father at His word just as Harrison had to trust mine.

Once you put your faith in Jesus, who died to pay the penalty you deserve because of your sins, the Bible says you're saved (Romans 10:9). Because of that, you can be certain you are God's child, once and for all. Your salvation is sealed with God's personal seal, the Holy Spirit (Ephesians 1:13). So take heart. Jesus assured us in John 14:18, "I will not leave you as orphans; I am coming to you" (HCSB). If you've accepted Him, no one can keep Him from your side.

How do you know for sure you are saved?

Be a Good Student of God's Word

Incline your ear to wisdom,
and apply your heart to understanding.
PROVERBS 2:2 NKJV

The storybook character Curious George would rather act first than investigate and learn the best way to approach a "problem." One day, for instance, he waves to a lady leaving packages on doorsteps. Assuming she's forgetful, George decides he'll help and gathers up all the boxes. After a lot of unnecessary work, somebody tells George she's the mail lady.[5]

In New Testament times, some Christians were a lot like George. They liked the Jesus the disciples preached about and quickly signed up to follow Him. But rather than taking the time to investigate the apostles and the truths they preached, they took verses of Scripture out of context. They failed to see and apply their true meaning. In the same way that Curious George creates messes because he fails to seek understanding before he acts, these Christians got themselves into all kinds of problems.

Jesus wants you to be a good student of His Word. Pay attention to the wisdom in the Bible, getting to know how its truths fit together, rather than trying to apply random verses without grasping what they mean. Ask God to give you understanding, so you can please His heart and avoid causing messes like George does.

How can you make sure you are being a good student of God's Word?

---

5 "Out of Order," Curious George, season 1, episode 1, directed by Scott Heming and Steve Socki, aired September 5, 2006 (PBS).

A Tale of Two Innkeepers

She brought forth her firstborn son, and wrapped him
in swaddling clothes, and laid him in a manger;
because there was no room for them in the inn.

LUKE 2:7 KJV

We don't know the name of the innkeeper who turned Joseph and Jesus' mother, Mary, away that night in Bethlehem. But we can assume he wasn't a man who thoughtfully cared about the needs of others. After all, why couldn't he give up his own room?

I can hear Mary and Joseph now, sitting around the dinner table, answering seven-year-old Jesus' question about the night He was born. They probably looked at each other laughing as they recounted how the innkeeper sent them to a stable—a fact that was probably anything but funny when it happened.

I love that Jesus, who could've had a grudge against innkeepers given His birth story, took the opportunity to mention one favorably eight chapters later in Luke's gospel. In the parable of the good Samaritan, an innkeeper provides shelter and medical care to a wounded man (Luke 10:35). At the Samaritan's request, this innkeeper welcomes an unexpected guest. By mentioning it in the gospel, we can see that the Lord notices when we make others feel at home.

Sometimes, life events test our willingness to be uncomfortable, so someone else might find comfort. For instance, your parents may invite a distant relative who asks to take over your room for a month while she gets back on her feet. Don't miss a blessing. Make room for those who need it; the Lord is watching.

Discuss why it's difficult to give up our own comfort to make someone else more comfortable.

A Baby Changes Everything

A virgin ... shall bring forth a son,
and they shall call his name Emmanuel,
which being interpreted is, God with us.

MATTHEW 1:23 KJV

When Jesus came to earth, God physically lived among us. That incredible moment is the centerpiece of human history, a fact reflected in our modern calendar. Every time you register for school, make a play date, or schedule an appointment, you deal in dates. And every one can be traced to the year when Jesus was born.

History books separate time into BC and AD. BC refers to the years "Before the Child" or "Before Christ," meaning those years that occurred before Jesus' birth. We know Jesus always existed, because He is God (John 1:1–3), but His physical coming was such a world-changing moment that it reset the human calendar. The year of His birth is generally agreed to be 1 AD. (AD is an abbreviation for the Latin phrase *Anno Domini*, which means "in the year of our Lord.")

While the years before Christ decrease in number (300 BC happened before 200 BC), the years since His birth grow larger (2015 is followed by 2016, and so on). BC is remembered in terms of a countdown to Christ's coming, but every year that passes now—and your every birthday—is one year closer to His return.

What was so special about Jesus' birth?

Center Peace

For unto us a child is born, unto us a son is given … and his name shall be called Wonderful, Counselor, The mighty God, The everlasting Father, The Prince of Peace.

ISAIAH 9:6 KJV

Augustine said around 400 AD, "You have formed us for Yourself, and our hearts are restless till they find rest in You."[6] Truly, our hearts were meant to beat for more than twinkly lights and roasted chestnuts. But it's easy to get tangled in the tinsel of holiday fun and traditions. Soon we find we're rushing, instead of savoring, the Christmas season.

Not long after I was married, I was planning to host my new in-laws for Christmas. My mother arrived to assist me in making final preparations. Frantically I raced between the kitchen and the dining room. After placing a casserole into the oven, I grabbed a bunch of Bells of Ireland flowers and began shoving them among the dahlias, roses, peonies, and hydrangea in the porcelain container on the center of our dining room table.

My mother gently placed her hand on my shoulder and whispered, "Don't forget Jesus."

When I looked at her quizzically, she confessed, "I used to do the same thing you're doing. I got so caught up in making sure all the details of my centerpiece were perfect that I forgot to focus on the Center Peace of my life—Jesus."

While it's easy to think the Christmas season is about gifts, pretty decorations, carols, and baking, it's really about Jesus. Make Him the Center Peace of your life this Christmas season.

What can you do to make Christ the center of your holiday?

---

6 Modern reading of the Confessions of St. Augustine, Book 1, Chapter 1.

The Gift

*Yet to all who did receive him, to those who believed
in his name, he gave the right to become children of God.*

JOHN 1:12

My friend Tessa and I went out for dinner around Christmastime. We discussed our family traditions and the excitement of opening gifts. Then I asked, "Isn't it sad to think of all those who have rejected Jesus, the greatest Gift of all?"

Tessa looked surprised and asked what I meant.

I explained all about God's gift of His Son on Calvary's cross, about how Jesus willingly died to redeem us from our sin nature. "Just imagine the Lord wrapping up a package to you with your name on it, Tessa," I said. "Inside is a ticket for the forgiveness of your sins. God places this personal gift of love for each of us under the Christmas tree. Our gift is Jesus, God's Son. Through Him we become God's children. But rather than accepting the present, so many people ignore it and decide to leave it there, unopened. We don't claim the gift."

That very night, Tessa prayed to invite Jesus into her heart, accepting and receiving her personal gift from the Lord. The memory reminds me that every moment is a gift-giving opportunity for those who willingly share God's plan of salvation.

How can you make your next conversation with a friend one that leads them closer to God?

Rudolph, the Prodigal Reindeer

"I can do nothing on My own."

JOHN 5:30 NASB

In the Christmas classic *Rudolph the Red-Nosed Reindeer*, Hermey the elf wants to be a dentist, but the other elves laugh at his goal. Meanwhile, Rudolph is bullied out of the reindeer games because of his shiny red nose.

"I don't need anybody," Hermey declares. "I'm independent."

"Me too," Rudolph insists. "I'm what you said … independent."

And so, rather than appreciating the unique way they've been created, Hermey and Rudolph allow the opinions of others to define them. They leave their homes and set out on a dangerous course.[7]

Our sinful nature pushes us toward independence too, prodding us to run away when things get hard, to disrespect authority, and to think we don't need anybody. But as Rudolph and Hermey discovered, no one is designed to be completely independent. We need others. That's the way God wired us. We need relationships and benefit from them.

Our friendship with Jesus is the most important relationship we can have. When we put our trust in Jesus by asking Him to forgive our sins and inviting Him to live in our hearts, He takes us on the most exciting adventure in friendship of all.

Did you know that Jesus didn't go solo? He relied on His Father and the Holy Spirit. He also surrounded himself with the Twelve, His friends and disciples.

Who do you depend on to help lead you the way God would want you to go?

---

7 *Rudolph the Red-Nosed Reindeer*, directed by Larry Roemer (Rankin/Bass Productions, 1964).

Spread Good News and Great Joy

When they had seen him, they spread the word concerning what had been told them about this child, and all who heard it were amazed at what the shepherds said to them.

LUKE 2:17–18

My children pack Operation Christmas Child shoe boxes every November, filling them with goodies and God's Word to spread "the good news of great joy" about Jesus' coming and purpose around the globe (Luke 2:10). The work of Operation Christmas Child reminds me of the gift the shepherds gave to Bethlehem the night our Savior was born. It's a gift every Christ-follower can share.

That night, shepherds were keeping watch over their little lambs. God chose this group to be the first to hear about the birth of His Son, "the Lamb of God, who takes away the sin of the world" (John 1:29). The shepherds hurried to see baby Jesus for themselves. Then "they spread the word concerning what had been told them about this child" (Luke 2:17). They talked to everyone they passed about Jesus' arrival and purpose.

Enthusiastically sharing the news that Jesus has come is the best gift you can give. As sure as the shepherds' testimony was met with amazement, your words of good news and great joy can lead people toward accepting Him as Lord and Savior.

What will you do to spread the news and joy of Jesus' coming this season?

Give Him Your Treasure

Opening their treasures, they offered him gifts,
gold and frankincense and myrrh.
MATTHEW 2:11 ESV

Led by a star after Jesus was born, wise men traveled to worship little Jesus and present Him with gifts. Just like today, gold was one of the most valuable resources in the ancient world. It was a gift fit for a king, a sign that the humble child, Jesus, really is King of kings. Frankincense was a tree resin used in temple incense. This costly gift was a nod to Jesus' role as high priest over God's people. Myrrh was also a fragrant perfume, but one associated with death. This sweet-smelling present hinted that Jesus would one day give His life for our sins.

Did you know Jesus desires and welcomes your treasure too? Sure, you can show your devotion by placing money in the offering plate on Sunday. But more precious to Him than cash is the gift of the jewel that beats in your chest. Proverbs 23:26 makes His most-wanted item clear: "My son, give me your heart" (ESV).

You see, Jesus wants the gift of your love and loyalty. He wants the one thing that—better than gold, frankincense, or myrrh—declares the truth of who He is. He is the Lord, who stepped into human history to set our hearts free from the curse of death, so we might live with Him forever. So if you haven't done so already, offer Him your treasure.

How does it feel to know Jesus considers your heart a treasure more valuable than gold?

Amazing Faith

Then Jesus said to the Roman officer, "Go on home.
What you have believed has happened!"
And the boy was healed that same hour!
MATTHEW 8:13 TLB

A good soldier must settle the issue of authority before he goes into battle. He needs to know who's in charge and agree to follow that leader's instructions, regardless of where they lead. One day, a captain in the Roman army came to Jesus and asked Him to heal his paralyzed servant. Immediately, Jesus agreed to go to his house and heal the boy. "Jesus," the soldier said, "you can stay right here. All you have to do is say the word and he'll be healed. You're the general and what You say goes" (Matthew 8:8–9). Sure enough, Jesus honored this man's sincere willingness to take Him at the power of His Word. Right then, from right there, He healed the servant.

We too are soldiers who should trust the authority of our Commander in Chief. We need amazing faith that trusts Jesus can do as He wants and that He responds to our prayers. The captain's request was rewarded because he genuinely knew God was able to do what He asked. He didn't waver in his trust.

Keep count of how many times a day the Lord gives you opportunities to trust Him—and remember that there's nothing our God cannot do. Believe that He'll come through for you, meeting your needs and solving relationship struggles. It may not come naturally at first, but work to allow Jesus an opportunity to marvel at your faith as He did with the Roman captain.

Why do you think faith pleases Jesus?

Listen to Your Blind Spot Buddy

Fools think their own way is right,
but the wise listen to others.
PROVERBS 12:15 NLT

Technically, a blind spot is an area that a driver cannot see clearly when using the car's standard mirrors. Once a driver realizes he's got a blind spot, he needs to either purchase an additional adjustable mirror or a back-up camera to reveal what's going on behind him, or he'll need to travel with an alert passenger who can stay on the lookout. To boldly switch lanes without receiving input from one of those aids is foolish.

Each of us has figurative blind spots in our lives. For example, we don't always see our faults or notice when a bad attitude allows us to confidently swerve into poor decisions. One of the greatest blessings that comes from surrounding ourselves with godly friends is that they can act as alert copilots and adjustable mirrors that lovingly point out our issues. When we listen to what they have to say about us, rather than assuming that we're always right, we can save ourselves a lot of damage.

Pay attention when Dad warns that you have a stinky attitude. Take notice when your sister says you're stomping on her feelings. The people God puts in your life can be important "blind spot buddies" who can help you better navigate life and stay on a path that honors Jesus.

When has your parent or friend been a "blind spot buddy" for you?

The Purpose of Pruning

"He cuts off every branch in me that bears no fruit,
while every branch that does bear fruit he prunes
so that it will be even more fruitful."

JOHN 15:2

If you visited Walt Disney World, most likely you would encounter a tree that looks like Pluto or a bush in the shape of Mickey Mouse. Not only does Disney hire some of the most learned engineers in the world to create amusing rides, but they employ brilliant horticulturists and landscapers to help grow their breathtaking gardens. These men and women train shrubs and trees to grow into different shapes. One way they do this is by taking time and care to cut branches and trim limbs to fit the shape of the character they are trying to form.

Jesus, the Master Gardener, has a certain shape He sees in us too. And to get us to look like Him, He must train us to go in the direction of His design. He does this by a process called pruning, which is painful for us, but is necessary in keeping us healthy and in shape.

Perhaps you are experiencing the sharp snips of Jesus' pruning shears in an area of your life. Rejoice in the closeness of your Father's loving care and in the coming fruit He's preparing your life to bear. Pruning may be painful, but it is always productive.

What is one of God's promises to us that holds true during the pruning process?

He Sinks Our Sins

You will tread our sins beneath your feet;
you will throw them into the depths of the ocean!
MICAH 7:19 TLB

The best way to lose something so it can never be recovered is to drop it into the middle of the ocean. The Mariana Trench, the deepest part of the sea, is an estimated seven miles down, and explorers don't know for sure if even that incredible depth is the seafloor's rock bottom. If your backpack goes down there, even the world's best dive team can't bring it back.

The Bible tells us that when we put our trust in Jesus, our sins are gone forever—He throws our mess-ups into the depths of the ocean. Not only is He serious about forgetting them, but He's serious about moving them beyond our reach. He tosses them so far away that it's pointless trying to retrieve them or worry about them anymore.

Our enemy loves to shame us into thinking that things we've done are too big and bad for God to forgive. He tries to get us to doubt Christ's forgiveness. But you can stand free and forgiven in the knowledge that your sins are no longer remembered by the Lord. And you can rest in the truth that there's no point in going fishing for what's been forgiven.

What should you remember the next time you start to worry about sins you've already confessed to Jesus?

Tomb Raider

"Where, O death, is your victory?
Where, O death, is your sting?"
1 CORINTHIANS 15:55

Lazarus had been in the grave four days when Jesus arrived. Mary and Martha were heartbroken, because they knew if Jesus had been there, their brother would have been healed. However, Jesus had something better planned than a healing. The crowds had seen Him perform many of those. Now He wanted everybody to witness a resurrection, removing any doubt about His identity. As Isaiah 25:8 foretold, He was preparing a preview of how He will one day "swallow up death forever."

"Lazarus, come out!" Jesus commanded, as He stood near the entrance to His friend's tomb (John 11:43). As soon as He did, Lazarus sat up in his grave clothes and started hopping toward the entrance! When he joined Jesus, completely well and whole, everyone watching knew beyond a doubt that Jesus wasn't just an entertaining teacher. Jesus was God. Only God has power over death. His words were so forceful that if He hadn't called Lazarus specifically by name, all the dead might have been immediately brought back to life by this divine Tomb Raider!

You and I need not fear death: Jesus has promised to resurrect us. But He's also given us a little taste of new life now. We are born dead in sin. Yet, when we answer His call to come out from its bondage, we are dead to sin so we can be alive in Christ.

How would you explain why those who love Jesus don't need to be afraid of death?

Construction Will Be Completed

*He who began a good work in you will
carry it on to completion until the day of Christ Jesus.*

PHILIPPIANS 1:6

One day, Billy Graham's wife, Ruth, was driving along and came upon a construction site. Careful to follow the warnings and stay within the orange cones of caution, she eventually approached the last sign, marked "End of Construction. Thank you for your patience." Laughing, she scribbled down that inscription to one day have carved into her tombstone.[8]

Ruth knew that we Christians are works in progress. Once we give our hearts to Jesus, He saves us and makes us new. But He also sends us through a lifelong series of tests and trials that are meant to sanctify us, that is, to slowly change our hearts so our attitudes and actions reflect His.

Sometimes, however, that shaping hurts, as Jesus calls us to let go of selfishness and pride and bad habits. And as Ruth's memorial reminds us, we can get testy along the way. We may even take it out on others, making their patience with us necessary. But God's Word promises that the good work He began in us at the moment of salvation, and that He continues in us through the ongoing process of sanctification, will one day be complete when we step into heaven. The Lord always finishes what He begins.

What do you think it means to be a work in progress?

---

8 "This Date in History: June 14, 2007 – Remembering Ruth Bell Graham," Billy Graham Evangelist Association, http://www.billygrahamlibrary.org/this-date-in-history-june-14-2007-remembering-ruth-bell-graham/.

ACKNOWLEDGMENTS

This devotional was a team effort. Thanks first belong to my Lord and Savior, Jesus Christ. Not only is He the star of this book, but He provided me with Lee, my dearly-loved husband, who kept encouraging me when I wanted to quit. A big thank-you must also go to our children: Caroline, Daniel, and Harrison. They provided both inspiration and loving support, tolerating many leftovers and extending me grace. I love y'all!

I'm thankful, too, for all the friends and family members who have faithfully prayed from this project's inception. Pastor Bobby Blanton, you preached the Word faithfully, helping me to stay on track. My Thursday morning Bible study buddies, your fellowship warmed me each week. Kris Cichelli, Amy Laws and Deborah Johnson, you babysat so I could maintain focus. My sister, Christa McClary McElveen, for her love and prayers, and her children, John Thomas and Madeline, for their questions that kept my wheels turning. My in-loves, Dan and Pam Reeves, you raised a great man. Conyers and Jennie O'Bryan, you helped me laugh when I wanted to cry. Jason and Taylor Gibbs, with Caroline and Daniel, you were my carpool of creative ideas as we drove to school. Carlton Garborg, David Sluka, and Brian Mitchell, you graciously encouraged me to create a resource to help moms and dads shine the spotlight on Jesus. And Bethany McShurley, you kept me moving. Without you, I would have focused on the mountain and not the Mountain Mover.

Finally, a special tribute belongs to Clebe and Deanna McClary, whom I am so blessed to have as my wonderful parents. Your commitment to each other and to Christ never fails to point Christa and me—and everyone else—to Jesus.

ABOUT THE AUTHOR

Tara McClary Reeves is a wife, mother, speaker, award-winning children's book author of *The Pirate and the Firefly* and *The Knight and the Firefly*, and passionate teacher of the joys and challenges that come with being a committed follower of Jesus Christ. Tara lives in North Carolina with her husband, Lee, and their three children. She considers it a privilege to point Caroline, Daniel, and Harrison to the Lord every day.

www.photographybychanda.com